What people are saying about *Your Keys To Heaven:*

."The spiritual secrets my daughters and I have learned from Gary Spivey through God are invaluable and life changing. The peace and joy I feel from being able to connect with God, Jesus, my Angels and loved ones in Heaven, is overwhelming! *Your Keys to Heaven* has changed our lives for the better and we are forever grateful and blessed to have the ability to receive guidance from Heaven. By reading this book, you will be on your path to the spiritual enlightenment that you deserve."

Angelique Homm, Las Vegas, Nevada

"Thanks, guys. This book is a great reference tool; it made my life a lot easier."

Zack Brown, age 12, Minneapolis, Minnesota

"This book is a Godsend! *Your Keys to Heaven* is an awesome tool for parents. They should memorize this, especially if they have a teen."

Christina Auman, Minneapolis, Minnesota

"You are holding in your hand for consideration an uplifting book that, when read, will drastically improve your life and, perhaps, direct you to help others in their daily lives. What are you waiting for?"

Carolyn Scibetta, Portland, Oregon

"Now that I have connected directly to God and can receive spiritual gifts, I know what it feels like to truly live in my spirit, which is always fearless, powerful, and can move forward in full confidence even in toughest of situations or the unknown. The techniques outlined in this book, along with the guided meditations, are so simple that *anyone* can use them to, not only feel fantastic daily, but also co-create the life they want to live and fulfill all of their dreams at God Speed."

Alex Hernandez, San Jose, California

"*Your Keys to Heaven* is a direct connection to God's light. Even with the smallest amount of daily effort, you can expect to see amazing changes in all aspects of your life. This book will enlighten the world?"

Brad Davis Jr., Richmond, Virginia

i

Secrets From God

Your Keys To Heaven

Unlocking the Gates to Personal and Spiritual Enlightenment

Gary Spivey
and
Dean Hymel

G. S. Limited Inc.

Your Keys to Heaven
Unlocking the Gates to Personal and Spiritual Enlightenment

G.S. Limited Inc.
248A N. Montgomery St.
Ojai, CA 93023
Ph.1-805-640-8368
http://GarySpivey.com
www.yourkeystoheaven.com

Copyright © 2006 by Gary Spivey and Dean Hymel
All rights reserved
First Edition
Printed in U.S.A.

ISBN 0-9778716-0-6
All rights reserved. No part of this publication may be reproduced or used in any form or by any means-electronic, mechanical, photocopying, or recordin without written permission from the publisher.
Every effort has been made to obtain permission for the material in the book. Theauthor, editors, and publishers sincerely apologize for any inadvertent errors oromissions and will be happy to correct them in future editions.
Publisher's Cataloging-In-Publication Data
(Prepared by The Donohue Group, Inc.)

Spivey, Gary (Gary June)
  Your keys to Heaven : unlocking the gates to personal and spiritual enlightenment / Gary Spivey and Dean Hymel ; edited by Patricia L. Fry.— 1st ed.

    p. : ill. ; cm + 1 sound disc (digital ; 4 3/4 in.)

  Includes bibliographical references and index.
  ISBN: 0-9778716-0-6

  1. Spiritualism. 2. Self-realization—Religious aspects. 3. Spiritual healing. 4. Angels. I. Hymel, Dean. II. Fry, Patricia L., 1940- III. Title. IV. Title: Spiritual secrets revealed

BF1275.S44 S65 2006
133.9

Edited by Patricia L. Fry
Book design by Dennis Mullican
Cover design by Nils Lawrence

Your Keys to Heaven
Unlocking the Gates to Personal and Spiritual Enlightenment

Table of Contents

Acknowledgements vii

Foreword ix

Your First Step xi

Introduction xv

1: A Child's Life Less Ordinary 1

2: Angels 13
   And how they affect us.

3: Demons 33
   And how they affect us.

4: Spiritual Gifts 89
   And how they work.

5: How to See and Hear Spiritually 107

6: Healing 123

7: Spirit Replacement 193
   How to replace your worn out spirit.

8: Soul Unlocking 209
   How to unlock heaven's knowledge hidden within you.

9: Gifted Children 227
   Understanding earth's precious cargo.

10: Using Your Spiritual Gifts 275

11: Messages From God **283**
    More Spiritual Secrets Revealed.

12: More Testimonials **299**

13: A Perfect World **339**

The Final Step **341**

Acknowledgments

First and foremost, I want to thank God and all of my Heavenly family of Angels. If it were not for them and their loving patience I would not have any spiritual secrets to share with you.

Next, I would like to thank my very best friend, manager and co-author, Dean Hymel, for his friendship and the same type of loving patience that God and the Angels gave to me. It took that loving patience to write a book with an organizationally-challenged person like me.

I would like to thank my assistant and one of the most creative people I've ever met, Nils Lawrence. Nils has the patience of a saint; he needs that working with me. I would like to thank him for his over-the-top creative talents. Those talents made it possible to figure out how to illustrate what I have in my head and to arrange it into a legible book for you to see.

I would like to acknowledge that both Dean and Nils are extremely spiritually gifted. They're able to see, hear and talk to God and Angels, receive spiritual gifts, remove Demons from people and see in all of the spiritual dimensions including heaven. They have contributed to this project in so many ways. Not only did Dean help write the book and Nils design it, they both gave me messages from God and Angels that were important for the completion of this book. It's a lot easier for the dark spirits of the universe to trick and confuse one spiritually gifted person, but to trick and confuse three was impossible for them. I can't thank Dean and Nils enough for all of their hard work and long hours. Without them, there would be no book. All I have to say is, I love you guys. You're the best.

I would also like to thank Michael Scott for his editing talent and for being the first person to read the book and say it was great. I would like to thank Corey Worden for drawing many of the pictures in the book. His talent and attention to detail is amazing. Thank you Corey for your patience and for drawing pictures when you were burned out and had nothing left to give. I would like to thank Patricia Fry, my second editor, who my Angels lead to me. We both live in Ojai, California and it was meant to be that we meet. She is an amazing editor and person. I would like to thank Dennis Mullican, who also lives in Ojai California, for his creative talent. Dennis designed the layout of the pages in this book. This is a very creative, time-consuming and detail oriented job.

Again I would like to thank God and all the Angels who patiently guided me through the spiritual lessons I needed to learn—and, believe me, I had a lot to learn so that I could present this book to you and the world.

FOREWORD

There are many books about spirituality on the market today, but once in a lifetime a book comes along that truly teaches us something new. *Your Keys to Heaven* is that book. Within these pages you will be taken on an extraordinary journey. There will be times when you think you are reading fiction. Rest assured, it's real. *Your Keys to Heaven* has the power to change the lives of its readers.

Your Keys to Heaven has been years in the making. It is a highly anticipated book written by one of the foremost authorities on spirituality: Gary Spivey. In this book, he explains how many of the physical, mental and emotional illnesses that people suffer from today are, in reality, spiritual blocks. He describes how spiritual blocks can cripple every facet of your life. More importantly, he has the unique ability to teach others how to heal these illnesses by removing their spiritual blocks. Through a simple daily spiritual regimen of prayer, meditation, and the process of using your spiritual gifts, you, too, can rid your physical and spiritual body of all illness.

Learning to receive spiritual gifts is just one of the spiritual secrets revealed within this book. *Your Keys to Heaven* unveils many ancient spiritual secrets that religious leaders around the world don't talk about or teach. Why is this? Is it because they don't know about the secrets, or are they afraid to give people the power to reach total spiritual enlightenment? Whatever the case, within this book many spiritual secrets will be revealed guiding you to personal and spiritual enlightenment.

Your Keys to Heaven is a book you will return to over and over again (throughout your lifetime) and each time, you will learn something new.

We are all spiritually gifted. God's light shines within each of us. Let Gary Spivey teach you how to turn it on.

Disclaimer

The information and experiences in this book are the author's own or were told to the author with permission to publish. The opinions are the author's unless otherwise indicated. The exercises and activities in this book are designed for everyone. However, they are not meant to take the place of appropriate and necessary medical treatment.

Results of success will vary from individual to individual depending on one's needs, condition and approach to the processes outlined in this book.

YOUR FIRST STEP

From the time we are born, we are on a journey through life. We constantly search for answers to our questions. Whatever the question, there is always an answer. If the answer doesn't satisfy us, we continue to search. I believe that, if you're reading this book, you're still searching for answers to some of your questions.

This book is designed to take you on a journey of self discovery. I will share with you information that you will not find in any other book; information that will help you in your search for answers.

First, I'd like you to respond to the following questions with total honesty. There is no right or wrong answer, just your answer. The importance of answering these questions will be revealed to you later in the book. Keep in mind that this is the first step in the discovery of whatever it is you are searching for.

Complete the following:

1. Religion is…

   _____

2. Spirituality is…

   _____

3. Heaven is…

   _____

4. God is…

   _____

5. Angels are…

   _____

6. Demons are…

   _____

7. Spiritual Gifts are…

   _____

Complete the Questionnaire:

Rate yourself from 1-10.
10 = 100% agreement with the question or statement
1 =100% disagreement with the question or statement

1. 10 God does exist.
2. 10 Angels do exist.
3. 10 Demons do exist.
4. 10 In history, people have been able to see God.
5. 5 I can see, hear and talk to God.
6. 10 God has spiritual gifts for everyone.
7. 5 In history, people have been able to see, hear and talk to Angels.
8. 5 Only select people can see, hear and talk to Angels.
9. 10 Angels can help guide your life.
10. 10 Demons cause havoc in everyone's life.
11. 5 I have the ability to heal myself from physical, mental and emotional illness.
12. 5 I can see, hear and talk to Angels.
13. 10 Heaven does exist.
14. 9 I have to die to see Heaven.
15. 10 Demons cause mental illness.
16. 10 In history, people have been able to hear God.
17. 8 I can visit heaven whenever I choose to.
18. 10 I have a physical and spiritual body.
19. 1 No one can see God and Angels.
20. 10 Demons cause physical illness.
21. 10 I have a spirit and soul within me.
22. 10 Spiritual gifts are given to me by God.
23. 10 I can receive spiritual gifts.
24. 1 There are a limited number of spiritual gifts I can receive.
25. 10 Everyone on Earth belongs to the same spiritual family.

26. _!_ Spirituality is a waste of time.
27. _lo_ In history, people have been able to talk to God.
28. _/_ Given my past, I can't be spiritual.
29. _/_ I don't have time to be spiritual.
30. _/_ God doesn't exist.
31. _/_ Angels don't exist.
32. _/_ Demons don't exist.
33. _/_ Spiritual gifts don't exist.
34. _!_ The only way to heal yourself is through medication.
35. _!_ Spiritual healing is for suckers.
36. _/_ I don't need to be spiritual.
37. _lo_ Demons cause emotional problems/illness.
38. _/_ No one can see, hear or talk to God or Angels.
39. _lo_ Children are spiritually gifted.
40. _!_ I don't want the responsibility of being spiritual.
41. _!_ My religion is the only correct religion.
42. _lo_ There are other dimensions that I can'see with my physical eyes.
43. _8_ There are other dimensions I can see with my spiritual eyes.
44. _8_ Someone has to be specially selected to see, hear or talk to God.
45. _/_ I have a physical illness.
46. _!_ I have a mental illness.
47. _!_ I know everything there is about spirituality and religion.
48. _!_ Meditation is a waste of my time.
49. _S_ I never meditated in my life.
⨍ 50. _!!_ I meditate every day.
51. _!!_ I don't know how to meditate.
52. _!_ I can't find my soul mate. I DID B/c I ASKED GOD FOR HU
53. _!_ Soul mates don't exist.
54. _8_ I have fear.
55. _!!_ I have anger.
56. _5_ I have guilt.
57. _5_ I believe luck has to do with spirituality.
58. _!!_ I live in denial.

59. _10_ Truth is important.
60. _10_ Truth is important in being spiritual.
61. _10_ Faith is important to me.
62. _10_ Being in a relationship is important to me.
63. _8_ Spirituality is important in relationships.
64. _6_ I have problems I need to fix in my life.
65. _1_ I know everything about everything.
66. _1_ Everyone diagnosed with mental disorders should take medications.
67. _1_ Everyone diagnosed with emotional problems should take medications.
68. _2_ I believe that people have the ability to diagnose physical illness with their spiritual abilities.
69. _10_ In medical school, doctors should also be trained to diagnose physical, mental and emotional illness with spiritual abilities.
70. _5_ Earthbound spirits exist.
71. _1_ The only way to stop being a drug addict is to go to rehab.
72. _1_ I can see, hear and talk to my dead loved ones in heaven.
73. _8_ I can manifest my dreams ond desires.
74. _10_ Children can see earthbound spirits.
75. _6_ I can see earthbound spirits.
76. _1_ I think this questionnaire was a waste of my time.
77. _10_ God loves everyone.

INTRODUCTION

In the beginning, we were all created equal; not our physical bodies here on earth, but our spiritual bodies that once lived in heaven. Everyone on earth has a physical and a spiritual body living together as one unit.

Your spiritual body resides within your physical body. Of course, you are aware of your physical body because you can see it and you use it on a daily basis. From the time you wake up until the time you go to sleep, you are totally aware of your physical body and the physical world surrounding you. However, most people are not aware that the spiritual body is living within the physical body.

Throughout this book I will demonstrate that whatever happens to your spiritual body, directly affects your physical body. I will prove to you that all physical, mental and emotional illness first occurs in your spiritual body and that the physical body is only suffering the negative side effects.

Your physical body—your mind—can only comprehend what you are taught, but your spiritual body has the ability to comprehend everything in the entire universe. Your spiritual body is connected to heaven and it has all of the secrets of heaven locked inside. Once you awaken your spiritual body and release this knowledge, you will be able to comprehend in your physical body—your mind— everything that your spiritual body knows. Awakening your spiritual body is the single most important thing that you can do in your lifetime. Awakening your spiritual body is the first step to understanding the spiritual world around you. By not awakening the spiritual body, you are only living half of a life—just a physical existence.

This concept may be difficult to comprehend at first. But, if you continue reading this book, you will come to a complete understanding.

The first spiritual secret I will teach you is how to awaken your spiritual body. I will also reveal many other spiritual secrets throughout this book—the secrets that religious leaders from around the world don't teach. These secrets really do exist.

One of the most important spiritual secrets you will learn is how to communicate directly to God, Angels and other Heavenly Hierarchy. I'm not talking about just praying to them: I'm talking about actually seeing, hearing and talking to them using your spiritual eyes, ears and voice.

I have always been interested in how people who have so much faith in a religion which is based on God's teachings, continue to have so much doubt and fear in their minds and hearts about communicating directly with God, Angels and Heavenly Hierarchy. There are people who think it is sacrilegious, but let me assure you it's real and anyone can do it. You don't have to be of any particular religion or faith; you just have to be open-minded and willing to learn something new.

According to many ancient religious texts, God and the Angels directly communicated to the people of that time and they passed along some very important messages. It is written in the Old Testament that God talked to Noah and warned him of the Great Flood. It is also written that God talked to Moses and gave him the Ten Commandments. It is written in the Muslim religion that the Angel Gabriel talked to Muhammad and dictated the Qur'an for him. It is written in the Mormon religion that the Angel Maroni talked with Joseph Smith and guided him to find the Book of Mormonism.

I ask you, if these people were able to hear and talk directly with God and the Angels, why should you not be able to directly communicate with them also? Well, you can! Let me show you how.

The spiritual secrets revealed in this book are very important. I ask you to approach each of them with an open and inquiring mind. Only then, will you discover the spiritual truth that lies within you.

How do I know these spiritual secrets?

Well, I was lucky enough to be born with my spiritual body already awakened within me. Throughout my life, I was taught many spiritual lessons by God, Angels and Heavenly Hierarchy. I will now teach you what I was taught and I hope, one day, that you will pass on to others what you will learne.

I work with people from all walks of life: Doctors, lawyers, politicians and celebrities as well as housewives, postal employees, and factory workers. They all have one thing in common: they are all spiritual beings with amazing spiritual capabilities. In this book, I have included many testimonials reflecting some of their spiritual experiences.

I have placed these unedited, personal testimonials throughout the book so that you can see just how different and how similar we are. Please do not skip the testimonials; there is much to be learned from each one.

I'm a single mother of two boys; long ago we dubbed ourselves the Three Musketeers. Together, we listened to Gary on the radio each Wednesday morning, every chance we could. When we couldn't listen together, either because of the boys' schoolwork or my work, we would share the stories of what we heard over dinner that evening.

Recently we had a couple years of bad luck and we were searching for answers, reasons, or lessons that I thought we must have to learn to turn our "luck" around. I was raised Episcopalian and yet I had trouble aligning my beliefs with the behaviors I'd seen displayed by those involved in organized religion.

My oldest son, Brian suggested that I ask Gary for help. Not long after that, we discovered that Gary was coming to Portland for a weekend seminar. The seminar was more than we could afford, but my eldest son, who had saved the money to purchase new hockey equipment, offered it to me so I could spend the day with Gary. I took a'ioan and he made my reservation.

On November 1, 2003, I entered a room in a hotel in downtown Portland that had the most amazing energy in it. You could feel this positive charge in the air. There were about twenty excited people sitting at tables, whispering quietly amongst themselves, getting to know one another. They were all, waiting for Gary to arrive. I guess I knew that on that day, my life would change forever.

The group was very diverse: a gentleman in his 80s, a woman who had lost her daughter to suicide, another woman whose husband was terminally ill, a hospice nurse, a wife in a nowhere marriage feeling insignificant and invisible, a mother and daughter who already knew the answers to their questions, a woman wanting desperately to conceive a child, and me wanting to rid myself of the Demons that were causing me to nearly self-destruct my life. And, of course, we all had questions about the more mundane things like love, income and jobs, lost items and our relationships with our friends and family.

That day we all had our questions answered but more importantly we learned about God, Heaven, Angels, Spiritual Gifts and Demons. We learned how to meditate and how to see God, how to receive spiritual gifts, and how to ask our Angels for help and guidance. Gary rid us of our Demons and showed us how to keep them away. We all left that day, awed by what we had learned and, among hugs and goodbyes, we took home with us a single tool to help us continue on our path: A meditation CD.

Personally, I had big questions regarding my sons, Brian and David; specifically, how was I doing as their only parent? The answer I got from Gary (no matter how I phrased my questions, trying to make the answers different) was that I needed to teach my children the spiritual secrets I just learned. I needed to teach them how to awaken their spiritual bodies, how to receive spiritual gifts and how to meditate. Gary told me that many Angels surrounded me and both of my children and that they were very spiritually gifted.

Naturally, when I got home from the seminar, my kids wanted to know everything about my day. We talked for hours about all I had seen, done and experienced. I told them how Gary had taught us to meditate and I put the CD in our player and we listenedThat was the first night our family meditated together. That was the day our lives improved spectacularly. Our bad luck seemed to vanish overnight. Good things began to happen almost instantly. My business began to sign new accounts, my failing car hung on until we saved enough for a new one. My attitude became bright and sunny—having said farewell to a "Psycho Demon" that made me cynical, impatient, and frequently angry—even with my children, whom I adore.

Of all the spiritual gifts God gave to us, the most momentous came in a phone call from Gary's office in March—about five months after I'd attended Gary's seminar. Gary was back in Portland and he was taking appointments for private readings while in town. I wasn't sure how I was going to pay for the session, but I made my appointment figuring that if the boys wanted to, we'd go see Gary as a family. One thing I'd come to understand is that there are really no coincidences. I wasn't sure why I'd gotten the call that weekend about the personal session, but I knew that only good had come from my first meeting with Gary. I know that my prayers had been answered in some way or another since I began getting in touch with my Angels. I had come to look at every opportunity as a possible answer to a prayer.

On March 14, 2004, my boys and I entered the hotel where we were to meet with Gary. When we saw him, I reintroduce myself and introduced my sons. I told Gary that I attended his seminar in November. He remembered me. I told Gary that, my boys and I meditated together and that while I was having problems seeing and hearing my Angels, God, and my spiritual gifts, my children could see everything with ease and were able to tell me what our gifts were.

t didn't take long for Gary to realize that my eldest son was spiritually gifted with clairvoyance and clairaudience, meaning that he could naturally see and hear spiritually. Gary said he had a Jesus Heart inside of him, and that this meant he'd be a spiritual healer. My youngest was also spiritually gifted; we spent some time discussing his diagnosed Attention Deficit Disorder. Gary told him to ask his Angels for help when he needed to stay focused on schoolwork. Gary seemed confident that, with all the Angels around him and with his spiritual gifts, he would not have any trouble sorting out the different energies around him.

For myself, I wanted desperately to see my Angels and hear them. Gary told me that I would, in time. He told me that I used the other side of my brain in the long hours I worked and was unaccustomed to using the imagination part of my brain. He told me that if I exercised this muscle, I'd be seeing and hearing in the spiritual dimensions before long. In our meditations with Gary that day, God had given me the spiritual gift of new eyes. With Gary's help I placed them in my head with my physical hands. Before we left, we asked Gary if he could help us to try to heal a friend suffering from lung cancer. He asked my sons to assist him. They worked for many minutes, and Gary and my two sons saw the snakes that were causing her cancer. Together they removed the serpent-like snake entities from our friend.

If our lives were changed dramatically on November first—they were changed even more dramatically that day on March 14.

Today, our friend is feeling better and has more energy. Since that day, my youngest son has not taken his Ritalin to help his concentration in school. Each day he asks for concentration from his Angels and each day he's also able to pay attention and sort out his schoolwork in the physical dimension. Not taking the Ritalin was his decision. Very plainly, he told me that he no longer needed it after seeing Gary. The medication would always be available to him should he feel the need for it. I get "Friday forms" that his teachers complete each Friday that tell me what work—if any—is not complete for the week and the teachers give comments on how the week has gone. The slips were good while he was on Ritalin, but they are even better now. Also, I have my funny, happy-go-lucky son back. The Ritalin had taken this wacky, sharp-as-a-tack kid and drained him, leaving him frequently with headaches at the end of the day.

Both my kids are stretching their spiritual wings, so to speak, figuring out how their spiritual gifts work and what they need to do and how to discover the best way to use them. We have all come to see or sense Demons in people, rooms and the world. Together, as well as separately, my sons and I work to rid them first from family and friends then the neighbors. As for me, my new spiritual eyes seem to have worked first in the physical sense. Several days ago, I was at my office very early in the morning. I put on my reading glasses to read my e-mail and discovered, to my surprise, that I couldn't focus. I took my glasses off and cleaned them, then put them back on. I still could not make out the words on the computer screen. As I flipped them up to the top of my head, I realized that I could focus without them. I haven't worn them since that day. I don't need them. My vision wasn't perfect right away. At first I had trouble focusing between written words on my desk and the words on my computer screen, but in about a day, that was gone, also. Now I read like I did when I was in my 20s. I pray that soon I will be able to see God, the Angels and all of my Spiritual gifts. I have confidence that I will.

It seems to me that Gary Spivey became the instrument for us to find our path to God, the Angels and our Spiritual gifts. We're ready to share our experiences and do our share to "pay forward" what Gary did for us.

T h a n k   Y o u   G a r y .
Carolyn Scibetta
Portland, OR

I wanted to share Carolyn's testimonial because it shows how a family learned to communicate with God and Angels. It also demonstrates how the members of this family changed their lives for the better once they learned how to receive their spiritual gifts and use them

You, too, have these natural, God-given spiritual abilities, but they are locked up inside your spiritual body. It is now time for you to awaken your spiritual body and learn how to unleash your own natural spiritual abilities.

It doesn't matter what religion you are or your spiritual beliefs. It doesn't matter what personal issues you are struggling with. You will benefit from this book. I've helped many thousands of people throughout the world to create more positive lives and now, if you are ready and have an open mind, I will teach you the following:

- I will teach you how to awaken your spiritual body.
- I will teach you how to ask your Angels for guidance and help.
- I will teach you how to receive your spiritual eyes and ears.
- I will teach you how to communicate with God, Angels and Heavenly Hierarchy. And when I say "communication" I mean you will be able to see, hear and talk to them.
- I will teach you how to receive spiritual gifts and how to use them to change your life instantly and forever.
- I will teach you about Demons and the havoc they cause in your life. I will also teach you how to get rid of the Demons by using your spiritual gifts.

- I will teach you about the spiritual dimensions around you and how they affect you here in the physical dimension.
- I will teach you how to use your spiritual gifts to heal yourself and others.
- I will prove to you, by using spiritual artwork, that what I'm teaching you in this book has existed throughout history: The secrets were always in front of our eyes.
- I will use quotes from many different spiritual texts to back up my teachings.
- I will share with you the personal messages given to me by God—messages that he wants me to pass along to you.
- You will receive your very own Keys to Heaven.

This list is only the tip of the iceberg. There is far more spiritual knowledge and many more secrets contained within these pages. As you will notice, this book is designed so that you read the lesson, first. I will then ask you to stop and play the CD, so I can personally guide you through each step.

I want to stress that I learned everything that I am teaching firsthand from God, Angels and other spiritual beings. The information in this book does not come from other books. But I have added quotes from ancient religious texts and I've used some ancient religious artwork in order to prove that the truth has always been there.

I've always had God and Angels guiding my life and my spiritual growth. Now it is time for God and Angels to guide your life and your spiritual growth. I believe that you are an amazing spiritual being who is searching for spiritual enlightenment. I hope the journey we take together will lead you closer to your personal and spiritual goals.

It's time. Let your journey begin…

Philippe De Champaigne (1602-1674)
The Nativity
Musee des Beaux-Arts, Lille, France
Photo by: Herbert Joss

Permission granted by Abbeville Publishing Group

A Childs Life
Less Ordinary

One day, when I was in my mid thirties, I was lying down meditating when suddenly, I saw all of these Angels that I hadn't seen before. They gathered around me in a circle. They were looking at me and saying, "Are you sure that's him? Why doesn't he look like the rest of them? Why is he so different? Do you think we made a mistake?"

Then I heard another voice. I remembered this voice from the trances I experienced as a child. It was the *bright light* being. He told the Angels, "No mistake. He has the keys; they are inside of him."

A Childhood Less Ordinary...

Me (Gary Spivey) 3 years old.

My childhood was very much the same as any other kid I grew up with, with one exception—I was always able to see, hear and talk to my Angels. Other than that, I was perfectly normal!

For the most part, I enjoyed all of the same activities that every other child in my neighborhood did; hanging out with friends and cousins, going to the occasional drive-in movie or going swimming in the family's swimming hole in a little section of Cedar Creek. Cedar Creek was about two miles outside of the small town of Biscoe, North Carolina where I grew up. The swimming hole was damned up so that it was deep enough for all of the kids in town to go swimming in. No one, where I lived, had a swimming pool in their backyard in those days.

I remember growing up on my Grandmother Eula Lee Spivey's farm in rural North Carolina with plenty of land, lots of animals, a lot of love and not much money. I didn't know we were poor because everybody around us was poor, as well. All I knew was that we always had plenty of good Southern cooked food to eat and we were very happy most of the time.

I remember my grandma sitting in the middle of her living room by the wood heater while she popped popcorn in an old black cast-iron skillet and told stories. We would pop popcorn and she would tell stories. That was the norm for my family back then in the early 1960s, because my family couldn't afford a television. Later, we got a television, my family's first one. And I remember that they were really excited to get it.

My grandmothers, Eula Lee Spivey and Nola Parsons, always had interesting stories to tell me. The stories I remember most clearly were those that Grandmother Parsons told me about my Grandpa Lancaster Parsons, who died before I was born, and his spiritual abilities. She said, "He was adventurous, fun and enjoyed life to the fullest." I always remember her saying, "You're just like your Grand dad!" He knew things before they would happen and could see lights around people. This made sense to me because, at the time, I started knowing things before they happened and I could always see a light around everyone's head. Sometimes it would glow a little and sometimes it glowed a lot. I noticed that the people who had the biggest glow were the people that I liked the most.

My grandmother told me that people came from near and far just to ask my grandpa questions. She said he tried to keep his abilities secret because it was the 1930s and many people didn't understand

and, in fact, feared them, but people still knew that Lancaster was different. Word of his abilities always seemed to get out and the people who didn't fear "them" always showed up looking for answers to their questions. Remember, this was the time of the Great Depression and many people had questions about their future. My grandmother said, "His abilities came in handy all the time, especially in the business your grandfather was in." I would ask, "What business was he in?" She would just smile and laugh. Later, I found out that my grandfather was a bootlegger. He made moonshine liquor and he had a liquor still out in the woods. He always knew when the authorities were about to catch him, so he would box up the liquor and hightail it out of there before they caught him. He was known to be spiritually gifted, but he was also known as one of the best bootleggers that Montgomery County, North Carolina had ever seen. My grandmother said that, not only could my grandpa see the future, he was also able to diagnose what was going on with people's health. The lights he saw around people, he referred to as their Angels.

I enjoyed these stories the most because I was able to realize from an early age that whatever I was going through was normal. My Grand dad could do it! Too bad he had already died and wasn't around to tell me how everything worked. Too bad no one else really knew, but at least it was a piece of comforting information knowing that someone was like me and that I shouldn't be scared of my abilities.

The Gift...

I was my mother, Eunice, and father, Coy's, only son. My sister, Joyce, was ten years older than me. I came to them later in their life, so it was a lot like being an only child. I was a very positive child, very sensitive, loved everybody and I just loved to laugh and make other people laugh.

I was born spiritually gifted and could always see with my spiritual eyes (clairvoyance) and hear with my spiritual ears (clairaudience). Since becoming aware of my spiritual abilities of clairvoyance and clairaudience as a small child, I always had a sense of not being alone. I had with me what I referred to as *my pals*. My pals, as a child, were my Angels. I was lucky because my mom, Eunice, never told me that my Angels didn't exist. Whenever my pals had a story to share with her, she always listened, maybe because she was interested in what I had to say or maybe because she really loved me a lot or maybe because her dad, my grandpa Lancaster, had many of the same abilities that I have and she knew what to expect.

Sometimes I think my mom had a hard time deciding if I was being serious about talking to my pals—my Angels—or if I just had a really vivid imagination. Nevertheless, she never scolded me either way; she just listened to my stories. At the time, I wasn't aware of just how close she was listening. I found out later that she was keeping track of what I would say. She always kept it to herself and just listened to me, never telling me that I couldn't talk to my Angels or that they didn't exist. If anyone told me that I couldn't see Angels or talk to them, I would tell my mom and she would ask me, "Can you see them?" I always answered, "Yes." She would say, "Well they must be there then. Just because someone else can't see them doesn't mean they don't exist." At that time, in the early 1960s, Angels were a subject that you only heard of in church, or an ornament that topped the Christmas tree. Nevertheless, I grew up with my very own staff of Angels that only I could see, hear and talk to.

The Trance...

Many times throughout my childhood, I would go into an involuntary trance-like state.

While in the trance I would see this *bright light* being looking over me making sure I was okay and, while I was in the trance, I would see other beings that would talk to me in different languages. I was always able to understand them and speak fluently in their language. This always baffled my family, especially when I would talk out loud articulately in different languages that were totally unrecognizable to my family.

With a few exceptions, the trance was always the same: I would experience shortness of breath and physical pain. I would be crying and screaming at the top of my lungs because I would see this darkness surrounding and engulfing the earth. It felt as though the darkness was trying to extinguish all life on earth. I would sit up in bed with my eyes wide open trying to show my parents and sister something that they could not see. In the trance state, my Angels always handed me a set of keys and directed me to put one key in the earth.

As a young child, I collected old skeleton keys. I couldn't get too many of them. I was fascinated by them. Sometimes they were gold and brass colored. Those were the ones I liked the best.

As the key would fit into the earth, I would turn the key unlocking the earth then I would see this blanket of light surround and engulf the earth removing all of the darkness. Instantly, everything would be better and the earth would glow with this bright gold energy. While this energy blanket was surrounding the earth, the *bright light* being would always tell me, "Just allow the light to do its job." The voice would always comfort me and tell me, "One day you will understand what this all means. For now, you're still too young."

Sometimes, while I was still in the trance, my parents would wake me up before I got the key into the earth. When this happened, I would just be distraught, screaming to the point of physical illness and throwing up. If I did not get the key into the earth and release the bright gold energy to remove the darkness from the earth, then my physical body would be in tremendous pain because of the dark energy. After a few hours, the pain would eventually pass. However, every time I got to release the gold energy, I would awaken without any pain in my physical body.

My family called my strange trances, *fits*. I remember my mom saying, "He's having another fit again, get some cold water, wash his face, and tell him we get it." Patronizing me was the only way to wake me up from my trance without me throwing a fit for the next couple of hours. Eventually, my family would awaken me by agreeing that they saw what I was trying to show them. In their naïve way, my parents would say, "Yes, we see everything, too."

These experiences went on throughout my childhood. As I got older, I would ask my Angels, "What does this vision mean?" The vision was of an overwhelming darkness ready to overtake everything that is good, which made me feel like, if I didn't do my job this would occur and, "Who is this light being that is talking to me?" They would always tell me, "It's not time for you to understand the vision, but you must never forget it for one day you will understand its importance."

Psychic Abilities…

As a child, I began to Demonstrate psychic abilities. I knew things before they happened; these things were usually small and unimportant, but inexplicable to a child of 4 to 5 years old. I could see things other people couldn't see.

I remember when I was about 7 years old warning my father, Coy of a tractor that was about to fall over on a man who was plowing his field. I saw the accident before it occurred. I also felt the man's pain before he felt it. I was empathing his pain: An empath is someone who can feel someone else's energy. I felt as if someone ripped my arm off, kicked me in the head and punch me in the stomach all at the same time. I did the natural thing that a 7-year-old child would do if they had been ripped, kicked and punched: I began to cry, "Help him! Help him now!" I was holding my stomach and screaming, "It hurts! It hurts really bad!" My father, thinking that I was physically ill, wanted to help me because I was obviously going through something. My father made no effort at all to rescue the man on the tractor because, in his world, nothing had occurred yet. Seconds later, when the tractor turned over on the man, the pain and fear I was feeling instantly left me. At this point, my crisis seemed to be over while everyone else's was certainly just beginning. I'll never forget the puzzled look my father gave me as he rushed to pull the man from underneath the tractor. Later that day, he asked me how I knew the tractor was going to fall over. I told him that my Angels had showed me a vision.

As I got a little older, my family would always ask me questions. At family gatherings they would play a little game called, "Ask Gary a question." I would be put in the middle of the floor and everyone would gather around and take turns asking me questions. I remember being around 9 years old and one of my uncles was asking a question about work or something, but the answer he got didn't have anything to do with his question. The answer he received was about his girlfriend. Kids that young will say what they see! Everyone in the room went silent because my uncle was married. And that was the end of the "Ask Gary a question" game. They still asked me questions, of course, but it was always in private, now.

There were many other occurrences that happened throughout my childhood. For example, one day during high school I was called into the guidance counselor's office. I remember thinking that I was probably in trouble. I was wondering, "What did I do that was so bad?" I walked down to the office and sat in the chair outside the counselor's door for what seemed an eternity, running through every possible scenario, wondering what I had done. The door finally creaked open and the guidance counselor asked me to come in and sit. Then she pulled her chair closer to mine and said, "I have just one question. I just took a really important exam at night school. Did I pass?" "Yes. But barely," I told her.

Two weeks later, she found out that she had passed… barely. She met me walking down the hallway and said, "I am forever in your debt for putting my mind at ease for the past two weeks." At that moment, I sensed not only her happiness, but mine as well. I was thinking to myself that I really enjoyed helping her and that maybe this is what I'm suppose to be doing with the spiritual abilities that I was born with.

As fate had it, I was still an ambitious teenager full of fun and with many life lessons to learn. At that time, even though I had these abilities to help people, my passion was playing music. This is where my crazy hair-do started; I would color it silver and white when I played music. I played bass guitar in a very popular band and I had rock star dreams, so helping people with my spiritual abilities was certainly not my priority, yet. I played music throughout the state of North Carolina and Florida for a short period of time after high school, but I didn't want to be a starving musician, so I went into sales. In sales, my psychic abilities really came in handy and so did the crazy hair-do and white clothes. Anyone who saw me would always remember me. It wasn't long before I was one of the top salesmen in my company. Eventually, I went into business for myself and, since the crazy look was already working for me, I kept it.

However, all the time I was in sales and in business for myself I always had a sense of missing something, even though I was successful from a material point of view.

Even though I've had an extremely busy life, I always meditate and talk to my Angels daily. In my meditations, I always saw the same vision that I saw as a kid: the key that would fit into the earth removing the darkness allowing the earth to glow. I always ask my Angels for the meaning of this vision and they always give me the same answer, "It's not time for you to understand yet."

I always had a sense of missing something in my life, but I couldn't put my finger on what it was.

Psychic Meets Psychic…

And then, one day, I met a psychic named Ruth Rogers and we became good friends. One day, Ruth, who had a radio show in Tampa, Florida, invited me to be a guest on the show. It was a show where we would take phone calls and answer the callers' questions. I found myself thinking back to the time when I helped the guidance counselor in high school and how good it made me feel. I was getting the same feeling every time I answered a question and helped someone. When I sorted out people's problems, I would feel better, too. The feeling that I was missing something was gone and I knew right then that I was suppose to help people with my spiritual abilities and insight.

Right then and there I knew I wanted to start doing radio shows; taking calls and helping people. I became a guest psychic on many radio shows across America. Since my crazy look was working for me already, I kept it. I soon became known as the psychic with the crazy white hair who dresses in all white. For about two years, I had my own radio show in Tampa, Florida until the station was sold and they canceled all the programming. I eventually started doing TV interviews and talk shows and, of course, I kept the look, but not without a challenge. Every TV producer and director I've ever worked with told me the same thing, "No one will ever take you seriously with that over-the-top, eccentric look." Sometimes the producers and directors would make me doubt my look. It did seem like a huge hurdle for people to get over when they first meet me. Every time I had the slightest doubt about my look, I would ask my Angels what they thought. They were always quick to respond in a loud voice "NO, DO NOT CHANGE YOUR LOOK!" Then they would say, "Everything is perfect and you are about to mess everything up by letting other people's opinions influence you." They explained to me that, even my look is part of God's perfect plan. I always respond by saying, "Ya'll are the Angels and I'm only human, I'm sure ya'll know what's best for me." They would smile and chuckle saying, "How would we recognize you, my 'Wooly Lamb.'" It was nice to know that I could entertain my Angels by looking like a lamb to them.

Doing radio and TV lead me into doing private sessions with people where I could help them with any problem they may have. This is where my Angels came in handy because they would always tell me how to help the person I was working with so that I could resolve their problems.

I knew I was doing what I was suppose to do, but the one thing that still bothered me more than anything was my vision of the key fitting into the earth. Every time I asked my Angels about this, they would always tell me the same thing, "It's not time for you to understand."

The Visit...

And so it was that, when I was in my mid thirties, I was lying down meditating when, suddenly; I saw all of these Angels that I hadn't seen before. They gathered around me in a circle. They were looking at me and saying, "Are you sure that's him? Why doesn't he look like the rest of them? Why is he so different? Do you think we made a mistake?"

Then I heard another voice. I remembered this voice from the trances I experienced as a child. It was the *bright light* being. He told the Angels, "No mistake. He has the keys; they are inside of him."

All of the Angels stepped aside while this being came in and introduced himself as God. I was in disbelief because, even though I remember seeing this *bright light* being throughout my whole life, I wasn't sure of this whole God situation. I mean, in a religious sense, I was sure there must be a God: It made sense that there was some supreme power to control everything. I was always able to see Angels, so I was thinking to myself, why wouldn't God exist? I'll admit that seeing God freaked me out a little because I never thought that, if He did exist, He would visit me. But there He was.

One of the first things He said was, "I see you listened to the Angels and kept your look my wooly lamb." I began laughing because I realized God had a great sense of humor. At this point in my life, I now realize God has a plan for everyone and, if His plan calls for me to have white wooly hair and dress in all white, then that is what I'm going to do.

In the years following my first visit from God, He taught me many secrets about spiritually and how the spiritual world directly relates to and affects us here in the physical world. I used all of the information He taught me in my private sessions with people so I could sharpen my skills. Every time God taught me something new, I used it to help people. He taught me how to receive spiritual gifts, how to heal people from physical, mental and emotional illness, how to visit heaven and teach others to visit heaven. He taught me how to teach someone to talk with Him, see Him, and hear Him and much more.

Everything God taught me is in this book and I will teach you.

I was able to ask God questions about anything. One of the first questions I asked him was about the recurring vision that I had from my childhood and throughout my entire adult life. The vision of this key fitting into the earth and a blanket of gold energy removing the darkness was forever imprinted in my mind. His answer was, "I will reveal the meaning of your vision when it is time. Now is not the time. I will tell you this about your vision: it pertains to every man, woman and child on earth."

I often thought God would get impatient and tired of answering questions for me, but He never has. God has taught me many spiritual secrets and given me many messages that He wants me to pass on to the rest of the world.

God Speaks…

God said that He has much to teach about true spirituality and the spiritual world that exists around all of us. God wants everyone to awaken their spiritual body and release their spiritual knowledge that's locked up inside each and everyone of us. He also wants everyone to be aware that there's a spiritual war of Good verses Evil going on around us each and every day.

God said, "Look at what the Demons have done to religion throughout history—making man fight and kill in the name of religion."

God said that He doesn't like it that different religions are fighting over whose beliefs are right or wrong, and that people are dying over religious beliefs.

God said, "In the beginning, it was simple: Everyone had one belief." It was in Him and His divine goodness. As time progressed, the true meaning of religion was diluted because of the Demons and dark energies that possessed the minds of man and turned their egos against one another and made them turn religion into the mess it is today.

God wants everyone to know that they have free will to do and believe in whatever they want to believe in, but this same free will is also mankind's vulnerable point. It is free will that the Demons and dark energies infect and attack, turning people and nations against one another.

God said, "Demons and dark energies have been affecting man's decisions for many generations. Every generation is shaped by the previous generation and your generation will shape generations to follow." He also said that now is the time for everyone to start believing in Him and not in the stories passed down from generation to generation. The true meaning of many of these stories has been influenced by Demons and dark energies. Believe in the firsthand knowledge you can get by communicating directly with Him.

With God working directly through me, I have put together this book so that you can discover what God wants you to know firsthand through your own eyes and ears.

If you want to learn the spiritual secrets God shared with me, then please continue reading. It will change your life and enlighten you.

By Permission of the British Library
Figure of an Angel
Royal 19 C. I f. 204v

ANGELS

AND HOW THEY AFFECT US

ANGELS!
Who are they? What do they do? How many are there? Does everyone have Angels?

As I travel from place to place, people from all walks of life and different religions always ask my opinion and question me about Angels. When God said that He wanted me to write the first chapter about Angels, I thought to myself, what an appropriate chapter to begin with.

Many cultures from all over the world and for thousands of years have believed in Angels. Angels are written about in many religious texts around the world including *The Bible* (Christianity), *Zohar* (Judaism), *Quran* (Islamic), *The Vedas* (Hinduism), *The Dhammapada* (Buddhism), *Tang Shi* (Confucianism), *The Book of Mormon: Another Testament of Jesus Christ* (Mormonism).

Angels are written about in many other spiritual texts such as *The Book of Enoch the Prophet* (one of the "Lost Books" of the Bible found in an Ethiopian Monastery), and *The Dead Sea Scrolls.* You can also go to a bookstore and buy hundreds of books written about Angels. Some show you how to receive messages from your Angels, some show you how to figure out your Angel's name and some even list all of the names of Angels. Many people are confused about Angels and what to believe about them. With all of these books talking about Angels, how do you know what's correct and what's not?

Ever since I was a small boy, I was always able to communicate directly with Angels. I don't know what it would feel like not to be able to ask Angels questions. They have always been there for me, especially when I need their divine guidance or just a friend to talk with. Believe me, there were many times in my life when I would have made the wrong decision without help from above.

I will teach you how to get in contact with your Angels and always have their guidance when you need it. I will teach you how to communicate (see, hear and talk) with God and Angels, so that you will be able to ask them any question that you may have.

Now, concerning all those questions people ask me about Angels: I thought that since God is helping me write this book, who better to ask? So I asked Him to answer the same questions I am asked.

What follows are some of the many questions I'm asked. Remember, there are many more questions you may have. I will teach you how to see, hear and talk to God and Angels so you can ask them your questions.

Question and Answers

Q) Gary: What are Angels?

A) God: Angels are beings of light created by me from my energy and they help protect heaven and all God planets from Demon and dark energy attacks. They also help guide souls to enlightenment.

Q) Gary: Angels come from you?

A) God: As I said, Angels were created by me; they were created with my energy. In the beginning, I used my energy to create all Angels. Then I gave the Angels the power to reproduce.

Q) Gary: Angels can reproduce?

A) God: Angels do not give birth like humans. They reproduce themselves, first by removing part of their energy field that makes up their spiritual being. They bring this part of their energy to me and they tell me why they need to reproduce. They don't reproduce because they feel an urge like women and men on earth. Their reproduction is mainly for the protection of heaven and other God planets such as earth. You see, the more people there are on earth and on other planets, the more Angels we need to protect and keep watch over people. Reproduction in heaven is nothing like on earth. When an Angel removes part of his energy from himself, that piece of energy makes up the life of the new Angel to be created by me: Just like the way I used my energy to reproduce Angels in the beginning. Reproduction is instant. Once the Angel tells me why they need to reproduce, I grant them permission and the new Angel appears instantly. All Angels have the right to reproduce, but they only reproduce when it is absolute necessary. There's one thing you should know, all Angels are united as one in heaven, so there is no such thing as parental feelings toward the Angel they helped create. All Angels feel the same toward each other. Angels live in heaven and their purpose is to help protect heaven and other God planets and guide everyone's spiritual body to enlightenment.

Q) Gary: How many Angels are there?

A) God: Every spiritual being on every God planet throughout creation has thousands of Angels watching over and protecting them.

Q) Gary: How big is creation?

A) God: No one would ever be able to conceive in their mind the size of creation.

Q) Gary: Are Angels born into human form?

A) God: No, Angels are not born into human form. People whom you think may be an Angel in the human form are actually just human souls that have reached enlightenment (awakened their spiritual bodies before dying) and have decided to return back to earth to live again and guide others to enlightenment. Once someone has reached enlightenment, then it is their decision to return to earth and guide others to enlightenment. Until you reach enlightenment, you will return over and over again—living lifetime after lifetime—until enlightenment is reached. On your path to enlightenment, there will always be Angels there to help guide you.

Q) Gary: Are Angels women or men?

A) God: Some people see them as women and some as men. They appear to you in whatever form you feel more comfortable seeing them in.

Q) Gary: Have Angels ever crossed into the physical dimension?

A) God: Do you mean in their Angelic body or in their human body?

Q) Gary: Angels have an Angelic and human body?

A) God: Yes, their Angelic body is the body everyone sees when they present themselves to you. When they need to appear on earth without drawing attention to themselves, they can take on human form and look like anyone on earth.

Q) Gary: Well, have they crossed in either body?

A) God: Yes, to both. Angels will cross into the physical dimension from time to time when it's absolutely necessary. Many times people catch glimpses of Angels while they are in their Angelic form and these are the sightings people talk about. But when they cross in a physical form, no one ever knows the Angel was there. He could be the person on the street asking for food or a stranger asking for directions, but they are always there for a reason. I'm sure many people have come in contact with one of my Angels without realizing it. The way you can tell if you came in contact with an Angel is if you can't stop thinking about that person: that's the effect an Angel has on you.

Q) Gary: What do Angels do, I mean what are their jobs?

A) God: There are different Angelic categories, so depending on what category they're in, depends on what their job is.

Q) Gary: What are the different categories? And who assigns them?

A) God: In the beginning I assigned them. Now, they're assigned to the same category from which the Angel who reproduces them is from. There are different categories of Angels, all with different jobs to do. These categories of Angels are:

ARCHANGELS

These are the most powerful of Angels. They were created with all of my powers and abilities. They stand guard over heaven and protect it from Demons and dark energies that are always ready to attack. They also watch over earth and other God planets to help keep the Demons and dark energies from attacking. The Archangels control all of the armies of heaven; they are in charge of all of the battles that are fought and they only answer to me (God).

WARRIOR ANGELS

These Angels are heaven's soldiers and they answer directly to the Archangels. Their main purpose is to protect heaven and other God planets from Demons. These Angels do not have all of my powers, but are the second strongest.

PEACEKEEPER ANGELS

The Peacekeeper's job is to try to keep peace between heaven and Demons in the universe. The Peacekeeper's job is to go out into any part of the universe where Demons are attacking God planets and interfering with the light beings (people) on that planet. The Peacekeepers are always the first to arrive. They give a warning not to interfere with any light beings on the planet. If the Demons do not comply, then the Peacekeepers will inform the Archangels and the ArchAngels will wage a war against them.

I want everyone to be aware that all of the battles going on throughout the universe are because the Demons are trying to possess and keep dark as many light beings as possible. Light beings exist on many planets; everyone on earth is a light being. Demons are afraid of light beings awakening their spiritual bodies; because, once a light being awakens their spiritual body, they have more power than the Demons. There is always a continuous battle for earth. The Demons are trying to keep everyone on earth dark and possessed while I (God) want everyone on earth to awaken their spiritual body and become the light being they are meant to be. There can be only one winner— Demons or Light Beings (You).

HELPER ANGELS

Helper Angels are not what you might think of as a helper (someone running around getting things for you). Helper Angels are the Angels that keep heaven running. They take care of all the various jobs there are in heaven. For example, one of their jobs is to take care of people's souls after they die. They assist these souls through their transition so they can get adjusted to their new life after death. Another job of a Helper Angel is to meet the soul at heaven's gates and show them around. There are many jobs in heaven and they all have a major function in keeping all of creation running smooth.

Q) Gary: What about Guardian Angels?

A) God: Guardian Angels fall under the category of Helper Angels. A Guardian Angel's job is to watch out for the people on earth and try to guide them to enlightenment and also keep them out of harm's way while on earth. Remember, there's always a battle between good and evil or Angels and Demons, and your Guardian Angels are there to help protect you. They help guide you to awakening your spiritual body, plus they also help you accomplish your dreams and goals while in your human form on earth.

These are only a few of the questions I asked God about Angels. I know that every one of you have questions. As you learn, in the chapters ahead, how to talk to God, you will be able to ask him any questions you may have.

> *"It is said that Joan of Arc started hearing voices at the age of thirteen and a half years old and these voices guided her into her military career. The voices were then accompanied by a great light. She acknowledged the voices as those of St. Michael and other Angels. When Joan was going on her first campaign, St Michael told her of a sword buried behind the altar in the chapel of St. Catherine-de-Fierbois and that sword is the sword she should use. The sword was found exactly where St. Michael told her it was."*

I would like to share with you a testimonial from Brad Davis, an attorney who got a little help from a Guardian Angel just when he needed it. This story has two parts.

Testimonial by Brad Davis

Part One: The First Time

Dear Gary:

I just wanted to drop you a note to tell you how much I appreciated the opportunity to have spent time with you and attend your spiritual retreat. I can honestly tell you that, when I traveled out to Ojai California, I did not know exactly what to expect and, based on my education and background, I felt like I would have to witness something on my own to fully understand the overall scheme of things. Lucky for me I met others who apparently have the same type of background as I, and I could see that they had the same skepticism. I knew that there was more to spiritually than what I was fully aware of and I had the impression that this weekend would open the door to a lot of new areas for me. I was not disappointed.

Before the retreat began on Saturday, I felt a bit out of place, having never meditated not even having an idea on how to meditate, which I felt put me at somewhat of a disadvantage. I felt that I may have some skills, but I have never exercised them and, therefore, I was just unable to see what a number of the other participants did. Since the retreat, I have been trying to meditate for at least a short period of time everyday with the hopes that things would open up for me, as well. The most difficult part for me is to relax and allow it to happen as opposed to trying harder and harder to make it happen, which I am sure makes it even that much more difficult. I look forward to spending time with you in the future.
Your friend,
Brad

Part Two: Angel Help

Dear Gary,

Over the period of time that we have been in contact, I have concentrated on meditating and hearing my Angels; communicating with them periodically. I thought you might find what happened to me recently somewhat interesting, considering the environment in which it occurred.

I was hired to defend a homeowner whose daycare nurse had allegedly slipped and fallen off his back porch, injuring her finger. I felt, after the initial investigation into this matter, that her credibility was somewhat low, but I did not have a definite course of action in which to positively win the case. I met with my client and got his version of the facts, but, unfortunately, shortly before the trial, he passed away under somewhat unusual circumstances. It appears that the plaintiff (the nurse) in this matter, who was still caring for him as the case was pending trial, had mistakenly or neglectfully caused his medication to fluctuate, and he died. There was insufficient evidence to show that she actually tried to kill him, but there was quite a bit of evidence developed during the pretrial phase to indicate that she was trying to use the best efforts she could to get him to give her the house and, in fact, before he died, he had been to his lawyer to change the will. Based on these facts, I not only wanted to do well for my client, but I wanted to make sure she got nothing.

I was well prepared for trial and prepared to try the case before a jury. On the day of the trial, midway during the plaintiff's case as she was testifying, I began to hear my Angels and get the same sensation I get when I'm meditating; however, this was actually in the courtroom in the middle of the trial. Although I felt like this was not the time to be diverted, I listened to what my Angels had to say. They told me that I needed to show two Polaroid pictures that I had in my possession that the plaintiff had given to my client before he died. The pictures allegedly show the way the porch was before and after she fell. Against what I considered was my better judgment, but listening to the Angels, instead, I pulled those photographs out and reviewed them while she was testifying. I noticed something about the pictures that I hadn't noticed before. They showed the rug and chair in one position on one photo and, on the other photo, the rug and chair wasn't there. I was convinced that she would testify that the pictures were taken at the same time which, based on the photographs themselves, would have been impossible because of the chair and rug being on one photo and not the other. Nevertheless, I went against my lawyer logic and did what the Angels told me to do.

She was extremely cocky and really playing it up for the jury. When I asked her about the first photograph, she identified it. I asked her about the second photograph, if it was taken at the same time. She smiled and looked at the jury saying, "Of course, you know that it could not have been taken at the same time because a Polaroid can only take one picture at a time." It was pretty obvious the type of attitude she had and I apologized for my error and asked if they were taken within a period of about thirty seconds. She acknowledged that they were. I continued that line of questioning for the next five to ten minutes, pinning her down tighter and tighter to her answer. Finally, I asked her how the chair and rug had gotten onto the second photograph if it wasn't on the first photograph.

It was blatantly obvious to me and apparent to everyone else that she was caught dead in a lie. The silence in the courtroom was almost scary as she paused, trying to collect herself to come up with another lie to help cover statements. I swear at that time I heard someone in my head say, "Gotcha!" I continued my cross examination for a few more minutes, but I felt, at that time, I had proven, thanks to a little help from my Angels, that she was clearly lying and I felt no reason to give her a chance to rehabilitate herself. After the presentation of my evidence, the jury went out and came back in a rather quick period of time, giving us a defense verdict.

Although I prepared very well for trial, I have got to thank my Angels for their assistance. Because of them, I got to clearly catch her in a lie that she couldn't talk her way out of, which was instrumental in obtaining the defense verdict. I thought you might find the use of my "co-council" interesting.
Your Friend,
Brad

Brad was very skeptical in the beginning, just as you may be, but he knew there was more than just this physical life we have. With a little dedication on his part, I was able to teach him how to communicate with his Angels.

This is just one example of how Angels can help you in your everyday life. If it weren't for Brad's Angels, he may not have won this case. Life is always a little easier with Angels on your side.

William Bouguereau (1825-1905), The Virgin with Angels, 1900
Musee du Petit Palais, Paris
Photograph by Hubert Josse

Angels are in every aspect of our lives, from the time we're born until the time of our death. They are always with us; guiding us and helping us.

I would like to share with you another quick story of a Helper Angel at work. This one pertains to me.

In July of 2004, Dean, one of the people who works for me, came to work and handed me an *Architectural Digest Magazine*. He told me that his Angels had told him to stop at a newsstand and buy it for me. At the time, I said, thanks, but really couldn't figure out why the Angels wanted me to have an *Architectural Digest Magazine*. I asked my Angels and they said, "You'll see." Over the next few months, there were many times I would run across this magazine and think of throwing it away. Every time I thought about it, my Angels would say, "Don't throw it away, just keep it." So I would just put it back in the stack of magazines.

In October of 2004, a young lady who worked for me as my housekeeper, informed me she was going back to college and I had to replace her. In November of 2004, I hired another lady to take her place. A couple months later, in January of 2005, I walked into a room that she was cleaning and there she sat on the floor looking at the *Architectural Digest Magazine*. She looked up at me and asked if she could please have this magazine. At that time, my Angels said to me, "Give it to her, but ask her why." So I said "Yes, you can have it, but why do you want it?" She started to explain to me that the house on the front cover was a house she used to clean and take care of, but when the magazine came out she could not find it on the newsstand anywhere.

Then it all made sense why the magazine came to me: The Angels knew ahead of time that the young lady working for me was going back to college and I was going to hire the lady that I did. The magazine was really for her—not me!

My Angels started laughing and said, "That's what we do: If people could just learn to pay attention to us, we could help them more." I teach everyone around me to communicate with their Angels and they really pay attention to them. If it wasn't for Dean paying attention to his Angels, he would not have bought the magazine in the first place and, if I would not have paid attention to my Angels, I would have thrown it away and my housekeeper would not have received her magazine.

Angels work in many mysterious ways. Just think, if they can get a magazine to someone or help an attorney win a court case then what can they bring to you? Angels are always working to help you, you just need to learn how to see, hear and talk to them. I can guarantee you that your life will be much easier with the help of your Angels. As human beings, we can't see everything our Angels see, so why not listen to them? They really do know what's best for us.

Manifesting...

One of the questions I get asked most often is, "How can I manifest my dreams and desires?" Well, it's very simple. First, you must know exactly what it is that you dream or desire. Second, your dreams and desires must have a vibration of truth, honesty, love and selflessness. What you're manifesting must not only benefit or help you, it must benefit and help others. Thirdly, when your dreams and desires are coming from a vibration of truth, honesty, love, selflessness and they benefit others as well as yourself, you just have to ask your Angels and they will bring your dreams and desires to you.

Later in the book, when I teach you how to see, hear and talk to your Angels, you will be able to ask your Angels to bring to you your dreams and desires. You will see many different Angels. Ask to see your Helper Angels and they will appear to you holding a golden notepad. Tell this Angel what it is you're trying to accomplish. You will then see them write it on the notepad. After they write it down, they will leave. At this point, they will align everything in the spiritual dimensions so that you may have your dreams and desires come true in the physical dimensions.

This is a testimonial from someone who manifested their dreams and desires.

Testimonial by Chris Donato

My name is Chris Donato. I met Gary Spivey December 1990. I met Gary by chance, or was it? At the time, my sister lived in Florida and went for a psychic reading from Gary. In her reading, he picked up on my energy and told her that I was spiritually gifted and he wanted to read me the next time I was in town. He showed me how to meditate and how to work with my own energies. Meditation allowed me to focus on life's important questions and answers. At a young age, I felt I had an extrasensory awareness. I knew things before they manifested. As time went on, I developed my awareness of the universal life force energy that connects us from physical to spiritual levels.

Every time Gary learned a new meditation, he would share it with me. The most important thing was when he showed me how to connect and communicate with God and my Angels. In meditating, God and my Angels would give me answers to my questions. The tough part is to know what question to ask because the answers come so quickly and easily. The answers to my questions would come in many ways. For example, sometimes I would hear the answer. Sometime I would see it like a slideshow or TV in my head. Many times something in the physical world would draw my attention to physically see a sign that would give me a hint to my answer.

My Angels and God lead me to the right place at the right time as long as I am willing to talk and listen to them. This has been so for all of my life decisions, at least when I paid attention. The latest life decision is a good example. As a dentist of ten years, I was recently searching for a dental practice to purchase. I worked for many years and was ready for my own practice, so I meditated on where to look. I asked my Angels to help. My Angels showed me an area map of where I lived in Florida and the surrounding cities. They told me that Tampa was the city where I would buy my business. A few days later, I ran into an old colleague whom I hadn't seen in years. I told him what I was looking for. He put me in touch with someone who introduced me to an older dentist looking to sell his practice. The practice consisted of special needs/mentally challenged patients. Special needs patients sometimes have greater needs and can be even more demanding than in a normal practice, so I felt Angelically led to help them. The place and time felt very right. My Angels showed me a tree with money and love—not just one, but an orchard. Since the purchase of my practice, I have been very successful and expansion is occurring.

Currently, I have a beautiful wife and three fantastic children. I share with them everything Gary has shown me and I teach them about their own ability to talk with God and Angels. Each of my children have their own talents. In time, they will realize their potential. It is amazing to see the world through the eyes of a child because there is a lot of magic. I would say that if people want to feel the vibrant energy within, then they should watch how a child experiences things. I personally don't think I've ever stopped being a kid. Everyone has the ability to communicate with God and the Angels. You just need to be shown how.

Thank you Gary.
Your Friend,
Chris

As you can see, the Angels brought to Chris the perfect dental practice when he truly desired it. All he had to do was ask his Angels for help. That is how easy it is to manifest what you truly desire.

This next testimonial is from Brad Davis Jr. At the beginning of this chapter, you read a testimonial from his dad, Brad Davis Sr., telling how his Angels helped him win a court case. Brad Sr., after attending my spiritual retreats, taught Brad Jr. what he had learned about God, Angels and the spiritual world around him which made Brad Jr. interested in learning more. Here is Brad Jr's. testimonial.

Testimonial by Brad Davis Jr.

I first met Gary Spivey just after my 18th birthday in January 2001, although he had touched my life a few years before that. I've always known things were a little bit different. When I was 16, I had a deep feeling that something awful was about to happen—to be more specific, that I was going to die. This is not exactly something most 16- year-olds think about. I had told my girlfriend at the time about it, and she couldn't figure it out either. I was happy, I was in a good home, there were no problems in school or life. I had what some would say to be a perfect life in everyway, except for the pronounced feeling that I was about to die.

My father had heard Gary on a local radio show and decided to call in to set up a reading for some fun. His first reading went over pretty well. Gary channeled his dead grandmother for him and, later in the reading asked if one of his son's drove a black SUV. Dad said "Yes". At the time, I was driving a Jeep Wrangler. Gary had seen me slide on black-ice into an on-coming truck—a fatal crash. My dad, not quite sure how to tell me this, sat me down a few days later just before I got ready to go on a ski trip and told me to drive very carefully. I asked why, and he told me I was going to be in a life altering accident. Two days later, I sat down with him again and asked if it wasn't going to be life altering, it was going to be fatal.

We had a freak ice storm that Sunday night and my father and I both agreed I shouldn't drive anywhere. The next week he called Gary back while he was on the radio and asked if I had made it past that fatal accident in my near future. Gary replied, "Yes, he'll be fine." Thanks to Gary's vision, I was able to avoid that fatal accident. And I also found a person who could help me unlock my own spiritual gifts.

Throughout the next few years, my father and I grew closer and closer with Gary. He would have readings with Gary about once every six months and would let me speak with him for the last five or ten minutes. When Gary started offering spiritual retreats, I was unable to go because I was attending school, although my father went and was able to come home and explain Angels, Demons, and Spiritual Dimensions to me.

I went to my first spiritual retreat the summer of 2004, and my life hasn't been the same since. I learned how to see dimensionally, how to clear my God Cord and all of my energy. I also met a new friend in the spiritual dimension, St Germain. After the retreat, I returned to Richmond, VA; back to my everyday life equipped with the spiritual tools I needed to help protect my friends and family. I lasted about a good three months before I was so completely blocked that I didn't know where to start clearing myself; my dad lasted about a month. Just skipping one day of meditating is seriously detrimental to your spiritual well being, a lesson that I continue to struggle with on a daily basis.

In early October of 2004, I decided that we needed to go out to see Gary for Halloween. I asked my dad about it and he said there was no way he was going. He said, "It costs way too much to fly all the way out there, especially for one weekend, and you don't even know if he'll be there." I worked on him for about another week or so trying to get him to agree to a trip, but his answer was still "NO!" I looked him in the eye and said "Fine then, I'm going to find a way to get us to the west coast for free!" He said, "Well you do that. You get us out there for free and I'll go see Gary."

At the same time, unknown to me, a local rock radio station was giving away two tickets to go see a promotional Halloween concert in Los Angeles: airfare, hotel and tickets to the show. I heard about it the next day on the radio, which also happened to be the last day to enter the drawing. In order to enter, you had to be the tenth caller whenever you heard the promo on the radio. I listened for the promo and called in. As I was dialing the buttons on my phone I said, "I am going to win this trip." At that point, I felt it. The only thing I can compare it to is a lightening bolt; it was so sure and so fast. The phone rang, the DJ picked up and I was the tenth caller. I had filled the fifteenth spot—a one in fifteen chance to fly to Los Angeles. At that point, I knew it was all over, I wasn't sure what I had done, but I knew it was over. I immediately took some time to lay down for a few minutes to go see God. When I saw him in heaven, he pointed down. I looked and I could see my name in the DJ's hand lit up in gold. I looked back at God and said, "It's really over isn't it?" He said, "Yes." I went on with my day. I had a friend flying in from Atlanta at 4:30— the drawing for the name wasn't until 5. I picked him up and told him about how my dad and I were heading out to Los Angeles for Halloween. About forty-five minutes later, the DJ called to let me know that I had won.

Now I use manifestation in everything I do. I currently work as a realtor. I bought my house when I was 21 years old; I'm now 22. I've owned the house for one year. It was the first house I listed and my friends and family had been hounding me for months to get it on the market. In early summer, I told my mom and dad not to worry about it, I talked to my Angels and they said I was going to sell the house in three days. I finally listed it in November; not a good time to sell a house. It was on the MLS system for three days and was posted on the market for twenty-five hours before I had a full price contract. I made a profit of $85,000.

Most recently, I was shown a foreclosure listing by my Angels in the local paper. I normally look at the foreclosures, but this particular one happened to be a *little out of our (my father and my) price range. The amount due on the note was $445K. Even though I knew it was pretty pricey, I called Dad at work to find out how much money he could come up with in about two weeks. He said he could do half and would see what he could do to come up with a partner. He spoke with a friend and we were in. The day of the auction came. I went to the courthouse to meet his partner and I could see that the house was already ours. The attorney representing the lender was holding the paperwork and it was completely lit up in gold. I looked over at our partner and both he and I were completely covered in gold light. We bought the house for the price we NEEDED to get it for. I continue to use my Angels and God's Light to guide me on a daily basis.*

Much Light and Love,

Brad Jr.

As I said before, to manifest your true dreams and desires, all you have to do is ask your Angels for their help and, just like magic, they will manifest before your eyes.

In life, there is always an opposite of something. The opposite of happy is sad, good is bad, up is down, black is white and the opposite of Angels is Demons. In the next chapter, you will discover just how much Demons affect every part of our lives in a negative way and what you can do to get rid of them.

Saint Anthony being tormented by Demons
The Metropolitan Museum of Art, New York
Rogers Fund, 1920. (20.5.2)

DEMONS
AND HOW THEY AFFECT US

Deaf and Dumb Demon (Mark 9:25)

"When Jesus saw the crowd growing he rebuked the Demon 'O Demon of deafness and dumbness,' he said 'I command you to come out of this child and enter him no more.'"

Blind and Mute Demon (Matthew 12:22)

"Then a Demon-possessed man—he was both blind and unable to talk—was brought to Jesus, and Jesus healed him so that he could both speak and see."

What are Demons? How do they affect us? Does everyone have Demons? How can we get rid of them? What do they look like?

As I travel from place to place, people always ask my opinion or ask me questions about Angels. But now that everyone is becoming more aware of Demons, I find I'm being asked my opinion or questions about Demons, as well.

Different religions from all over the world believe that Demons do exist, but they don't teach or show people how to get rid of them. This is not because they don't want to, it's because throughout history people have been programmed to think that only certain members of their church or religion could get rid of Demons. This is not true. Everyone has the power within themselves to remove and banish the Demons and dark energies affecting their lives, the lives of loved ones and even strangers. This power comes from the spiritual body within; it simply needs to be awakened and released. Getting rid of or banishing Demons and dark energies is a spiritual secret that will be revealed to you within this book.

Everyone probably has as many questions about Demons as they do about Angels so I had a conversation with God about Demons, just as I had about Angels. I will share with you the questions and answers from that conversation.

When I reveal the spiritual secret of how to see, hear and talk to God, you will be able to sit and talk to him for hours asking him any questions you may have about Demons, Angels, things going on in your life or the life of people you know. I want you to realize that everyone on earth has the capability to see, hear and talk directly with God.

I'm not asking you to blindly believe everything that's in this book; these are my opinions from my life's work and from me talking to God and Angels. I want you to learn how to communicate with God and Angels so that you can ask them your questions and find your truth for yourself. One day God or Angels may reveal to you a spiritual secret that you can teach me and the rest of the world, so that we may all benefit from their knowledge.

God said, "Many people don't want to hear about Demons because they are scared of them or in denial that they really do exist." Don't be aloof and bury your head in the sand just because you don't understand Demons. I will show you that we all have Demons affecting us in some part of our lives. However, pretending that Demons don't exist, ensures they will continue to cause havoc in your life by keeping you spiritually darkened down and keeping your spiritual body from being awakened. This also ensures that whatever trick they are playing on you guarantees them victory over you every time.

Questions and Answers

Q) Gary: What are Demons?

A) God: When Angels were created, they were created in my likeness. I gave them free will to obey the laws of heaven. As time progressed, many of the Angels grew tired of following the laws and they challenged me. The Angels, who challenged me, were cast out of heaven not to be in my graces ever again. They were doomed to exist in the spiritual dimensions between heaven and other enlightened planets. The exiled Angels became what is written about and painted in art throughout history and what is known to man as Demons. Once these Angels were exiled from heaven, they started causing havoc on all enlightened planets trying to block heaven's energy from reaching the spiritual beings living on that planet. They managed to totally extinguish the light on some of the planets and dim the light on others. Earth is one of planets that is dim. But now it is the dawn of a new spiritual awakening on earth and the spiritual beings on earth will have the power to fight back and awaken their spiritual bodies so they can banish the Demons from earth.

Because the Demons didn't have any laws to follow after their exile from heaven, they managed to cause tremendous havoc on earth by possessing the minds and bodies of mankind. This is why it's time for mankind to fight back by awakening their spiritual bodies and taking back what's rightfully theirs, their mind and their physical and spiritual bodies.

It didn't take long for the Demons to realize they had the power to reproduce themselves, just as in heaven, all they had to do was remove a part of their energy and bring it to the head Angel (Demon) and they would reproduce it. They reproduced just to do it, not because there was a need and soon they outnumbered the Angels in heaven. Demons want to possess everyone on earth and I just want everyone to live on earth as in heaven.

Can the Devil Multiply? Grave question in the 15th Century!
This monster being a possible result, Popular etching

In the beginning, the fallen Angels had the same powers as the Angels in heaven, but the more they reproduced on earth, the weaker they became. One side effect of reproducing on earth is that the more they reproduce, the weaker and stupider the offspring became, but this didn't stop them from reproducing; each offspring, the further it extends out from the original source, the more it took on Demonic features. This is why some Demons are stronger than others. Today, they still reproduce and they just become dumber and dumber and weaker and weaker.

Q) Gary: Is everyone affected by Demons?

A) God: Every man, woman and child. There are no exceptions. If someone thinks Demons don't affect them in some area of their life, then they're wrong. For many thousands of years, the Demons were winning the war on earth but now it's time for you to awaken your spiritual body and do your part to help the Angels win this war. The Demons have always possessed the minds of man throughout time, thus the true meaning of the spiritual war going on between Angels and Demons was not put into spiritual doctrines. Demons would possess the minds of men while they were writing the spiritual text, making them think people wouldn't understand the true meanings of what's really going on in the spiritual world. Many teachings were not put into spiritual text. They are lost forever. The parts left out or edited out are the secrets you need to know in order to defend yourself and win this war. Everyone is engaged in this war—old and young alike. Everyone needs to awaken their spiritual body and start fighting for freedom. The Demons are trying to keep everyone suppressed to a spiritual awakening and I want everyone to become spiritually awakened.

I gave everyone free will to choose what they want to believe in or not believe in. You choose what side to fight on. By not fighting, you're joining the Demons side by default.

Q) Gary: How do they affect us?

A) God: They cause havoc in every aspect of your physical, mental, emotional and spiritual body. They attack your spiritual body which, in turn, affects your physical body. Every illness physically, mentally or emotionally is the result of thousands of years of Demons having their way with you. The physical body and the spiritual body was meant to join together as one and everything that was possible in heaven was supposed to be possible on earth. Before Demons (Angels) were exiled from heaven and began inhabiting the spiritual dimensions around earth, there was no such thing as illness within the physical body, mind or spiritual body. As you already know, people's bodies and minds have many illnesses. The Demons can cause major illness in the body, such as cancer or in the mind, such as depression. They affect every aspect of everyone's lives. They can cause someone to commit suicide or just get into a fight with a loved one.

Q) Gary: How do we protect ourselves?

A) God: In the beginning, when the Angels first fell, there was not much anyone could do to protect themselves, so I had to put rules into effect that the Demons were not to interfere with anything I created or my Angels would kill them.

Detail of the War in Heaven, c.1320. From The Apocalypse.
The Metropolitan Museum of Art, New York; The Cloisters Collection, 1968. (68.174 folio 20v)
Photograph, all rights reserved, The Metropolitan Museum of Art.

It wasn't long before the Demons outnumbered the Angels and began interfering with everything I created. My Angels can only kill so many; that's why it's time I show everyone how to kill Demons, themselves, so they can help the Angels fight this spiritual war. This war is for all mankind because Demons are not prejudiced. They want to possess everyone on earth and keep them spiritually darkened down. The way for you to protect yourself is to awaken your spiritual body and learn to receive spiritual gifts. These gifts will keep you safe and help you get rid of Demons. That is just the beginning. Once you learn how to get rid of Demons within, you teach others, and once they learn, have them teach others. Parents teach your children and they should teach their children. Every generation should pass this information down to the next and, one day, Demons will not exist anymore and heaven will be on earth.

Q) Gary: What do Demons look like?

A) God: Demons come in many shapes and sizes. Some are as small as a single cell in your body and others are bigger than the planet. Demons look similar to the Demons depicted in art throughout history. All Demons have one thing and one goal in common, the destruction of mankind. Do you think there would be any wars on earth if the Demons weren't here? The answer is, No. Demons make war, not mankind. Demons just possess the minds of men and turn them against each other, that's who causes wars. This is why people should learn to see spiritually so they can see the Demon that's affecting them and get rid of it.

One thing that I know from all the work I've done with people is that it's just as important to know about Demons as it is about Angels.

Growing up as a gifted child, I was always able to see Angels which made for very interesting times. But some of the most interesting times were when Demons would come into the picture. Not only could I see Angels, I could also see Demons. Throughout my childhood and early adult life, I would see Demons, but I never really understood the impact and chaos they caused on human life. As I grew older and became more and more aware of my spiritual abilities, I started realizing the affects Demons had on everyone. Every single person living on earth has a Demon in one form or another affecting them in a negative way.

Demons are the opposite of Angels. Angels are full of light. Demons are full of darkness, and their mission is to spread the darkness to as many people as they can, keeping everyone spiritually darkened down.

>   *St. Paul wrote that we:*
>
>   *"Should not let Satan take advantage of us by being ignorant of his devices."*
>
>   *2 Corinthians 2:11*
Bible

As you know, most religions teach their followers to believe in Demons in one form or another. The more I work with people, the more I learn about Demons. We all have them. They come in many different shapes and sizes, all with different functions to cause havoc in your life. There are Demons that attack us in the physical dimension—throwing things across the room, sexually assaulting people, holding people down, or just tormenting people mentally, emotionally or physically. Demons possess the minds and bodies of people, making them do horrible things such as killing someone or even killing themselves. There are Demons that attack us in the spiritual dimensions causing illness in our physical bodies. Get rid of the Demon and you can get rid of the illness.

>   *"By sunset, the courtyard was filled with sick and Demon-possessed, brought to him for healing, so Jesus healed great numbers of sick folk that evening and ordered many Demons to come out of their victims."*
>
>   *Mark 1:32-34*
The Bible

>   *"In solemn truth I tell you, anyone believing in me shall do the same miracles I have done, and even greater ones because I am going to be with the Father."*
>
>   *John 14:12*
The Bible

Just as Jesus cast out Demons from people—healing them from their illness—you can do the same. Jesus taught his disciples how to cast out Demons from people and they probably taught many people. But back then, you were looked on as a sinner or someone against the word of God and you were put to death for your healing abilities. Just look at what they did to Jesus. I'm sure that Jesus' mission was to teach everyone about God's power and reveal spiritual secrets to everyone. Because Demons possessed the minds of men and made them not believe in Jesus or even allow them to be opened-minded enough to hear him, they sentenced him to death. Just think of how great the world would be now if they would have just listened to Jesus.

I don't want anyone to think for a moment that I'm comparing myself to Jesus because I'm not. I was born with the abilities I have, and I also have the ability to teach others and that's what I want to do.

Please be open-minded enough to realize that we all have the power to get rid of the Demons that are within us.

Testimonial by Diana and Kevin

I just wanted to write and thank Gary for all the work he has done with my boyfriend, Kevin, and me. We had the opportunity to meet with Gary a few months ago when he was here in Minnesota. At the time, Kevin had been battling severe health problems that none of the doctors could diagnose. He was very ill and, in most cases, unable to work. He was suffering from asthma (which he never had before) kidney problems, aches and pains, weakness, face rash, vision loss, headaches, insomnia, fatigue. He even fell asleep driving a few times and crashed his car.

We were desperate to find answers and treatment. Of course, the many doctors he saw wanted to treat him for each individual problem and loaded him up with prescription drugs. He refused to take them, and we went to see Gary, instead.

Gary explained that what Kevin was experiencing was a spiritual crisis—he was basically possessed and doomed health-wise unless he "spiritually woke up."

Gary spent a great deal of time ridding Kevin of the Demons he had inside his body that were wreaking havoc on our lives. Gary also taught Kevin how to receive a gift to be able to kill the Demons himself.

Immediately after our session with Gary, Kevin's health improved. His energy was restored and he was as healthy as before. It was truly a miracle. A few weeks after our meeting with Gary, Kevin had a difficult time believing he was healed. He resorted back to his old reality where it didn't make sense to be perfectly well in a moment when doctors had been scaring him with another dark outcome. He began to question if his healing was real and slowly his health started to decline again. I kept reminding him that it was his responsibility to remain healthy by killing the Demons himself. Gary had given him a great gift, but he was relying on his one-time healing instead of treating himself daily to stay in his new-found state of health. It just goes to show how very powerful the mind is and how we can cling to the concrete reality that we are taught by our culture.

I reminded Kevin to pray and meditate and told him to use his spiritual gift to kill the Demons. I told him to have faith—something he never had before this. After many talks, cheer-leading sessions, and encouragement, Kevin started training himself to think differently. His health has returned again slowly day by day. This has given him more confidence in the fact that what Gary did for him and what Gary taught him was very real.

I think it is important to say that all forms of healing takes place from within and we all have to take an active roll in our own life—primarily with our thought patterns and attitudes. I'm so thankful to Gary for teaching Kevin how to heal himself. Kevin is now healthy, changing his life, changing his career, and we just became engaged. Everything is going well for us and Kevin is learning what faith is all about. He is setting a great example for his children. It's awesome that they have been able to see *their dad get better by opening up spiritually and becoming a different, better person and father.*

Thank You Gary!
We love you!!!!
Diana and Kevin

Everyone has the ability to heal themselves of physical illness: You just need to be taught and you need to believe it's possible. As in this case with Kevin, I was able to heal him of his physical problems by getting rid of the Demons that possessed him, but it was up to him to keep the Demons gone.

When I work with people, I always become more aware of how things all tie together and, no matter how bizarre the story or situation sounds, it always ends up making sense. For instance, most of us have some awareness of, when we were children, seeing monsters in our bedrooms. Our parents told us that this had to do with being afraid of the dark. They would say something like, "There's nothing that's going to get you, it's your imagination, there's nothing in there, now go back in your room and go to sleep." Well, this was partially true. While there may not have been anything in the room in the physical dimension, there were probably all kinds of Demons in the spiritual dimensions. Most kids are able to see Angels and Demons, alike. Many times, kids consider Angels their invisible playmates and Demons are considered monsters that are usually seen at night when they are going to sleep and in the alpha state—this is the in-between state right before you fall asleep.

As you may remember reading in my childhood story, I would call Angels my pals. I had no idea at that time that these guys would stay with me for the rest of my life; I never stopped seeing them and they were always there for me. Besides seeing Angels, I would always see the Demons that were trying to cause havoc in my life. Most of the time, as we get older, our practical minds take over and we quit seeing our Angels and the Demons.

There are many people who may not think or acknowledge that Demons exists, but rest assured they do exist and we all have them in one form or another. Just as Angels exist, so do Demons. People are always saying to me, "I'm very spiritual." or "I believe in God, so I know I don't have Demons." Believe me, we all have them. Some people are just tormented by them more than others, be it physically, mentally or emotionally.

What I've come to realize over years of working with people from all walks of life is that the people who are tormented the most by Demons are also the people with the brightest light or, as I refer to it, God energy—those with their spiritual body naturally already awakened like I was as a child. When I say *naturally awakened* I'm talking about being born with their spiritual body awakened, so the person didn't have the choice. There are many people who are born with their spiritual bodies already awakened and these people are the ones who get attacked by Demons—not because something is wrong with them, but because they are special and have so much God energy within them. When the Demons recognize someone with this energy, they realize that this person has the ability to kill the Demons that torment them or others. The only bad thing for that person is that they are not aware of their spiritual abilities or what's going on because society doesn't understand what's going on with them from a spiritual stand point and how it affects them mentally, emotionally or physically. As a society, we can't explain or teach these people what's happening. These people don't understand how to protect themselves from the Demons—until now that is!

There is a battle of good and evil or Angels and Demons and the battle is over our soul and our planet. By awakening your spiritual body, you are joining God's team.

I will show you how to defend yourself and others from Demons. I will teach you how to rid all Demons from your life, from the lives of those you love and even strangers. We must all join together in this battle. It's not about what your religious beliefs are. It's not about where you live, it's not about what race you are, it's about defeating the Demons that plague all mankind.

I've been talking about awakening your spiritual body and I will teach you that shortly, but I don't want anyone to fear this and think they will be attacked by Demons. When you awaken your spiritual body, you will start to become aware of the Demons that are attacking you and you will be able to rid yourself of these Demons, making your life better.

It is better to realize that Demons do exist than to live in denial.

Testimonial by Kristy M.

Hi Gary!!!

I must tell you how much better and completely different I feel from the instant you helped me!!! I went to your seminar just out of curiosity to see what I could learn and I learned a lot more than I bargained for. You were stunning me at how you were helping people and I felt comfortable enough to raise my hand. You came right over and asked me what was wrong I said, "Sometimes at night I see and hear things." Your immediate answer was, "Your Demon is sexual right??" As I grabbed onto the table so I wouldn't fall over, I got out the word, "Yes." I thought I was crazy before you answered me because I had been feeling intense energy at night which was angry and forceful with me. Then you asked me if I wanted to get rid of it or did I like it. Well, after all the laughter in the room quieted down, I said, "Yeah, I'm done with him." You began pulling it out. You were having a battle because you said he was a stubborn one and he didn't want to leave me. He kept saying that I was his girl. You said, "He's hissing and cursing at me—he really doesn't want to leave you, he's been with you for awhile." Then you said, "I almost got him… There, he is gone." The second you said, "There," my body felt one-hundred percent lighter (I never knew what that meant before to have your body feel lighter). I felt like I was floating internally for the first time ever. You also said that this was the reason I didn't have a boyfriend because this Demon would push them away as soon as they would get close. It was the most incredible feeling I've ever had and this proved that I wasn't crazy. I literally thought I was going insane hearing voices and being touched and molested by an invisible something.

Yeah, that's one to write home about. Gary, thanks so much and I'm going to start meditating and keeping this away from me.

Kristy M.

As you can see from this story, Kristy thought she was crazy because of this Demon sexually molesting her; but once I got rid of this Demon, she felt better. As I said before, Demons come in many shapes and sizes. Not everyone will have a Demon like Kristy's, but we all have them. One thing is for sure, we can all get rid of our Demons.

Now I would like to share with you another testimonial.

Testimonial of Tracy Mc Donald

I heard Gary Spivey on the radio for a couple of years now and I've always felt drawn to him. I have attempted to meditate and connect with God—a higher power, my higher self—for longer than I care to remember. Everything I have ever tried has failed. I thought it was me; I wasn't giving it my all, not teachable, etc. But a nagging little voice started me thinking that maybe I was being blocked somehow. Something was keeping me from finding the peace and serenity I'd been searching so desperately for.

I've heard Gary remove Demons from people on the radio many times. Finally, I decided to give myself a gift and I called and made an appointment with Gary. This is my story.. ...

My reading with Gary started with me asking him to check my body for Demons or entities. He started removing dark energies from my body and, as they were removed, I could feel the energy in my body shifting and changing, I was feeling lighter and very hot throughout my body.

Gary said that I had many Demons and entities blocking me from the light-not just in this dimension, but in five other dimensions, as well. He said that I was spiritually gifted and that is why these Demons attacked me-to keep me from seeing and knowing who I truly am. I have always known that I was gifted, but was never able to do anything with it. I have tried many different ways and modalities in order to feel connected to God and I've always given up, feeling defeated.

Gary saw God standing behind me. He said that God tilted my head back and poured holy water down my throat. Before Gary had uttered those words, the back of my throat got hot and I felt warmth down to my stomach. God, himself, had given me a healing!!! I then asked Gary, "Who am I?" God answered him and said "She is one of mine." I am still struggling to take it all in.

When I asked Gary about my daughter's health, Gary told me to close my eyes and look at my daughter with my spiritual eyes. I was able to see what he was seeing— dark energies swirling over my daughter's head. I saw him reverse the flow bringing bright light into it and then I saw it dissipate. I was able to see a huge Demon standing behind her, and J saw the Demon explode as Gary brought light to it. I saw him remove a snake-like entity from her throat. It, too, exploded in light.

Then we looked at my other daughter, who was lying down in her bed. A dark Demon was swirling around over her bed; he, too, exploded as Gary brought in light.

I was told by two different neurosurgeons that I needed two different surgeries on my neck. Gary saw entities there and removed them. My entire body was riddled with dark energies—all trying to keep me from the light. I now feel Angel's wings fluttering against my back. I feel surrounded by God's love and light.

Gary told me that my struggles to find and know God's love are behind me now and my future is full of bright light. All I need to do is seek God's light and know that I will find it. Not doubt it, but know it!

Tracy McDonald

"That is why I tell you, Lord that people who speak about what is invisible and hard to explain are like archers who shoot arrows at a target during the night. Of course, they shoot arrows like any other archers, since they are shooting at a target, but in this case, the target cannot be seen. When the light comes forth, however, and banishes the darkness, then what each person has done will become clear."

The Secret Teaching of Jesus
by Marvin Meyer, Random House, Inc.
The Book of Thomas
Chapter 3:1, 2, 3

Now I would like to share with you some of the many Demons that cause havoc in our lives on a daily bases. I see these Demons time and time again when I'm working on people. If you are still wondering who is affected by Demons and dark energies, the answer is simple: Start with yourself and then look at the person closest to you, and then the next person you see and the next and the next. It doesn't matter if it is a family member, friend, co-worker, or just someone you see walking down the street. Everyone is possessed by Demons. Some people want to live in denial that Demons even exist. If you are one of these people, let me suggest that, for a brief moment, you pull yourself out of denial and kill the Demon that's keeping you in denial.

Just as God said, "Demons come in many different shapes and sizes." Now I will share with you some of the many Demons I get rid of every day from people just like you and me. I am sharing these Demons with you so that you may realize that you or someone you know may have one or more of these Demons affecting them. Shortly, I will show you how to rid yourself of all Demons.

Drawing by Corey Worden, 2006

Present Moment Demon

Have you ever found yourself worrying about the past and what you have done or should have done? Or do you find yourself worrying about the future and what will or could happen? I'm not talking about just thinking about the past or future because everyone does that. I'm talking about obsessively thinking about the past and the future.

The Present Moment Demon makes you think of things from your past and makes you worry about the future at the same time. When this happens, you cannot be in the present moment enjoying your life. It disrupts your vibration and keeps you confused.

Have you ever been somewhere, but felt like you should be somewhere else? When you're with someone, do you ever feel like you should be with someone else—doing something besides what you're doing? Most people who cheat in a relationship, have this Demon.

Here's what's happening to you: This Demon is possessing the spiritual body that is within you; confusing it, making it think, "I should have, could have, would have"—making your physical body feel these same sensations. If you get rid of this Demon (and I *will* teach you how to get rid of Demons), you will feel better and you'll be in the moment and able to enjoy yourself.

In the spiritual dimension, you will see with your spiritual eyes (seeing with your spiritual eyes is another spiritual secret I will teach you.) two Demons stuck back-to-back. One is pulling your thoughts to the past and one is pulling your thoughts to the future. You will use your spiritual gifts to get rid of the Demon. (Spiritual gifts is another spiritual secret I will teach you.)

Drawing by Corey Worden, 2006
All Rights Reserved, G.S. Limited Inc, Ojai, California

Cannot Accomplish Anything Demon

Have you ever had a day, week, month or even longer when you just thought of everything that was going on in your life all at one time and you just stayed confused and not able to do anything? You felt or may feel as though you are paralyzed. When I'm working with people, this is a very common occurrence. The reason is because of a Demon that makes you think of everything you have going on in your life all at one time.

When this happens, your mind starts to race and you can't prioritize anything—making you feel stuck. You think you can't accomplish anything. When this Demon is around you, you will feel overwhelmed by everything that you have to do and you'll feel that it's better to do nothing than try anything.

All you have to do is clear your spiritual dimensions (this is another spiritual secret I will teach you shortly) and get rid of the Demon attacking your spiritual body. In the spiritual dimension, you will see with your spiritual eyes an ugly Demon-like, dragon-looking creature with multiple heads attacking your spiritual body. Each head of the Demon is thinking of something different, which makes your mind race and think of multiple things at one time.

Drawing by Corey Worden, 2006

Scared Demon

Have you ever found yourself scared for no apparent reason and you just couldn't get rid of that feeling no matter what you tried? Everyone has, at some time or another. It's just part of life. Or is it?

This Demon makes you feel scared when there is nothing really to be scared of. A couple of examples would be; talking in front of people, job interviews, talking to someone you're attracted to. Fear attacks everyone at different times and places. Not everyone has the same fear, but everyone who is feeling fear over something that they shouldn't fear has this Demon standing next to them in the spiritual dimension infecting them with his poisonous, dark energy.

In the spiritual dimension, you will see a Demon standing next to you shaking and trembling so fast it seems like a blur and slightly out of focus. Clear your spiritual dimensions and get rid of this Demon and your fear will go away.

Drawing by Corey Worden, 2006

Confusion Demon

Have you ever had trouble making a decision?

Many people have trouble making decisions about anything from what clothes to wear, what to cook for dinner, what career path to take or what car to buy, to who to date or marry. Many people suffer from indecisiveness; they can't make a decision about anything, and this torments their life.

This Demon keeps you confused; it makes you very indecisive about everything. In the spiritual dimension, you will see a Demon-like creature with multiple heads and also a head on its tail or butt. This Demon makes you feel as though you don't know which end is up. That's the reason for the head on its tail.

Clear your spiritual dimensions to get rid of this Demon and your decision-making skills will get better instantly.

Drawing by Corey Worden, 2006

Jealous, Envy and Greed Demon

Everyone has felt jealously, envy or greed at some time in their lives. This is because the Demon of Jealousy, Envy and Greed is around all of us.

This Demon makes you feel the emotions of jealousy, envy and greed toward other people and their possessions. This is a very common Demon. Any time you feel the slightest little bit of jealousy, envy or greed, you can be guaranteed that this Demon is with you.

As I said before, Demons attack your spiritual body making you feel emotions that aren't real. This Demon falls into the category of what I call, "psycho Demons." These Demons choreograph disasters. They can create such rages of jealousy within you that you just go psycho and even hurt someone else or yourself. You may even kill someone or yourself. When someone commits suicide, I always see a cluster of these Demons attacking their spiritual body.

In the spiritual dimension, you will see a Demon running back and forth between you and the person you feel these emotions toward. This Demon will be taunting and teasing you and pounding you in the chest.

All you have to do is clear your spiritual dimensions and get rid of this Demon, and the feelings will go away.

Drawing by Corey Worden, 2006

Communication Demon

Have you ever found it difficult to talk to someone and express your true feelings about something that is very important to you?

The Communication Demon makes it hard for you to express yourself through speech. It stops you from saying what's on your mind or giving your opinion on whatever the topic of discussion may be.

This is a very common Demon. Many people come to me and want to know why they feel restricted around their throat when they need to speak up. This could be in your professional or private life. If this Demon is around you, you will not be able to speak your mind—even though you should!

In the spiritual dimension, you will see a Demon holding a rope with a spiked dog collar around your throat pulling it tight. These Demons usually travel in groups of two or more.

If someone has a Communication Demon, the spiked collar is around their throat and the other end of the collar is around the Demon's throat. They will have a dark energy in their communication chakra located in their neck. At the same time, while they may have a hard time communicating in the physical dimension because of this Demon, something even more serious may be happening to them.

This Demon may be causing an illness within the neck area such as arthritis or even thyroid cancer.

Drawing by Corey Worden, 2006

Emotionally Numb Demon

Do you have or do you know someone who has absolutely no emotions toward anything, or their emotions are completely mixed up? They are sad when they should be happy or they're happy when they should feel sad.

The Emotionally Numb Demon affects your emotions, making you feel the wrong emotion at the wrong time or no emotion at all. For example, you may be in a great relationship where there is absolutely nothing wrong. You go on a romantic date, but, instead of feeling love toward this person, you're feeling not worthy, or you may hate or be irritated with this person for no apparent reason. This particular Demon makes you feel an emotion that you shouldn't feel. Some people have their emotions mixed up or they may not have feelings at all. I work with many people who find they don't have any feelings toward other people; they are completely devoid of feelings. This is the case, especially when people are taking anti-depressants or other mood altering drugs.

In the spiritual dimensions, you will see a Demon standing in front of you with a metal plate attached to its stomach. What happens is this Demon imbeds into your spiritual body causing a black energy in your stomach. Get rid of the Demon and you get rid of the black energy. Then your true feelings will shine through.

Your stomach or gut energy has to deal with your emotions. The Demons put this black energy over your stomach to block your emotions or stop you from having any feelings at all.

Drawing by Corey Worden, 2006

Obsessive Compulsive Demon

Do you or someone you know suffer from Obsessive Compulsive Disorder? This disorder is actually caused by Demons.

The Obsessive Compulsive Demons get into your head and make you think the same thought over and over and over and over again, or they make you repeat the same physical act over and over and over again, uncontrollably.

When I see these Demons with people, it's always the same: The Demons are in their head and around their body. The Demons look like little black paper doll cut-outs in the shape of Demons. They're holding hands and they wrap around the brain and the rest of the body all the way down to the toes.

This Demon is always present in everyone who has an addiction to drugs, alcohol, smoking, eating, gambling, sex or even co-dependency. It is also what I believe to be the core reason that people can't stop doing any of these hurtful things even though they try over and over again. For example, if you're a chain smoker, you will have hundreds of these little obsessive compulsive Demons on your arms and hands making you reach for a cigarette over and over again—telling you to, "smoke, smoke, smoke!" Finally, your conscious mind gives in and you smoke a cigarette again and again and again. This is true for anyone who has an addiction to anything: This Demon makes you do it over and over and over again—making you become addicted to it.

There are two things going on (1) spiritually you have these little Obsessive Compulsive Demons affecting you and (2) mentally you have a habit. Once you get rid of the Demons, the habit will be very easy to break no matter how bad it is. Usually, when I get rid of someone's Obsessive Compulsive Demons, they can break the habit within a few days and never return to their addiction again.

There are other cases of Obsessive Compulsive Disorder. A person who may circle the block four times before he pulls into his driveway or someone who has to straighten out all of the objects on her countertop before she can go to sleep at night. As I said before, clear the spiritual dimensions and get rid of these Demons around you and in you and the problem will go away.

Testimonial by Christina Auman

I was out in California in September 2004 with my three children and we went to see Gary with one of my girlfriends who had lost both of her children. My friend was having an appointment with Gary for her own personal reasons and I about mine. One of the reasons I went to see Gary was to see if he could do anything to help me stop smoking because, more than anything, I wanted to quit. I had tried everything possible to quit smoking including having most of the side effects of Zyban, which could have been fatal. I wanted nothing more than to quit by my 30th birthday. Well, today is my 30th birthday and today is my forty-first day without smoking. I just wanted to thank you, from the bottom of my heart, for what you did for me by getting rid of my Obsessive Compulsive Demons. I have not had a cigarette since my meeting with you in September.
May God Bless You.
Christina Auman

Sleepy Demon

This Demon will make you fall asleep or get extremely drowsy for no apparent reason. Many children in school have this Demon: The Demon causes the child to get very drowsy in class. They try to stay awake, but since they're trying so hard to stay awake, they can't pay attention to the teacher, and their school work suffers. This Demon also attacks when you're driving—trying to cause you to have an accident. If, for example, you have to be up early one morning for a really important meeting, this Demon may cause you to sleep through your alarm.

In the spiritual dimension, this Demon always stands next to you blowing sleepy dust in your face. The dust is a grey color and, when it's blown into your face, it creates heaviness within your whole body, especially your eye lids.

Just think, if teachers would learn to rid this Demon from their students, how their schoolwork would improve. How many children, who are diagnosed with attention deficit disorder, may not have this disorder at all?

Depression Demon

According to the World Health Organization, 121 million people worldwide suffer from depression. I've worked with people taking as many as two, three, four or more anti-depressants a day just trying to feel better. If the medical society would learn to treat depression from a spiritual standpoint, many of these people would never need any medication. If you want to feel instantly better, then just get rid of the Demon causing the dark energy in your head.

I see the spiritually-crippling effect that anti-depressant drugs have on people. If you learn to get rid of the Demon that is causing your depression, you will be able to get rid of the drugs.

In the spiritual dimension, you will see a large Demon standing behind you with his hands around your head compressing and projecting dark energy into your head. When this happens, it forces all your God light and happiness out of your head causing your depression.

Testimonial by Keith Cochrane

My name is Keith Cochrane; I'm a 36 year old man with two kids. I was in a very dark place in my life. I was at a point where I just wanted to shoot myself—my mind was cluttered with dark and depressed thoughts. Then I heard Gary on a radio show in San Francisco and thought maybe he could help me.

I talked to Gary over the phone. Gary said that, in the present, if I were to continue as I was, he saw me waking up one day and blowing my head off. He got rid of the Demons that were keeping me depressed, mummified and trying to kill me. He showed me how to look into the spiritual dimensions and receive spiritual gifts so I could get rid of the Demons myself, if they were ever to come back.

At that time, I was on 60mg of Prozac a day. I learned how to keep the Demons away and, three weeks later, I'm off the Prozac and feel great. From the time I put down the phone until now, my life has completely changed. I got more help in one phone call with Gary than all the shrinks combined.

Thank you so much Gary, you really changed my life.
Keith Cochrane

Drawing by Corey Worden, 2006

Anger/Rage Demon

Do you have a bad temper or do you lose control for no apparent reason? This Demon causes people to get mad and lose control. I'm not talking about getting mad for a good reason, for example, if your purse or wallet is stolen. I'm talking about the people who are mad at the world about everything, even when they don't have a reason to be mad. This Demon will make you get mad over nonsense things—the weather, your team loses, too much traffic, or your spouse looks at you the wrong way.

The Anger/Rage Demon makes you rage at things you can't control.

In the spiritual dimension, this Demon jumps into your physical body totally possessing and taking control of you for a while. Once this Demon gets done with you, it will leave your body and you will stop raging, but it may be too late—the damage may already be done. You may have hit a loved one, quit your job, run someone off the road in a moment of rage, killed someone, or even killed yourself. Once this Demon leaves you, it goes on to its next victim creating more havoc, leaving you behind to deal with the mess that it created.

In the spiritual dimension, you will see a Demon that's black in color with large fangs. This Demon is very intelligent and can manipulate you and others around you all at the same time—creating the perfect disaster. This Demon has pointed ears, evil eyes, sometime horns and fang teeth and it also has claw hands. When these claw hands get a hold of you, it is hard to shake loose. People, who are addicted to drugs or alcohol, are many times more susceptible to these Demons.

I know I must sound redundant at this point, but you must clear your spiritual dimensions and use your spiritual gifts (I will teach you how to receive them) to get rid of the Demon, in this Demon's case, before it gets rid of you or someone you love.

I was doing my regular once a week radio show in Las Vegas when we got a call from a listener. I sensed an importance in the DJ's voice as he said, "Gary, you've probably heard about this." I hadn't heard about it because, sometimes I'm so busy that I don't pay attention to the news. This was a horrible situation that took place in Vegas where a lady came home to the most unthinkable tragedy that could ever be. Her husband, her daughter and her nephew were all murdered. That was about all the information I had to go on and, the next thing you know, we are live on the air. With a crying and shaky voice, she began to ask me her questions as if I were an old friend and the only one who could know the true answers to them. She was desperate for these answers as her husband, her little girl and her nephew had all been ripped away from her in a single blow and for no apparent reason. As I tapped into her energy, I felt a depth of pain in my chest and it was all I could do to keep from crying.

I tried my best to comfort her and to read some sort of sanity into this horrifying tragedy that had fallen on Kimmie and her loved ones. This more than horrifying tragedy had only happened a few days before hand. This is her story:

Testimonial by Kimmie Kuivinen

My name is Kimmie Kuivinen (the mother of Johnna and wife of John). I was driving on my way home from work on 6-18-05 and called my husband, John, on the phone, who was sitting at the apartment with my daughter Johnna and his brother, Carleton, and his son, Kameryn. As we finished our conversation, he said, "I'll call you back in a minute." He didn't call back, so I called him back. I said, "What are you doing?" He said, "Going crazy, I'll call you back." But he never did. I got to the apartment about nine minutes after I got off the phone with him. I got out of my car and started walking toward the front door. As I was walking down the sidewalk, my brother-in-law (Carleton) was walking out of the front door. Once he saw me, he turned around and took two steps back toward the front door (like he forgot something), then he turned back around and walked to the parking lot. I walked in the door to find my husband on the kitchen floor with a shotgun wound. My daughter, Johnna, age, 6, and nephew Kameryn, age, 5, were in their bedroom. They had also been shot. I was frantic and called 911. Within minutes, the police and emergency services were there.

When I spoke to you a few days after the shooting, you said that Carleton had a multiple personality and another spirit (Demon) entered his body and made him do all of these horrific killings, and then left his body. You said a Psycho Demon entered his body and this is why it happened. You said that Carleton didn't even know what he'd done or why he did it. As crazy as it sounds, there couldn't have been any other reason why he did this other than a Demon taking over his body. For my brother-in-law to be the one who did this, is mind blowing to me because he has been nothing but good to us. I have never seen him and his brother fight or argue at any time, so it made no sense to me that he had done this horrible thing of killing his brother, his niece and his own son.

You said that you saw one of the children was earthbound and you believed it was the little boy. You told me to tell Kameryn to look up and go with the Angels. You then told me that you would need my help to coax him into the light with the Angels so he could ascend to heaven with my husband and daughter. You then told me to call his name out loud. I said, "Kameryn, take the Angel's hand. Go into the light." He then let himself go because he recognized my voice and trusted me.

When I saw Carleton outside the apartment, he was walking out the front door. He turned around and took two steps back toward the front door and then turned around and walked back toward the parking lot. You said that *my* husband, in the spiritual dimension, got in his way and was screaming at him to leave me alone and leave now as he did instead of going back into the house to kill me, too. You then said that you could see my husband and my daughter and they were crying tears of joy because they were talking to me. John (my husband) said to tell me that Johnna's head was okay and that he (my husband, John) could breathe. You then said that they both loved me and they said they were okay. At that time, an Angel took my nephew to them in heaven and he was also there but very confused because he just arrived. You said an Angel is taking them and walking away now. After I hung up the phone, I was still listening to the radio and I heard you talking to the DJs (Chet and Amy). You stated how the little boy (Kameryn) listened to me because he trusted me. When he heard my voice, he listened and went with the Angels to the light. You said that he was very scared and freaked because he was the last one to get shot and he saw everything that happened. That's why he was earthbound.

After I spoke to you, everything that you had said was exactly right. You said, in the reading, that John said to tell me, "Johnna's head is okay," and that he could breathe. The part where you said he could breathe made sense to me, because no one else knows what I said to John when I saw him shot lying on the floor. I repeatedly kept saying over and over to him, "Baby just breathe! Just breathe! I'm here." For you to say that he said, "Tell her I can breathe, I'm now in heaven," was amazing to me. But the part that you said about Johnna's *head being okay, I did not understand. I had the reading with you on the radio on Thursday 6-23-05 and did not see my husband and daughter until their wake on Friday 6-24-05. When I saw them, they had done my daughter's hair different than I normally do it. Johnna had cut her bangs about six months prior to this happening and her hair was short in the front. Over the next six months, her hair had grown out a bit and was getting longer. When the funeral home did her hair, they had layed her hair across her forehead. That was completely different than the way she normally looks, so I moved her hair back and discovered a big red bump on her head. You had told me about her head a day prior to me even seeing them. I was completely amazed and I believe that John knew I was going to move her hair and he didn't want me to be surprised when I saw the bump on her head.*

I want to thank you for all of your help with this tragedy that has happened in my life. I can agree with Kameryn (my nephew). As he joined my husband and daughter in heaven, he told you, "Thank you. You are a nice man."

Thank you so much, Gary, for being there in my time of need.

Sincerely,
Kimmie Kuivinen

Drawing by Corey Worden, 2006

Mutilation Demon

The Mutilation Demon gives you the urge to cut yourself.

This Demon has the capability of jumping inside of your physical body, gaining control of your central nervous system and making you think that the most important and practical thing in the world to do is to slice the top of your arms, legs, wrists or chest over and over again. It makes you believe that it is attractive to cut yourself.

For example, one day you may be sitting around watching TV. You go into the kitchen to get something to drink and suddenly the Demon jumps into your physical body, telling you to take out a knife and cut yourself. So you reach into the drawer, pull out a knife and cut yourself. When this Demon is through with you, it will exit your body leaving you with the bloody, scarred mess it made of you.

Once this Demon is done, a Depression Demon may take hold—making you go into the bottomless pit of depression wondering why and how you could mutilate yourself. Then, a Suicide Demon may take over—driving you to even commit suicide. I've noticed that this Demon affects mostly young girls starting at the age of 11-13 years old. A telltale sign that this Demon is present may be that the young girl is writing on her hands and arms or even on the walls of her room. This Demon is also empathable or contagious as all Demons are.

This is an example of how one Demon affects you and then another Demon joins in the fun of destroying your life.

In the spiritual dimension, a Mutilation Demon has long knife blades for fingers and a dagger for a tongue.

Here's a letter from a lady who had one of the most possessed daughters that I have ever seen. This child was diagnosed with many disorders; she was on lots of different medications. I'll let her explain to you what it was like before and after I used my spiritual gifts to help her daughter.

I then helped her to receive her very own spiritual gifts so that she could continue helping her daughter and get rid of the Demons that would attack her.

I should emphasize that this is an extreme example.

Testimonial by Susan

This child was born C-section. She was stuck. She wasn't coming out either way and they had to pry her out of my stomach. She was a very quiet baby, didn't cry very much and liked to sleep. At 18 months, she took off her diaper and said, "I'm not wearing this anymore." And she didn't. She was very content; she could watch Disney movies for hours. When she was about 2 years old, I was dressing her for a birthday party—I wanted her to wear a cute dress and she didn't want to. I could not believe that someone so young and small could become so angry and violent. I thought, at the time, that this is what they meant by the Terrible Twos. When she was 3 to 4 years old, she bumped her head and needed stitches. When it was time to stitch her up, they could not hold her down. They had to call in a male nurse. They put her in a papoose (strapped her head and body to a board) and the male nurse also held her head. It was not the stitches that freaked her out, it was being held down. At that time, her father and I knew that she was very strong-willed. As she entered school, she was quiet—she didn't have a lot of friends. She mostly played with her sister. She liked to watch movies, read and write stories. She also played sports. She didn't really have any close friends.

We battled off and on about normal stuff; she was always very determined to get what she wanted. She was interested in palm reading, crystal balls, Black Magic and spells—she wanted a Quiji board, and she brought home a voodoo doll. Life started to get much tenser when she turned 12. I thought it was the age, maybe it is, I don't know.

That is when the suicide attempts started. She has been hospitalized twice for suicide attempts and self harm. She has cut herself several times with many different objects—anything sharp will do, and some of her injuries required stitches. She has also burned herself, carved words on herself and dislocated her thumb. The list goes on and so do the medical bills. She has pierced herself several times and given herself tattoos. She can sleep for hours and hours, day after day. She works everyone to get what she wants— hurting herself if she does not get what she wants. New Year's Eve 2002, she didn't get her way. She wanted to go to a party and she threatened us: If she couldn't go, she was going to kill herself and carve 2002 in her chest. When we got home, she was sitting on the couch watching TV. She looked okay. However, she had destroyed her bedroom. A red blood-like substance was thrown all over the walls and floor and she had spray-painted nasty words on every wall. We called the police, but they couldn't/wouldn't do anything. The doctors prescribed an antidepressant; however, she never took them.

She talks and writes about killing herself and she has threatened to kill me, her father and sister. She says she hates herself and does not know how to be happy. She likes feeling mad and angry: That is normal and comforting to her. She will scream at us, "I wish you were dead, I hate you." She would not let us touch her or hold her. She would always say, "Don't touch me."

For Mother's Day, she had taken photos of her bloody cuts, smeared the blood on an old Mother's Day card (saved by me) then had the film developed and gave them to me for Mother's Day. This broke my heart. She attempted to run away. She wanted to move into a foster home where no one would know her so she could start over. Her grades in school have been D's and F's for three years. She has been offered help in school, however, she will not take it. She has been offered alternative schooling, but will not go. She says she does not care about anything because she will die. She has been seeing a therapist off and on for the last one and a half years (she has the therapists snowed). We have done everything to help her. We started to look for residential treatment centers for her.

Then we called Gary.

When I talked to Gary about my daughter, he said she was very angry, very dark, did not like herself, thought she was ugly, very angry at her father and hated her sister. She felt like a man—had split personalities, and a traumatized soul.

When Gary looked at her in the spiritual dimension he saw armies of Demons, hundreds of them—more than he had ever seen with anyone. He removed all the darkness and all of the Demons; he said she was now glowing. Gary asked if I would document some details about what happened to her after the Demons were removed.

That night, she was very quiet. We were going Christmas shopping. She picked out a couple of items, but was almost zombie-like; she didn't really talk and did not even get angry with her sister, when she normally would have. She said that she was tired and ready to go home. The next day, she said she did not feel good (throwing up all day and she had a headache). She wanted to stay home from school. She often would do this; however, this time was different. She said that she wanted to sleep in our bed. This was very odd for her, there was a lock on our bedroom door for obvious reasons. I let her sleep there for the day.

The next couple of days were just quiet, a huge welcome relief for the family. She asked me to sleep with her one night and tell her stories—any stories about anything, so I did. She said she felt like she was dying but couldn't explain anything other than that. She said she felt empty. About two weeks later, she was with a friend and said, "I feel very content; I've never felt this way before." I used this opportunity to get in a couple of hugs from her.

Things were quiet for a month or so, then a Demon showed up. Her father could see it in her eyes. She was yelling, screaming, swearing and threw a pan at him. This was caused because he would not give her a ride. She calmed down and went to her room—we found out later, to cut herself. We sat and prayed to God and the Angels to get rid of the Demons.

Things were quiet for a while, but I think the Demons are creeping back little by little. This past week, she said she's going to kill herself, but first she is going to stab a knife in my chest because she said she hated me. She scared her sister so much that she won't sleep in her own room. She was screaming and swearing at her father and throwing things at him. During this, she tripped and fell. Later, she said she dislocated her thumb. I don't know if she did it to herself or not, however, she blames her father. She said "The F'er broke my thumb." After that, she said she was going to slit her wrist.

Gary was in my hometown and I needed to see him. I needed Gary to save my child from the Demons and herself. When I met with Gary, he said, "There are still a lot of Demons with her." He was able to work on her darkness and remove more Demons; he said they are very strong and did not want to leave her. Gary said she had a split soul, half-white and half-black. This would explain a lot of her behavior. Gary also said she makes Linda Blair (the child in The Exorcist movie) look like a cupcake. Gary removed the Demons and darkness.

The next day, once again she was sick, throwing up, had a nosebleed, and pain and pressure in her head. She lay around the house for a couple of days, but she was much calmer—life did not seem so crazy and it was almost pleasant. There were few times when I could sense the darkness was still there, but things were much, much better.

I knew that Gary had an upcoming spiritual retreat and Gary thought it would be a good idea for me to attend. I'm going to Gary's retreat to learn all I can to help my daughter stay Demon-free. My daughter asked if I would ask Gary if she had any Demons, I said I would.

It was retreat time, and, yes, she did have some Demons still hanging around. During the retreat, I learned how to receive spiritual gifts: I received a spiritual gift from God of a huge dagger/sword to kill them and keep them away. At first, I could not see my spiritual gift; however I kept swinging that sword until Gary said they were all gone.

Weird stuff has been happening in my house since my return from the retreat. My husband is seeing Demons, but doesn't believe it; he says it's his imagination and that I'm messing him up. I told him to kill them with the dagger that he can see, but again he thinks it's his imagination. He had us running to a lower level of our house because he saw a huge Demon on our bedroom ceiling; it swooped down and went into our bathroom. I asked him if he killed it and he said, "No, I just told you to get out and then followed behind *you." Then my daughter—who used to be Demon girl—called from her bedroom, screaming to come quick, there were Demons in her room. I grabbed my husband and ran to her; she was under the covers shaking and crying. What she saw was real. She said it came out of the electrical socket and looked like it had wings that were on fire. It stood at the foot of her bed and then moved to the side and just stood there. She said to me, "I thought Gary got rid of all the Demons."*

I told my daughter, "Gary can get rid of them, but they will always come back one after the other on a daily basis; that is why Gary stresses the importance of meditating. To clear yourself every day is essential. That way you will always be Demon-free or as, I like to put it, 'meditation is like Demon bug spray.'"

I now have an incredible daughter—one I have never known.

I have Gary to thank. I will continue to meditate and project light to her everyday.

Thank you so very much.

Susan's daughter is doing much better now. She was extremely possessed when I first started working with her, and she still has Demons that come around. But now she knows when they're messing with her and she understands how to use her spiritual gifts to get rid of them.

The most important spiritual gift I have is the gift to remove Demons from other people, and to show them how to receive spiritual gifts and remove Demons from themselves. Everyone has the ability to get rid of Demons; it's not hard to learn and I will be teaching you in the upcoming chapters.

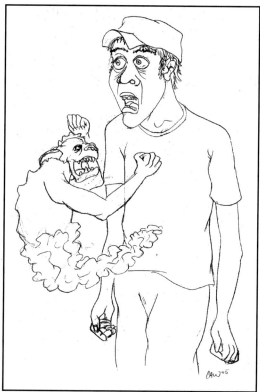

Drawing by Corey Worden, 2006

Panic Attack Demon

The Panic Attack Demon is one of the most common Demons that I come across. Many people have Panic Attack Demons, it's a very ugly-looking Demon in the spiritual dimensions that pounds and beats you in the chest causing you to freak out and panic in the physical dimension. Just get rid of this Demon, and the panic attacks will go away.

If you had something that suddenly popped out of nowhere and started screaming and yelling and pounding you in your chest or head, you'd probably freak out in a panic. Well, this is exactly what most people do when faced with a Panic Attack Demon because, in the spiritual dimension, this is exactly what's going on. People who have this Demon in their spiritual dimensions are clinically diagnosed with panic attacks.

There are many different medications for panic attacks and there are many different theories for what's really going on—none of which I think makes much sense. However, I'm not a doctor. All I know is that I can make a person's panic attacks simply evaporate within a few minutes of working with them and clearing their spiritual dimensions and spiritual body. I can also show them how to get rid of any future panic attacks.

What's the recipe for this? Simple: Spiritual gifts. There is a spiritual gift given to you by God to remove any Demons or dark energies that are affecting your spiritual body which, in turn, affects your physical body.

Here's an example of what happens when I get rid of a Panic Attack Demon. When I get rid of a person's Panic Attack Demon they start explaining how warm their head feels or, "Wow! It feels like my heart is on fire." The reason they feel this warm sensation is because I'm getting rid of their Demons and allowing God's energy to enter into their physical body. It doesn't matter what type of Demon you get rid of, you will feel this warm rush come into your body because you're removing the Demon that is blocking your God energy from entering your spiritual body. Once the Demon is removed, the energy will enter your spiritual body causing warmth within your physical body.

Testimonial by Jennifer Lenzen

My session was with Gary on June 7th 2003.

My reason for having a session with him was because I had been suffering from panic attacks and depression for years, but the last three months before my session with Gary was the worst. I had severe generalized anxiety along with panic attacks and depression. It was a challenge just to get out of bed; all I wanted to do was die. My heart was constantly beating a million miles an hour and I really thought I was going crazy. It was the scariest time of my life! I saw many doctors and was on medication for the anxiety and depression, but nothing worked.

In my session with Gary, I told him about my problems and he told me that I had Panic Attack Demons around me and depression energy in my head. First, he asked if he could get rid of the Demons and I said, "Of course." Instantly, my chest got really warm and my heart went back to beating like it used to three months ago. I felt calm, relaxed and warm. Next, he worked on my head—removing negative energy. My head felt warm and super light. What a great feeling!

That night after my session, I was able to go to my friend's wedding—something I thought I couldn't do because I was afraid to leave the house.

Life is actually fun again. I am still off medications and don't have any more panic attacks or problems with depression. I feel that I am a better mother, wife and all-round person.

I thank you.
Jennifer Lenzen

One thing that's very important to understand about Demons is that they attack your spiritual body causing many problems that manifest into panic attacks, depression, anxiety, maybe even causing mutilation. The list goes on. But this is not the only problem Demons and dark energies cause when they attack your spiritual body.

They can also cause serious illness in your physical body such as cancer, hepatitis, multiple scleroses, Alzheimer's, bi-polar disorder, and this list also goes on and on.

When I get rid of a person's Panic Attack Demons—these Demons attack the chest area—I then look further into their physical body. At this point, I may see this person suffering from asthma or some other chest related illness. It always seems to hold true that, whatever Demon you have attacking you in the spiritual dimensions, is causing you an energy block in your physical body. These energy blocks will usually manifest into some form of illness. If allowed to go on long enough, then the illness will decay your physical body even to the point of death. This is why you must learn to get rid of the Demons in the spiritual dimensions before they cause irreversible damage to your physical body.

Anytime you remove a Demon that is attacking your spiritual body, you will notice a tremendous surge of warmth or lightness—some people describe it as tingles—within your physical body. This is your natural God energy rushing back into the space that had been darkened down within your physical body by the Demon.

I'm always amazed at how the Demons work in such synchronized tandem to destroy our spiritual and physical bodies. They always have the same goal: To totally destroy our God energy.

Drawing by Corey Worden, 2006

Suicide Demon

One of the most treacherous Demons is the Suicide Demon.
This Demon's goal is to take you out of the game, putting you in one of the most horrible spaces there is: "The Earthbound Dimension."

If a Suicide Demon can talk you into suicide, you will usually continuously relive that moment of death, whether you are hanging from a garage rafter, have a bullet wound to the head, or whatever horrible thing the Demons talked you into doing to mutilate your own physical body. These suicide victims are in much need of rescue as they cannot proceed to heaven because they've cut their spiritual learning process short at their own hands. Suicide is totally against all spiritual rules.

The way a Suicide Demon works is that it will be embedded into your aura line gaining control of your central nervous system, making you think, first, of having a glass of water, then turning on the television, maybe then taking your shoes off, and then blowing your brains out. Many times, there is not a lot of thought involved when people kill themselves. Often, when people kill themselves, the people around them weren't even aware they were thinking of it. The fact of the matter is, they weren't. They just thought of it and did it all at the same time. There's a good reason to check yourself for Demons!

Some of the feedback I get from people after working with them to get rid of their Demons is, "I owe you my life." Well you don't owe me your life, but you probably do owe God and your Angels your life. For you see, they showed me how to receive spiritual gifts and I simply use my gifts on you to get rid of your Demons.

Now, you simply have to receive your own spiritual gifts to keep the Demons away. Remember, as a child you may have been able to see monsters (Demons) in your bedroom and your biggest dilemma at that point was just trying to convince your parents you were really seeing the monsters (Demons). However, as an adult, you may have forgotten about being able to see the monsters (Demons)—dismissing them as simply a child's imagination and being afraid of the dark. Well, guess what, they really do exist.

All of our physical problems come from some Demon or dark energy that is affecting our spiritual bodies in the spiritual dimensions causing problems within our physical bodies. It seems simple to me: Get rid of the Demons in the spiritual dimensions and the physical problems will simply evaporate, if caught early enough.

I work with many doctors on hard-to-diagnose cases and I've noticed, over the years, that more and more of them are coming around to this type of thinking. They are now realizing that there's more to us than just this physical body we live in.

Then Jesus spoke to the Demon within the man and said, "Come out, you evil spirit."

Mark 5: 7, 8
The Bible

Sometimes, in my private sessions, I meet people who are so far off track with what they think is going on with them.

I recently read a young man. He was a 32 years old and was brought to see me by his mom and his sister. When he walked into the room, the first thing he said was, "I saw you on television!" He remembered me from a talk show some time back. I smiled and said, "Well, I'm glad to see you and I hope I can help you." His mother started crying immediately and said, "My son is in so much pain. I want you to help him, if you can. We've tried everything. We've carried him to many doctors, therapists, psychoanalysts, psychiatrists and we've only been able to help the problem but not really cure it. You see, my son is diagnosed with schizophrenia. He hears voices in his head and they tell him to do horrible things, like kill himself."

At that point, I started smiling. The mother looking quite concerned, and asked me why was I smiling. I said, "Well, this is a recurring story that I hear a lot. Many times, people do hear voices in their heads and the voice simply tells you to kill yourself. Well, if you trace it back to what the voice really is, the voice is a Demon. I call them Suicide Demons. Suicide Demons are in a family or group of Demons that I call Psycho Demons. They make you mutilate yourself. They make you hurt or kill other people or even kill yourself. This is what your son has." I told her I found that many times Demons attach themselves to spiritually gifted people—you see, where there's a lot of light, there is also a lot of dark trying to extinguish the light.

At that point, she started crying violently. I thought, well, I have to work on her first to calm her down and then work with the son. As I worked with her, her energy started to feel very calm. She told me that she felt a sense of lightness going over her body and she asked. "Can you help my son?" I said, "I'm sure of it."

I started working with her son and, to my surprise, he could see everything I was doing in the spiritual dimensions. I then said to him, "Above your head there is a dark energy."

He smiled.

I asked, "Do you see it?"

He said, "Yes."

I said, "Can you see the face on the dark energy?"

"Yes."

"Now then, what happened?" I asked.

"It exploded in a big ball of light," he replied.

I smiled. At that point he said, "And I feel warm down my back and in my head. Why is that?"

I said, "Well, that was a Demon that was talking to you and telling you to do horrible things to yourself and kill yourself."

The young man said, "I feel much better. However, I feel like there is something else."

At that point I realized that he was sensing some other Demons that were also attached to him. As I got rid of two more Demons, he saw both of them explode in light.

I then realized, because of his Angels, that he was naturally a very gifted person and able to do amazing spiritual work with getting rid of Demons for himself and others. You see, some people are born with the ability to kill Demons and, while they may not be the most intelligent scholastically, they may be absolute rocket scientists with their ability to get rid of negative energies. It would be in everyone's best interest to learn what they know. They have the power to brighten the whole planet with a single thought and a single projection of light because they are born with very powerful spiritual gifts of healing from God. These are gifted children and many times these special children grow up to be wrongly diagnosed adults, placed on severe medications. I asked him at that point, "Are you on any medications?"

He said, "Yes, I'm on a heavy dosage."

I was very surprised that, even on the medication, he could still see and feel because certain medications will usually make you numb and dumb and disable your spiritual abilities to where you cannot see or feel anything spiritually.

I realized that, if he was not on the medication, he would probably be as spiritually gifted as I am—or more. At that point, I told him that he was amazing. He smiled and a tear came to his eye. I think it had been a very long time since anyone told him that he was amazing or that he was anything good. He probably only hears, "He has a problem." "He's a schizophrenic." "Something is wrong with him." "He has a disorder." And he had to be sedated on drugs because of his disorder.

I then worked and showed him how to receive spiritual gifts. I brought him up to heaven where ArchAngel Michael greeted us and said, "He is one of mine and I present him with my sword." Michael showed him a huge Demon and told him to kill it. He killed a Demon larger than the planet, and then two more, and then another. He said he was feeling lighter than ever and better—he was able to talk to

God, he was revered in heaven as a hero, and given the sword of Michael. His mother was smiling and there were tears running down her cheeks when she saw him smiling and glowing. He knew he had done something really amazing and really good, not for only himself and his family, but for everyone alive on earth. The family all left happy with a new focus and the realization that his mental illness was nothing more than a misinterpretation by the doctors and that he had been born spiritually gifted.

This case is an extreme scenario. He has some serious problems that few of us have to deal with. Maybe your problems aren't this great. Maybe they are. Maybe they're worse. However, if you use your spiritual gifts to get rid of your dark energies, many times, all of your problems will just evaporate with the dark energy.

You're probably very tired of hearing about dark energies and Demons, but this is probably the most important subject I can talk about and that you can hear about.

There is one main rule and one thing that you have to realize: There are spiritual wars and spiritual battles being fought everyday in different heavenly dimensions. The spiritual war is always between good and evil—between Angels and Demons. Once you understand there is a war going on, you must understand the number one rule of battle, "Know your enemy." The more you know about your enemy, the further you'll go in any battle. This includes the ongoing spiritual battle we all fight on a daily basis.

As I become more blessed with spiritual gifts, and I use these gifts to remove people's Demons, I become more sure of my theory. I see it being proven to me time and time again as I work with people and teach them how to understand, receive and use their very own spiritual gifts.

By Permission of the British Library
Detail of Daniel in the Lion's Den, Add .35254B

SPIRITUAL GIFTS
AND HOW THEY WORK

"Now concerning spiritual gifts, brethren, I would not have you ignorant."

1 Corinthians 12:1
Bible

"I long to see you so that I may impart onto you some spiritual gifts to make you Strong."

Romans 1:11
Bible

"Follow after charity, and desire spiritual gifts, but rather that ye made prophecy."

1 Corinthians 14:1
Bible

When God presented himself to me for the first time, I was in my mid-thirties. Ever since that day, I maintained a communication with Him daily. I communicate with Him in my meditations, while driving my car, walking the dog, eating breakfast: If fact I'm in touch with God and my Angels all day. They are in every aspect of my life. Once I teach you how to get in touch with God and Angels, you will also have a direct communication with them all day and in every aspect of your life. It's great to have divine guidance in every aspect of your life. It makes everything a lot easier.

God has taught me many things about the spiritual world around us. God said that his goal is for us to live in bliss here on earth as it is in heaven, free from all the chaos.

*"Have not those who disbelieve know that the heavens and
the earth were one connected entity then we separated them."*
Quran
21:30

He taught me about the spiritual dimensions around us and how they
are of vital importance in our lives. He taught me about spiritual gifts
and how important it is for all of mankind to understand how simple it
is to change your life by learning to receive spiritual gifts. He taught
me how to use my spiritual gifts to heal people and he gave me the
simple spiritual recipe to show everyone how to heal themselves. He
taught me how important it is to maintain a perfect spirit and how to
unlock the knowledge our soul contains. All of these things will be
taught to you in the same order they were taught to me. The first
thing I will teach you is about spiritual gifts.

I asked God, "Why doesn't any spiritual text explain or teach us
how to receive spiritual gifts?"

God said, "That's one of the many spiritual secrets that was not
put into spiritual text or it was edited out because the Demons
possessed the minds of man and made them think it should not be
taught to the masses. But it was taught at one time on earth." God
also said, "This is a spiritual secret that should be and needs to be
revealed to everyone on earth because spiritual gifts have the power
to change anyone's life for the better, instantly."

After God explained spiritual gifts to me, I really wanted to receive
one, but he said, "In time, I will show you how to receive your spiritual
gifts, but now is not the time."

A few weeks later, as I was running out the door to catch a flight
that I was already late for, I heard God say, "Now is the time. You're
ready to receive your first spiritual gift."

I was thinking to myself, "This is not good timing," but he is God
so I listened to what he had to say. He said, "Sit down, shut your eyes
and look up into the spiritual dimensions."

I sat down, shut my eyes and looked into the spiritual dimensions.
I saw God handing me a staff made of gold and a necklace. On the
necklace there was an amulet made of gold with a big red ruby in the
middle. God said, "Take these, they're yours. Reach up with your
hands and receive your spiritual gifts." When I did, I felt a warmth
in my fingers that I never felt before. The warmth went throughout
my whole body. I asked God, "Is this warmth what I'm supposed to
be feeling?"

God then explained to me that when someone receives a spiritual gift, they will feel a warmth in their fingertips, hand or even their whole body will light up because they are allowing a piece of God into their spiritual body.

God then explained to me what the spiritual gifts I've just received were to be used for. He said, "The staff you received is for healing and getting rid of darkness. The necklace and amulet is for abundance."

Of course, at this point, having never received a spiritual gift but only having heard of them from God, I had many questions. But before I could ask my first question, God said, "I will answer all of your questions as soon as you get to your final destination because for now, in the physical world, you may miss your flight."

After making the flight, I was sitting there doing nothing when suddenly God said, "You can ask your questions now."

I had many questions about spiritual gifts. I'm sure that you have many questions also. Here are some of the questions that I asked, and the answers God gave me. When I teach you how to see, hear, and talk to God yourself, you will be able to ask him all of the questions you may have about spiritual gifts and more.

Question and Answers

Q) Gary: What is a spiritual gift?

A) God: A spiritual gift is a gift from heaven given to spiritually enlighten beings so they can protect themselves and others from Demons and dark energies. Spiritual gifts may appear as a staff, sword, harp, crown, book, robe, dagger, shield or a heart, just to name a few.

There are thousands of spiritual gifts customized for use in every part of someone's life. Each spiritual gift is spiritually custom-made for the person receiving it and their spiritual needs and physical well-being.

Q) Gary: What is a spiritual gift used for?

A) God: Each spiritual gift you receive will enable you to get rid of any Demon or dark energy that is attacking your spiritual body causing illness or problems. For example, if you have cancer, you didn't get it in your physical body first. It was caused by a Demon in the spiritual dimensions attacking your spiritual body. If you prevent the Demons from attacking your spiritual body, the Demons wouldn't be able to cause cancer in your physical body. Demons stand in your way all day long blocking you from happiness. Demons are always present in your life. All illness and problems you encounter every day in your physical body, has first appeared in your spiritual dimensions; if you use your spiritual gifts to get rid of the Demons that are attacking you in the spiritual dimensions, you will never have to deal with illness or problems in the physical dimension.

> *"When evening came, they brought to him many possessed with Demons. He cast out the spirits with a word, and healed all who were sick."*
>
> *-Matthew 8:16*
> *The Bible*

Q) Gary: How does someone use a spiritual gift?

A) God: Once you receive a spiritual gift, just ask me I will tell you what it's used for. There's never a time when you receive a spiritual gift that I will not explain what they're used for and how to use it.

You may receive a sword; a sword is used for killing Demons. I will show you how to use the sword to clear your spiritual dimensions—to remove Demons and dark energies that are attacking you.

You may receive a dagger; daggers are used for cutting away dark energies that are affecting you in the spiritual dimensions. You may receive a harp. When you play the harp you will find that you start to giggle—for the harp is for joy and laughter.

You may receive a crown. The crown is given to you whenever you achieve higher levels of spiritual awareness. The more you understand about spirituality, the more I will teach you; the more I teach you, the more crowns you will receive.

You may receive a staff. All staffs are different: some have a jewel on top, some are made of pure silver, some are made of pure gold, and some are made of wood. All staffs have different functions.

You may have a problem with a Demon attacking you in your room at night, so I may tell you to touch the floor with your staff and you will see the Demon explode in a bright white light. You may receive a spiritual gift of a staff to get rid of depression; I will tell you to touch the staff to your head in the spiritual dimension. When you do, the Demons causing your depression will leave. Then in the physical dimension, you will notice a lightness in your head because you have just removed the Demons and dark energies that were causing the depression. I may say to put the staff inside your body in the spiritual dimension and you'll be able to notice little black Demons leaving your body and exploding in the white light around you. In the physical dimension, you'll notice a lightness and feeling of warmth throughout your body as the Demons leave. This is how your spiritual gifts work. Follow the instructions I give you and you will never have to suffer with physical, mental or emotional problems again.

Q) Gary: How do you know when to use a spiritual gift?

A) God: I will only give you spiritual gifts that you need; it may be for a physical illness, mental illness, emotional problem or to remove blocks. Whenever you receive a spiritual gift, you will know that you have the need to use it. Some spiritual gifts that you receive indicate that you have reached a higher level of spiritual knowledge. You will see these in the form of a crown, book or scroll. Open the book or scroll and read the message on it.

Q) Gary: After using the spiritual gift, what happens to it?

A) God: Once you receive a spiritual gift, it is yours forever to use whenever you have a Demon or dark energy attacking you. Once you use it, you must store it inside of your chest. Just touch your hand to your chest in the physical dimension and the gift will automatically be stored inside of your spiritual body for all eternity. Once you put the spiritual gift inside your chest, you'll notice your chest feeling brighter—larger than life. This is because you have a piece of me (God) inside of you. When you need your spiritual gifts just touch your hand to your chest and pull out your spiritual gift, use it and then return it again to its safe keeping place deep inside your being.

> *"Once you have received your gift from God, neglect not the gift that is in thee."*
>
> *1 Tim 4:14*
> *The Zohar*

> *"Stir up the gift of God, which is in thee… for God hath not given us the spirit of fear; but of power, and of love, and of a sound mind."*
>
> *2 Tim 1:6, 7.*
> *The Zohar*

Q) Gary: Can anyone receive spiritual gifts?

A) God: Yes! The young and old alike can receive spiritual gifts; no one is too young or too old. The sooner you begin receiving them, the sooner you can begin ridding yourself of all the Demons around you and everyone else.

Q) Gary: How can other people receive their gifts?

A) God: I will teach you a simple meditation that you can teach others so they will be able to receive their spiritual gifts. This meditation will teach everyone how to see, hear and talk to me. Everyone will be able to see their spiritual gifts and, when they see the spiritual gift, they need to reach up with their hand and grip the spiritual gift with their fingers, pulling the spiritual gift closer to them. They'll notice warmth in their fingertips, hands or even their whole body will light up as they received their spiritual gift. Once they receive their spiritual gifts, things will start to change for the better in their life. At first, many people may think this is their imagination playing tricks on them, but later on, as this peaceful feeling stays with them and they start to see the changes in their lives and the lives of the people around them, they certainly will realize this is not their imagination. They truly received a spiritual gift from God.

> *"I long to see you so that I may impart to you some spiritual gifts to make you strong."*
>
> *Romans 1:11*
> *The Bible*

"The lord is my shepherd, I shall not want ... Even though I walk through the valley of the shadow of death, I fear no evil, for you are with me; your rod and your staff, they comfort me."

Psalms 23:4

The Bible

Once God and I were finished with the questions and answers, God said to me, "I want you to start using your spiritual gifts to help others." The following day, I was due to appear on a radio show in Atlanta, Georgia where I was a regular guest. After the show, I had private appointments for the rest of the day. I thought to myself that maybe I would have a chance to use my new spiritual gifts.

The next day, when I showed up at the radio station, the producer met me downstairs to escort me to the studio. I noticed his head tilted over to the side and he was walking a little stiffly. About the same time, I noticed his problem. He turned to me and said jokingly, "If you really want to impress me today, make my neck feel better."

I heard God say to me, "Here is your first chance to use your spiritual gift of healing."

I told the producer that I might be able to help if he had a few minutes before we went on the air. He said, "Take all the time you need because this pain is almost unbearable."

Since this was my first attempt at healing a physical problem, I asked God to guide me. God said, "Look at his neck with your spiritual eyes. Do you see the little Demons biting it?"

I said, "Yes."

God said, "Take out your golden staff and touch the Demons and they will blow up because of the heavenly energy the staff contains. Darkness can't exist where there is light."

In the spiritual dimension, as soon as I touched the Demons, they exploded and in the physical dimension, the producer started moving his neck and said, "What did you just do? My neck has been stuck like this for two days and now I can move it."

I told him I received a spiritual gift of healing yesterday and that he was the first person I tried it on. He then said, "Well I guess it works because my neck feels perfect, like there was nothing ever wrong with it."

From that moment on, I realized that I may be on to something. If you get rid of the Demons that are attacking someone causing their physical problems, when the Demon is gone, the person's physical problems go away. We are all capable of healing one another and I will teach everyone.

God then said to me, "Yes everyone is capable of healing because everyone is made of light. You just need to remove the darkness and you can be healed." God also said, "There is one important rule about healing that everyone must know about: The person being healed must truly want to be healed, and the person doing the healing must truly want to heal that person or no healing will ever take place."

"There is light within an enlightened person, and it shines on the whole world. If the light does not shine, it is dark."

The Secret Teachings of Jesus
by Marvin Meyer, Random House, Inc.
The Gospel of Thomas
Saying 24

God said, "Now is the time for me to reveal to you the meaning of your ongoing vision about the world being covered in darkness. I know you've wanted the answer throughout your life. Now the time has come for you to understand."

I was excited to finally understand that vision that's been recurring since I was a young child.

God said, "Your vision was always of a darkness that would start to take over the earth and at the last second an Angel would direct you to use a golden key and insert it into the earth, unlocking it and releasing a beautiful golden energy that would engulf the earth removing all of the darkness. The earth would start to glow. The keys in your vision are a spiritual gift that you were born with. Because you were born with your spiritual body already awakened, you were able to access and use them without knowing what you were doing. The darkness in your vision was of the Demons and dark energy that attacks people on earth trying to block their spiritual evolution and enlightenment. The gold energy represents people using their spiritual gifts to stop the Demons. At this point in history, it can go either way—darkness can win or light can win; it's up to everyone on earth. The keys are a spiritual gift that everyone on earth was born with. They are just locked within their spiritual body. Now you must show everyone how to access their own personal keys by awakening their spiritual body. Everyone has a set of two keys within them. One of the keys fits into the earth, just like in your vision, and releases a gold energy which removes all the dark energy and Demons from the planet. You must teach everyone about this key because everyone must use their key to remove the Demons and dark energies that plague mankind. If everyone starts using their personal key, then the vision of the key releasing this gold energy and removing all the darkness from earth will happen and earth will evolve into its next spiritual evolution which is to bring heaven to earth. If they decide not to use their key, then the Demons and darkness will take over and extinguish the light on earth."

God also said, "The second key is the key to heaven. When the time is right, I will teach you how to use this key to access the doorway to heaven. For now, go out and teach everyone the importance of receiving and using spiritual gifts."

Many religious texts talk about spiritual gifts but none of them tell how mankind can receive them. Spiritual gifts are everyone's weapons against Demons and other dark energies. Since receiving my first two spiritual gifts, I have received thousands more and I've taught thousands of people how to receive their spiritual gifts. It's not that hard; God gave me step-by-step instructions on how to teach everyone and I will share these very important steps with you shortly.

The first thing God taught me was how to teach others to see with their spiritual eyes: This is the first step to receiving your spiritual gifts. I stress this point because, seeing spiritually happens instantly: One minute you sense there is something on a deeper spiritual level, the next minute you're able to see in the spiritual dimensions around you.

This is Mohammad's testimonial of what occurred when he received his spiritual eyes and was able to see in the spiritual dimensions and receive his first spiritual gifts. It helped him to understand what was going on around him and how to fix the situation.

Testimonial by Mohammad

I started questioning different types of energies a few years ago. It all seemed to begin with a woman who I was dating. Unknown to me in the beginning, she practiced black magic. After our relationship ended, I started to experience a lot of bad things in my life as well as bad spirits around me. I started to question things in my mind: why certain things are happening to me. Was it all coincidence? Was I unlucky? What in the world was going on?

Around this time, a friend of mine who was a spiritual minister gave me my first glimpse of spiritual warfare. I started to gather knowledge on this subject from books, friends, and anywhere I could in order to learn more and maybe find the answers to what was happening to me.

First and foremost, I am an extremely logical person. When I look at things, I analyze, process and try to find solutions. This was something beyond my comprehension, but, at the same time, all of the research was making sense. Once I began to put things together, I came to a sort of understanding about spiritual warfare and its role in my life and the lives of those around me. My knowledge and faith in God would end up being my biggest tools in fighting the day-to-day battles. After all, they were battles.

For many years, I had been an avid listener of a local radio station in Minneapolis, Minnesota that had you, (Gary) as a regular guest psychic on each month. The more I listened to you and the stories from other listeners, the more I began to think that you were far more than a psychic and that you could actually help me. You described things that I had been feeling and listeners calling in were having some of the same problems that I was. Was it possible that I wasn't the only one? The way you talked about different energies and how you use God's love was intriguing to me, but at the same time, I did not want to have false hope. My life had taken me down some very dark paths and I was in an extremely dark place. I didn't feel that I had the energy to fight. I was using it all to exist; the only thing I remained true to was my faith in God, which was steadfast.

In my life, when I have needed something, God has provided me with it. This time was no exception. I started dating a woman that I had known for some time; I was not expecting a relationship, nor did I think I was capable of one. But as love goes, it took hold of my heart and gave me the energy I needed to start seeking answers again about the bad energies I still battle with daily. I began to notice that the more I started feeling good about life and myself again, more and more bad things were happening to me and those that I love. I started to seriously consider calling you; I had nothing to lose. I thought about it for a long time, but my head would fill me with doubts. My girlfriend motivated me to call, but every time I was about to call, something would come up and I would find myself very busy. I finally was able to call and make an appointment with you and it was a long way from actually happening. The entire time before the session date, I was uneasy, apprehensive and bad things around me started to increase in frequency. My head kept telling me to cancel.

All night long, I had horrible nightmares. I felt uneasy and I didn't know what was happening to me. The other thing I have learned is that bad energies will not only attack me, but those that I love as well, as a way to get to me. For example, I had rescheduled my session with you for the next day and all I wanted to do was stay at home and watch television. I just wanted to lay low until I could speak with you. Then I got a phone call from my nephew who means the world to me. He started telling me that earlier in the day he had passed out and hit his head on the floor and ended up going to the emergency room. I couldn't believe what I was hearing; this was really starting to affect, not only me, but also those whom I love. Instead of staying home that evening, like I had planned, I ended up driving to my nephew's house and picking him up so he could come stay at my place for the weekend. Now, not only did I have my girlfriend at the house, I had my nephew there. I was very uncomfortable; I had wanted to speak with you in private. The bad energies were not making this easy, so I almost canceled again. They were fighting to make me cancel, to keep me ignorant and blind—putting more doubts into my head.

    The following morning arrived and my anxieties and doubts continued to increase. Then I received the call from you. In the beginning, I felt nervous and uneasy, as you can imagine. With all that I had been going through, I didn't know if this was going to help or not. I started to tell you my story. I told you that I used to date a girl who practiced black magic and that, ever since I broke up with her, I had a lot of bad things happen to me and I felt bad spirits around me. You said, "Dark energies moved from her to you." You ask me if I wanted to get rid of them; I said, "Absolutely!" You told me that I have a very highly evolved soul and great energy and that these dark energies were attracted to me. You started removing these dark energies and I felt extremely hot all over. You said I could remove them myself and you had me close my eyes and showed me how to see in the spiritual dimensions. I was able to see these dark ropes hanging from my feet that were attached to something even more massive—something that had big red eyes and was standing some ten feet behind me. You said these ropes have been hanging on for a long time and had nothing to do with my girlfriend. (Suddenly, this all made total sense to me as I had been having chronic feet problems for years and I even had two surgeries to help correct the problem.) You helped me remove these energies and also helped me see my Guardian Angels and receive spiritual gifts.

    This was the most amazing experience of my life. I thought I was losing my mind before I talked to you, but you showed me a world that I didn't know existed. I was sweating with a warm soothing spiritual heat the whole time I spoke with you. I saw many things during the session, these included dark ropes hanging on my feet, rows and rows of Angels, my Guardian Angels, and I received spiritual gifts. I was handed a staff and a necklace from a light source from above. After the session, I felt energized, rejuvenated, light and I could feel my spirit rise.

Since my session with you, I feel more empowered, and I have a better understanding of what is happening. With my new spiritual gifts, I seem to be more at peace and happy, and I now know I have power over the dark forces. With my gifts, I am able to connect to the light source above (God), and it feels awesome. Dark forces still attack me, but, with my spiritual gifts, I know I can keep them off. I continue to pray and meditate daily and I wait for God to show me what he needs me to do.

Mohammed

Just like Mohammed, you will gain sight into the spiritual dimensions and be able to see the Demons and negative energy affecting you. You will also receive spiritual gifts and learn how to use them to remove the Demons and dark energies affecting you.

I share this testimonial with you because I want you to realize that Demons and Angels really do exist and there is a battle for your spiritual body going on all of the time. Demons really cause havoc in your life and Angels are there to help guide you to spiritual enlightenment.

Mohammed questioned the energies he was feeling. Even though he didn't know what was going on in the spiritual dimensions, he knew things weren't going well in the physical dimension and he sensed a connection between the two.

Like Mohammed, if you realize things aren't going good for you or you have physical, mental or emotional problems, there are Demons around you affecting your life. Once you have the mental understanding that you have power over any Demon or darkness because you are the dominant spiritual being on this planet, then it becomes easy to get rid of the Demons. Remember, we are all powerful God beings made in his likeness.

Concerning spiritual gifts: I meet people all the time who have many spiritual gifts which they already posses, yet they know nothing about them. The reason these people have these spiritual gifts is that they were born with their spiritual body already awakened. When I see these people, I always take time to show them how to use their spiritual gifts and how to see, hear and talk to God and their Angels. While they may not be aware of their spiritual gifts, they are aware that something is going on with them. These people tell me that they feel different, but they don't know why and they always seem to have a certain sense of responsibility to change the world—to make it a better place, but they don't know how.

Some of you who are reading this book may already possess spiritual gifts because your spiritual body is already awakened. You may be one of the people who has the reoccurring feeling that you should be doing more to help people, but you just don't know what it is you're suppose to do or how to do it.

One day, after I had just finished doing a radio show in Memphis, Tennessee, I was walking past the office where my assistants answer the phones. I heard my Angels say go in the office, there's a phone call you need to take. At that time, one of my assistants was getting ready to hang up from a phone call and I heard him say, "Hold on, Gary just walked into the office." My assistant told me that the person on the other end of the phone had questions about spiritual gifts and visions that they've been having. My Angels said, "Take the phone call." On the phone was Patrick. Patrick had heard me on the radio; I was talking about spiritual gifts and being able to talk to God and Angels.

Patrick was having visions of God and Angels and was confused about what he was seeing. I worked with him for a while and realized that he was one of the most naturally gifted people I've ever had the pleasure of talking with. After a little while, I was able to help Patrick make sense of everything going on in his life. He had many spiritual gifts, but was confused about how to use them. I was able to sort it out for him, so he would understand exactly what was going on.

Testimonial by Patrick Culligan

Gary was able to identify certain facts and information that he had no way of knowing. My education, professional background and personality gave me an unrelenting preference for reality, facts and tangible evidence: My instincts and personal experience allowed me to accept, at face value, that which I cannot explain. I have no idea how Gary Spivey is able to do what he does or why he does it. He likes to explain how easy and simple it is. Perhaps it is easy. Mr. Spivey also exhibits great insight into the nature of spiritual gifts. Gary was able to clearly explain the concept of spiritual gifts to me, and explain to me the gifts I already possessed. His explanations translated into a far more profound understanding of my own gifts and spiritual abilities. He has enabled me to more completely let go and better develop and use these assets. With this new understanding of spiritual gifts, came a sense of peace and confidence, which has helped me push forward with changes that have resulted in a better life for me, my loved ones, extended family, friends and associates. A single moment of real insight has helped me change what will become a lifetime of activity. I feel that real truths are very simple and that they transcend religion, culture, intelligence, status, location and appearance. Gary was able to help me understand the nature and use of my spiritual gifts at a very important time in my life.

Yours,
Patrick Culligan

When people like Patrick already possess spiritual gifts, it is sometimes overwhelming because they have so many things going on around them in the spiritual dimensions that they often feel confused. It's easy for me to look at them and tell them what's going on because of my experiences. I just have to teach them so they can understand their spiritual gifts and teach others.

"There are different kinds of gifts, but the same spirit."
Corinthians 14:1
Bible

Many times, when I'm teaching people how to see spiritually, those who are the hardest to teach are the well-read ones who think they know everything already. We all know someone like this: You can't teach them anything because they already know it. If you are this person, try to suspend your know-it-all-knowledge and your ego while reading this book and you may learn something new that will be very helpful to you. We only use five to ten percent of our brains. Some people have a very intelligent five to ten percent of their brain. What would be wrong with using the rest of our brain? You can be highly intelligent and spiritually stupid at the same time. The reason is that many highly intelligent people only believe in tangible evidence of something real or something that occurs in the physical dimension first. Their thinking and their theory is exactly backwards. This is where they're tricked. Everything occurs first in the spiritual dimensions and then makes its way down to the physical dimension. That's the reason you want to get rid of the dark energies in the spiritual dimensions so that negative things never occur in the physical one.

People with huge egos are extremely hard to teach because their ego stands in the way of learning. These people usually want to learn for selfish reasons, and spirituality doesn't work that way. The other people who have a hard time learning about spirituality are people who are not on their vibration of truth. I don't mean that they are compulsive liars, but even a vibration of denial or drama is an untruth and all spiritual energies work on the vibration of truth. The easiest people to teach are children and people who are humble. I find, when I work with these people, that they are usually spiritually brilliant because their brain and ego don't stand in their way or create roadblocks for them. These people are usually very humble and childlike. I'm not saying that intelligent people or people with egos can't learn, but they just need to learn to slow their brains down and stop over-thinking for a moment or drop the ego and become humble. Spirituality is for everyone and, as God said, "Everyone can and must awaken their spiritual body."

"Seeing with your spiritual eyes
is the most important gift
you can give yourself."
- GOD

The Complete Woodcuts of
Albrecht Durer c.1498
Dover Publications, Inc.

HOW TO SEE AND
HEAR SPIRITUALLY

Ever since I was a small child, I was always able to see, hear and talk with my Angels and hear the messages they had for me. As I grew older, I started seeing, hearing, and talking with God. Since the first time I started communicating with God, he has revealed to me very important spiritual secrets that affect every man, woman and child on earth. The secrets include how to receive spiritual gifts and how, through receiving spiritual gifts, you can have a better life. Other spiritual secrets include a spiritual roadmap from earth to heaven—you just need to learn about the ten spiritual dimensions that surround us. God revealed vital information about our higher selves, our souls and spirits. He also revealed how to heal our physical bodies by clearing the Demons and dark energies attacking our spiritual bodies and He showed me the secret to awakening the spiritual body. All of these secrets are easy and available for everyone to learn. The first step is to be able to see and hear spiritually.

When I started on the journey of teaching others about these secrets, my biggest dilemma was: How am I going to teach others to see and hear the way I do? I must teach everyone how to see through their spiritual eyes not their physical eyes and hear through their spiritual ears not their physical ones.

One day I was thinking about this dilemma when I heard God ask, "What's the matter?"

I said, "I may have a problem teaching others."

God asked me, "Why?"

"Because everyone may not be able to see and hear spiritually as I do."

God said, "Everyone has the ability to see and hear spiritually. Some people will see clearer than others and some will hear better, but everyone has the ability. They just need to be taught. No one is teaching them; so teaching them is your job." God then added, "It's actually very easy to teach. You see, everyone has an imagination. People can imagine everything from a beach to a snow-covered mountain to a beautiful flower or a puppy, and this is the same muscle you use when seeing spiritually. Once someone can see spiritually, their hearing will follow."

I said, "People may think they're imagining what I'm saying and not really seeing or hearing it for themselves."

God then said, "You have to explain to them that this is just the doorway to seeing and hearing spiritually. Once they understand where the doorway is, they'll never have a problem finding it again."

God then taught me a meditation that I can teach to everyone who will open their doorway to seeing and hearing spiritually.

First, I would like to share with you a brief testimonial of someone learning to see and hear spiritually for the first time.

Testimonial by Sarah Eden

Good Morning Dear Gary,

I remember the day I received the gift of the staff so clearly. I had called to ask you for help because I knew something was wrong, but didn't know what. I couldn't concentrate clearly. I seemed to evoke strange and negative reactions from everyone around me. I felt "dark." My own daughter was even having symptoms that were requiring extensive medical testing with no clear diagnosis. You were able to see this darkness and you worked with me on the phone to get rid of it.

You explained Demons to me and taught me how to get rid of them. You told me that God was telling me how much he loves me. You asked me if I could see him and I couldn't. You then taught me how to see spiritually. Again, you asked me if I could see God. You told me to concentrate until I saw something then, *before I could explain to you what I saw, you described what I was seeing in detail before I could get the words out of my mouth.*

It took a little while in the beginning and, as I passed the frustration point, I saw a mountain and clouds. It was not clear at first, but as I studied it, I began to see more clearly. I described it to you as the scene from the Ten Commandments when Moses came down from the mountain with the tablets. God looked like Moses from that film in my vision. I could see him carrying a staff and holding it out to me. You told me to reach for it and take it. You told me to use it whenever I felt darkness around me. I took the staff from God's hand and, at that moment, the darkness cleared. It was amazing!

When I later visited you at your spiritual retreat in Ojai, California, you taught me to always place my staff in my chest for safe keeping where I knew it would be when I wasn't using it and, when I needed it to go there and pick it up. You told me to hold it out in front of me as God had that first day and clear the darkness.

When I was at your retreat in California, I saw a number of people receive spiritual gifts and learn to see spiritually. Their stories were as exciting for me as were my own. What was incredible was how so many people, when we were gathered together, could see their spiritual gifts and the spiritual gifts of others, and how separately, each was able to relate such intricately detailed information about the event without any knowledge from others in the group.

My staff is a gift from God that I will carry with me always. Thank you for opening my spiritual eyes and allowing me to see the spiritual world around us.

Love,
Sarah

Just like Sara, everyone has the ability to see and hear spiritually. You just need to learn how.

Testimonial by Tenoch Cebreros

Hearing Angels

I first heard Gary Spivey on the radio in San Francisco. He was talking about an upcoming spiritual retreat he was having. Gary was explaining that he would teach everyone how to communicate with God and Angels and how to get rid of Demons and dark energies that cause havoc in our lives and much more. Since I'm the type of person who loves to learn and is always searching for a deeper meaning of life, I decided to attend his retreat.

One of the first things he taught us was how to hear our Angels. He explained how easy it is and how everyone can do it. He said that many times when Angels are talking to us, our ears would get physically hot, turn red, and we would feel the heat. I remember this happening from time to time throughout my life, but I never knew what it meant and I didn't really pay much attention to it.

That was until Gary Spivey taught me that when my ears get hot, to sit quietly and listen because this meant that my Angels were talking to me. In my mind, I was saying, "Yeah right, Gary, whatever you say." But I thought I would humor him and try it anyway. Boy was he right! They really do speak to me and to you if you would just take the time to listen. In my personal experience of hearing Angels or, what some people call "voices in their head," these voices are the voices of Angels that help and guide us throughout our lives. Now, when Angels speak to me, it does not sound like some one else's voice, I hear it as my own, but it is distinctive and different.

I know it's a comforting voice that helps me when I'm down. It comes down to this, it's not whether you hear them; we hear them all the time, it's whether you listen and trust that voice. Call it otherworldly, call it intuition, call it Angels, call it what you wish but just remember to listen and to believe. Ssshhhh, what do you hear?

Your Friend,
Tenoch

Art Throughout History

Now is the perfect time for me to explain why I used certain pictures of artwork throughout this book, but before I do, I would like to share with you a testimonial from Fredrick Guess about my art background.

Testimonial by Fredrick Guess

My name is Fredrick Guess and I am an artist with a gallery and studio at 910 Royal Street in the French Quarter of New Orleans. Gary Spivey and I have known each other for many years.

Once, when Gary and I were in Washington, D. C. together, I brought him to the National Gallery of Art. Though Gary had no background in art or art history, I thought he might enjoy seeing the museum and that he might benefit from my years of study in those fields.

I wasn't expecting or prepared for what happened that day because, almost as soon as we entered the gallery, Gary began telling me about each of the paintings we viewed.

Having loved and studied art all of my life, I was amazed to hear this guy from North Carolina, who had no formal art background, tell me details about the paintings. Much of what he said I already knew, but he also elaborated on what the artist was thinking or doing at the time. And he wasn't limited to the artist, but also talked about the people featured in the paintings and what was happening to them at the time the work was created. Whether it was the personality or the personal history of a sitter in a John Singer Sargent portrait or the people portrayed in a landscape by Claude Monet, Gary always gave precise information about them.

At one point, he stopped in front of one of Monet's paintings and described, in great detail, the trauma a highly regarded, elder artist had bestowed on Monet and how severely the experience had affected him. Later, at home, I investigated the painting in one of my reference books and found that Gary had it absolutely right! I felt privileged to have heard about the meeting the two artists had in such detail. Any curator would have been stunned to have been there when Gary described the scene.

As we moved through the exhibit, different paintings gave Gary different levels of information. Some artists, like Vincent van Gogh, brought out incredible amounts of detail. For instance, one painting that we spent some time viewing was a van Gogh with figures in an orchard. The description Gary gave of van Gogh while he worked on this painting was astounding—and most of which I had already known, but also knew Gary wouldn't have.

Others, a painting by Cezanne for example, left Gary feeling that the artist did not want to be read. From what is known about Cezanne and van Gogh, those traits fit their profiles. Again, I felt that I was having an experience that the curators of the museum would have given an arm for.

At times, when we were in front of a painting of which I knew nothing, Gary would read it, then I would read the information card on the wall to verify what he said. He was dead on every time!

Gary showed the same level of ability in the Antique and Old Masters Art Gallery I had in Tampa, Florida. I remember once Gary mentioning, as he casually walked by a painting we had on consignment, that it was more valuable than we thought. Later, after I had sold the painting and before the consignee had been paid, the original owner discovered the true value of the piece and wanted it back. It took some time for me to recover *the painting and give it back to the consignee, but I did it, wishing the whole time that I had listened to Gary beforehand. I could then have researched it more thoroughly and avoided that messy affair.*

We both now have very busy lives and don't get to see much of each other anymore, but I often think back to those times I had with Gary before he became famous because of his abilities. To think that for more than two years, I practically had Gary and his abilities to myself to experience such incredible events!

Sincerely,
Fredrick Guess

From the moment I first went into the National Gallery of Art with Fredrick, I was hooked on art. I fell in love with psychically reading the paintings or piece of art and understanding and feeling what the artists felt at the time they were creating it.

I really became interested in paintings, carvings or any artwork pertaining to God, Angels and Demons. I've researched hundreds of paintings and sculptures: Even though they all vary and look different and come from different parts of the world, you have to wonder where and how did the artist get the images that they created their masterpieces from. Do you think God, Angels and Demons came down and posed for the painting or sculpture? I don't think so.

When I psychically read these pieces of art, I can understand what the artists were going through and where they were getting their inspiration from. What was happening to the artists is that they were using their spiritual eyes—getting a glimpse of what was going on around them in the spiritual dimensions. All artists use their imagination to create. The imagination is the doorway to one's spiritual eyes. Imagination is how you see spiritually.

Maybe these artists knew how to see spiritually and knew exactly what they were creating or maybe they didn't have a clue how to see spiritually or how they could come up with the beautiful images they were creating. But the one thing I'm certain of, having researched hundreds of pieces of art pertaining to God, Angels and Demons, I'm absolutely positive that people have been seeing with their spiritual eyes throughout history. In the spiritual artwork is where the spiritual secrets to all religions lie.

I want you to look back at page 13: The title page to *Angels*. That's a beautiful painting of an Angel. First someone had to see it and then paint it. The only way that could have happened is if the Angel came into the physical dimension and posed for that painting, or if the artist saw into the spiritual world—seeing the Angel and then painting what he saw.

On page 22, you will find a painting of the blessed Mother Mary surrounded by Angels and holding Jesus in her arms. Do you think the artist was there at that moment physically and witnessed this or do you think he got a vision into the spiritual dimensions with his spiritual eyes and witnessed this beautiful sight and then painted it? Most people don't give much thought to where the sightings that created all of this artwork throughout history may have come from. But maybe they should.

Look at page 33, the title page for *Demons*. From the time I was a little boy, I would see what I considered Demons lurking around in the spiritual dimensions and the Demons I saw looked just like those tormenting St. Anthony. I was very surprised when I came across this drawing because I realized that the artist who drew this in the year 1320, could see the same Demons that I could see as a child and still see now.

If you look at page 37, you will see a painting of Angels using their spiritual gifts to kill the Demons. This is exactly the way it works and the way I see Angels helping us fight our spiritual battles now. You are armed with spiritual gifts to help you get rid of the Demons and dark energies that attack you in the spiritual dimensions causing you tremendous problems in your physical world.

In the Demon chapter, pages 33 - 88, there are drawings of the Demons that I see all the time around people causing problems in their lives.

I had a friend, whom I taught to see spiritually, draw the Demons for me and, if you look at spiritual artwork throughout history, you will find Demons that strongly resemble these.

Also look at page 35. Can Demons reproduce? Well you know what God said about Demons reproducing. According to this painting, someone must have seen into the spiritual dimensions and saw what was happening.

Concerning the painting on the title page of the chapter on spiritual gifts, page 89, it looks like the Angels are giving Daniel spiritual gifts to help protect him from the lions. If you look at the picture on the title page of this chapter, *Seeing and Hearing Spiritually*, you'll see a picture of one of Albert Durer's wood carvings: It looks to me as if he was seeing into heaven with his spiritual eyes.

I can give examples from many spiritual paintings throughout history to back up the concept of seeing spiritually. Now, I've shown you through art that people have always seen spiritually. Maybe this was their way of painting the spiritual truths that they were very aware of, but not allowed, either politically or religiously, to openly talk about or write about in their day. But they certainly wanted future generations to not lose these teachings.

Why didn't these artists teach others to see spiritually? Maybe they were unaware that they were seeing with their spiritual eyes because they were taught that what they were seeing was coming from their imagination and, in a sense, it was. But the imagination is also the doorway to seeing spiritually. Maybe they were totally aware that they were seeing with their spiritual eyes, but were just afraid to teach others. Whatever the reason why they didn't pass on this secret, we will never know. I do know, however, that I can teach you how to see spiritually. The secret will be revealed to you now and you will be able to start seeing God, Angels, Heavenly Hierarchy and receiving spiritual gifts so that you can help kill the Demons that have been plaguing you and mankind for a long time.

All of the paintings used in this book, as well as many more paintings that I strongly feel have secret spiritual messages to tell, can be viewed in full color at www.yourkeystoheaven.com.

Three Steps to Seeing Spiritually

This is a simple three-step technique that I always use to teach people how to see spiritually. It may seem a little silly in the beginning, but it's the easiest way to get someone to see spiritually.

Step One: First, plan a time when you will not be interrupted by anything. Take time for yourself. Find a place to sit comfortably. Once you are seated comfortably, I want you to locate your imagination muscle or, as many of you may know it, your third eye. This is located in the middle of your forehead.

The way to find your imagination muscle is to close your eyes and place your fingertips in the middle of your forehead. Now, with your hand still on your forehead, you need to open your third eye. I want you to imagine gold energy flowing from your fingertips into your head. Imagine the inside of your head filling up with gold energy. Once your head if full of gold energy, remove your fingers from your forehead. You just opened your third eye, your imagination muscle.

Step Two: With your imagination or, as God calls it, your imagination muscle, I want you to do a simple visualization exercise to get used to using your imagination.

First I would like you to relax. Once you're relaxed and ready to begin, I want you to imagine a beach. Just imagine the soft white sand, blue water and sunshine. On the beach imagine a horse and an elephant walking together talking to one another (as silly as that may sound). Stop here for a moment and really visualize this image with all of your imagination. Really see that horse and elephant talking, laughing and having a good time. Imagine them playing in the water, listening to music and dancing in the sand.

God explained to me that, for some people, their imagination will be as clear and vivid as a movie playing in their head, others may just see an outline of the images and, to others, the image may seem foggy. Some people may have a hard time with their imagination, but they can sense what's going on. God explained to me that everyone's imagination works differently—some are more vivid than others, but everyone does have an imagination muscle, and the more you use that muscle the easier visualization becomes.

Step Three: Now that everyone knows where their imagination muscle or third eye is located and how to use it, we can get started on the meditation. Your imagination muscle or third eye is where everything will take place.

When seeing spiritually, you have to use the imagination muscle (or third eye) whichever you feel more comfortable saying. The key to seeing spiritually is to just relax and allow the visions to come into your imagination. In the beginning, many people will say and think that this can't be happening. Let me assure you that over the years I have taught many people to see spiritually and just about all of them thought the same way in the beginning. Once they understood the process, they never questioned it again.

I will teach you how to see God and Angels and how to receive spiritual gifts. Never be frightened by any vision you get because God is there with you, protecting you.

Meditation for Receiving Your Spiritual Eyes

Note: I would like you to read through the mediation so you can get familiar with it. After you have finished reading this section, I will ask you to stop and play the accompanying CD so that I can walk you step-by-step through the meditation which will teach you how to see God and how to receive your spiritual gifts.

This meditation was given to me by God. Once He gave me this meditation, He then explained that it was only four steps and that the last one was the most important step. God said, "Most people become totally lost with the fourth step."

I said to God, "I will teach it to everyone so that they can understand." I was eager to find out what I had to do. God then gave the four steps to me, and now I will share them with you.

Step One: Before you start, find a comfortable place to sit. Don't lie down because you may fall asleep. Once you are comfortable and relaxed, close your eyes. I want you to relax your body and get comfortable. I want you to shut off your brain by not thinking about anything. If you are an over-thinker, then just keep telling yourself there is no place I need to be at this moment except right where I'm at.

Once you shut down your brain, I want you to visualize with your imagination, soft white feathers surrounding your entire body.

Once you are surrounded by all of these feathers, you will feel the tension within your physical body leave you as it is absorbed by the feathers. Just release all of the tension and allow it to flow out of you and into the feathers. You're becoming as light and comfortable as the feathers that surround you.

Now, tilt your head back a little so that your face is pointing upward, but not so far back as to make you uncomfortable or hurt your neck. With the same imagination you used to visualize the feathers, think of a beautiful ocean: See the blue ocean with waves coming onto the pristine white sandy beach. Now, see yourself standing on the beach with the sand between your toes; just feel the warmth of the sand on your feet. Look up and see a beautiful blue sky with white fluffy clouds floating past you. I want you to relax and enjoy the ocean, sand and blue sky.

Now, imagine the blue sky turning to a pure golden sky. Now imagine the gold sky opening up and you can see a bright gold energy/light shining through the sky. Imagine this bright light shining down through the sky and surrounding your whole body. Let it surround your head, neck, shoulders, arms, chest, back, stomach, legs and feet. Just relax and allow this bright light to surround your whole body.

Now, imagine and allow that same light to enter in through the top of your head and into your body. Allow the light to fill up your whole body from head to toe. Allow this bright light to flow though your head, neck, shoulders, arms, chest, back, stomach, legs and feet. Allow this light inside your body to penetrate into all the muscles, organs, bones and cells.

Once this is done, look back up at that bright light shining through the gold sky and imagine yourself floating up through the sky, passing through the clouds and entering into that light.

Step Two: Now that you're in the light, look down and imagine that you're standing on a golden floor. Look around and you'll see that you're in a room with a golden floor and walls.

Look straight ahead. You will notice someone standing in the distance. Walk closer to that person until you reach him. At this point, you may just make out a figure or you may see his whole body clearly. The person you see may look like an older gentleman with long white hair and a long white beard. This person you're now standing in front of is God. If you look to your right and left, you will see thousands of Angels on both sides of Him as far as the eye can see.

You will see God lay His hands on your head; you will see a gold energy surround your body. This gold energy will awaken your spiritual body. You will see this gold energy blend in with your body, making you feel stronger and more powerful from within because of the awakening of your spiritual body.

The first thing you should do is to introduce yourself to God and you may hear Him say, "Hello," or he may have a message for you. Now you are listening for the first time with your spiritual ears, not your human ones. Sounds through your spiritual ears will sound more like a thought inside your head, but there are exceptions. Some people may hear with their spiritual ears as if they were hearing with their physical ears. At this time, you may talk to Him, asking Him questions and He will talk back to you.

Ask God for your spiritual gift or gifts and you will see Him hand them to you. Put out your hands and take them. You may see a golden staff, a harp, a dagger, a crown or one of many thousands of spiritual gifts, God has for you. Once you've received them ask Him what they are for and how to use them. Once He tells you about your spiritual gifts, put the gifts in your chest for safe keeping; you do this by touching your hand to your chest in the physical dimension.

Step Three: After receiving your spiritual gifts, it's time to ask God your questions. You can hang out with God and the Angels for as long as you want, asking them any question that you need answers to. Also, now is the time you ask for guidance in your life or reveal if you need help manifesting your dreams and desires. Remember not to have an ego or try to control the conversation because this will make you lose your connection to God and the Angels.

When you're finished asking questions; always thank God and the Angels for their time and patience.

Now onto the biggest step…

Step Four: There is no Step Four.

Stop there and just realize that you were standing before God and his Angels; talking to them and receiving spiritual gifts. Your spiritual body has just been awakened.

When you've finished meditating, don't go back and over-think or doubt everything you've just experienced. Know that it was real and that you can return to this place anytime you desire. Many people will think that what just occurred couldn't have just happened. Let me reassure you that you have just spent time with God and Angels. Your spiritual body is now awakened and you did, indeed, received spiritual gifts.

When God first gave me these four steps I thought, "Could it be this simple? Will everyone get it? Will people think it's too easy or will they think it's too complicated?"

I said to God, "You mean it's as simple as **Step One**, look up; **Step Two**, allow your (God's) golden energy to surround and enter your body; **Step Three**, see God, and **Step Four** doesn't exist?"

God then said in a stern manner, "NO, Step Four does exist. Step Four is the most important step; Step Four is, "there is no Step Four!" This is where people's logical minds want to take over and convince them that nothing has just occurred.

Finding Time in the Day to Meditate

We all know that there are twenty-four hours in a day.

Some people work eight hours a day and some people work twelve to fourteen hours a day or more. We also have to tend to different issues—our homes, our children, having our hair done, taking the dog for a walk, hobbies and so forth. With this being the case, we need to take at least twenty minutes each day to devote to meditating Not only will you be able to talk to God and your Angels, but you will also be able to understand the spiritual dimensions as they specifically relate to your path. If you could see God and your Angels in meditation, you really don't have to be concerned with learning too much else from other spiritual sources. God and your Angels will tell you what you need to know or do. Just ask them—it's a pure and easy way to learn spirituality.

God energy has so much power that every molecule in your body will sense a renewed vibration—a vibration of honesty, a vibration of truth, a vibration of strength and the vibration of power. You'll become totally fearless and also totally blissful and happy. If you can imagine these sensations running through your body, then meditate for twenty minutes each day and you will know what happiness is all about.

I assure you that, if you spend at least twenty minutes a day in meditation, there's nothing better that you could be doing with this time. Set time aside to work on yourself and meditate so you'll be able to see God, your Angels, Heavenly Hierarchy and receive your spiritual gifts. Your spiritual gifts will free you from your personal bondage created by the Demons and dark energies within your spiritual dimensions.

Remember, when God gives you a spiritual gift, always ask him what it's for and how to use it. As you learn to use your spiritual gifts, you will receive more and more, and these spiritual gifts will change your life instantly.

When God gave me this simple, yet important, knowledge of how to teach others to communicate with Him, I couldn't wait to teach everyone because now I had a hotline to God. As I shared this knowledge with other people, I found that it really works. Other people are seeing, hearing and talking to God and their Angels.

The excitement I get from seeing other people becoming excited because of their connection to God and their Angels, is overwhelming at times. I realize it's so simple; you don't have to join or be a part of any particular religion or study for a lifetime in order to get in touch with God or receive spiritual gifts. You don't have to meditate on top of a mountain for seventy-five years hoping to get a glimpse of God. Why would he make it so complicated?

He didn't. Societies did.

You may think, "This isn't enough information, I need more."

If this is how you feel, then remember Step Four. It is that simple. Remember that your spiritual gifts are divinely led to you. Your spiritual gifts may be different from anyone else's in the world because every single person is on their own spiritual path. If you just do one simple thing, meditate for twenty minutes every day to get in touch with God, Angels, Heavenly Hierarchy and receive your spiritual gifts, then your life will change instantly.

I have a saying that I use all the time: "Everyday you don't meditate, don't eat and don't drink." Pretty soon you're going to feel the sensation of hunger and thirst.

Meditation is food and nourishment for the spiritual body. It's just as important to feed your spiritual body as it is to feed the physical one. If you don't meditate, you'll feel a different sensation, not of hunger or thirst. Most people have a sensation of weakness, emptiness or that something is missing in their lives and they just cannot put their finger on what it is. I can tell you what it is: it's the need for spiritual nourishment.

The easiest way to start meditating is just to start and the easiest way to continue meditating is to build a habit.

I've put together a meditation journal so you can track your progress and build a daily habit of meditating. Tracking your progress is very important because you receive spiritual gifts daily and it becomes hard to remember what you received.

You also get important messages from God and Angels that you may not want to forget. You may ask God or your Angels for help in achieving something and it's always exciting to keep track of how long it took them to hook it up for you. If you would like to order one of my meditation journals, there is an order form in the back of this book or you can order it online at www.yourkeystoheaven.com. Remember, every day that you don't meditate, don't eat or drink. Sooner or later you will get hungry and thirsty.

Note: Some of you may feel like, "Wow that was easy! I got it the first time just by reading it and following the steps." Some of you may need a little more help. Now please stop and go to the track on the CD entitled, "Seeing and Hearing Spiritually." I will walk you step-by-step through the process of this meditation.

Remember, there is neither rhyme nor reason about who can see God the first time or who has to work on it a little more. Every one of you can see God. Sometimes the people who have the hardest time seeing in the beginning, end up seeing with the most vivid color and detail. Don't worry or over-think it. You're not racing or competing with anyone; you're on your own spiritual journey and spirituality is not a competition.

HEALING
HOW TO SPIRITUALLY HEAL YOURSELF AND OTHERS

If you have been following along in this book, you should have just returned from a magical journey where you learned to see and hear spiritually, came face to face with God and Angels, received your first spiritual gifts and awakened your spiritual body. Now this magical pathway to God is open to you forever. You may return whenever you would like, but this journey is just the beginning.

I am now going to show you how the spiritual and physical worlds are intertwined and how they directly affect each other.

In the world we live in, if you're sick you go to the drugstore and buy over-the-counter medications or you go to the doctor or hospital and they prescribe a medication for you to take. Sometimes the medications work and you get better and sometime they don't work. One of the things that bothers me with all medications is the known and unknown side effects on our body. I'm not saying, "Don't take your medications." What I'm saying is that there is a better way to heal yourself—one that, until now, no one has been teaching you.

There is a better and easier way to heal yourself and that is by allowing God's energy/light into your body and removing the Demons and dark energy within you.

We're all human and our physical bodies do break down and get sick, but I believe that, if you keep enough God light in your body, you can avoid any great illness. I'm not saying that a Demon can't slip into your spiritual body now and then causing you to become sick, but now you have the power to allow God light into your spiritual body to remove the Demon and heal yourself.

"Last of all I want to remind you that your strength must come from the Lord's mighty power within you. Put on all of God's armor so that you will be able to stand safe against all strategies and tricks of Satan. For we are not fighting against people made of flesh and blood, but against persons without bodies—the evil rulers of the unseen world, those mighty satanic beings and great evil princes of darkness who rule this world; and against huge numbers of wicked spirits in the spirit world."

EPHESIANS 6: 10-12
Bible

"...then I breathe into it and it becomes a bird with Allah's permission and I heal the blind and the leprous, and bring the dead to life with Allah's permission... most surely there is a sign in this for you, if you are believers."

Quaran - [3.49]

"And he spake unto me again, saying: Look! And I looked, and I beheld the Lamb of God going forth among the children of men. And I beheld multitudes of people who were sick, and who were afflicted with all manner of diseases, and with devils and unclean spirits; and the Angel spake and showed all these things unto me. And they were healed by the power of the Lamb of God; and the devils and the unclean spirits were cast out."

1 Nephi 11
The Book of Mormon

What is Healing?
Healing is getting rid of the Demons in the spiritual dimensions before they attack your spiritual body and create a dark energy within your physical body causing physical, mental or emotional sickness.

Illness in our physical bodies is the direct result of Demons and other dark energies that have been ruling over earth for thousands of years. These Demons attack everyone's spiritual bodies causing all of our illnesses. Our physical bodies are paying the price. If you don't believe me, then just look at all of the illness in the world: It can't be blamed on anyone and it's not anyone's fault that they are sick. Through thousands of years, many illnesses were created by Demons and these illnesses are sometime handed down generation to generation. The reason the illness is handed down from generation to generation is because the Demon that created the illness is also handed down from generation to generation. That is the reason you need to learn how to get rid of the Demons, so you can get rid of your illness or prevent yourself from getting an illness and maybe handing it down to a loved one.

You have the power to heal and prevent future illness within you or anyone else. God's light is the most powerful cure against all sickness.

When I was younger, people would often come to me and ask if I could heal them. At that time, I could not because I had not received the spiritual gift of healing, yet.

At that time, the only thing I could do was tell about the past, present, future or talk to a dead loved one, but I always knew that there was more that I could do to help people. Even though they would walk away from their sessions with answers to their questions, they would also walk away with their pain. From my view, I always looked at pain and illness as being a Demon or dark energy, and I always looked at health and happiness as being God energy.

One day I asked God to show me how to take away the Demons and darkness causing all this pain and illness within people. I knew that if I could get rid of people's darkness, their God energy (light) would be able to flow into their bodies. At that time, I was thinking that, if God showed me how to heal, then I would have to get rid of all the Demons in everyone by myself! I didn't realize that I would soon be able to teach everyone what God was teaching me.

Shortly after I asked God for help, I received my first two spiritual gifts. One of my spiritual gifts was for healing. God showed me how to use this gift to get rid of the Demons in and around myself. Then he showed me how to use this gift to get rid of Demons within others. Earlier in the book, I talked about how I used my healing gift for the first time and healed the producer of a radio show. With my spiritual gift, I could simply touch people's spiritual bodies and I would see Demons running out of them, then exploding when they touched the God light surrounding these people.

As these Demons would leave the spiritual body, the people would claim to feel lighter. Some would feel sensations of heat, some would feel tingles and others would even get dizzy and pass out.

When you see an evAngelist touch people and they pass out, it's because they are channeling God energy into that person's spiritual body chasing away the Demons. The person can't help but pass out. These evAngelists may not know what's happening in the spiritual dimensions and they may not be able to show you what they are doing, but it's possible for everyone to learn how to allow God light into their body.

I realized that my gift of healing was really working when, time-after-time, people would come to me and tell me how their physical illness went away after I worked on them spiritually. I knew, then, that I must teach everyone how to use their spiritual gifts to get rid of dark energy and Demons in themselves, family, friends, loved ones and even strangers.

I asked God if this was possible. He said, "Yes, I'll show you how."

I was a little nervous, so I asked, "What if they don't listen or believe it's true?"

God said, "I gave everyone free will, so it's up to them to learn or not, but it's up to you to teach."

From that day to this, I've been teaching people how to heal themselves and others.

Every person on this planet has the ability to learn how to heal themselves and others because we all have a spiritual body that lies inside of our physical one. Even the bad (possessed) people do. I know that everyone must get rid of the Demons and dark energies that are blocking God's energy from connecting to their spiritual body and healing their physical body from all illness.

When I'm working on healing someone, I'm working in the spiritual dimensions that exist all around us. These dimensions can only be seen with spiritual eyes. There are ten dimensions that I work in when healing. The first is the physical dimension where we all live and the tenth dimension is heaven where God lives. There are eight dimensions between heaven and earth where Demons and dark energies attack the spiritual extensions of your physical body causing you physical, mental or emotional illness. These spiritual extensions are known as your higher selves.

I will teach you about the spiritual dimensions shortly, but first, I would like to share with you some testimonials from people who were healed through the light of God. In these stories, you will find that I helped all of these people, but I'm only the teacher leading the way. I believe that every one of you can do exactly what I'm doing; you simply have to learn. I'm not trying to say I have all of the answers, but I do have some and I want to teach everyone God's power of healing.

I learn everyday from people whom I've taught; they call with their stories and I learn from them all, especially kids. Children are some of the most amazingly gifted spiritual beings on this planet. I have a chapter dedicated to gifted children later in this book.

Read through the testimonials and then I will show you how to heal yourself, your loved ones and even strangers.

Testimonial by Carol O'Conner

I would like to share with everyone how it was that I came to meet Gary.

I first heard of Gary a few years ago. He was a guest on a radio program in Las Vegas and he was talking about a spiritual retreat he was going to be holding in Ojai, California where he was going to teach everyone how to get in touch with God and Angels, how to receive spiritual gifts and how to get rid of Demons so we can heal ourselves and others. By the end of the radio program, I had decided to attend the retreat.

I went into the retreat open-minded and willing to learn anything that was taught. I never expected to learn what I did. Gary taught me and everyone who attended the retreat how to see, hear and talk to God and Angels, how to receive spiritual gifts and understand the 10 spiritual dimensions around us. He taught us how to see Demons and understand the havoc they cause to every one of us in our everyday life. He also taught us how to use our spiritual gifts to get rid of the Demons causing illness.

Not long ago, my mother had a stroke and the first person who came to my mind was Gary. I knew of his healing abilities and knew he could heal my mom. Here's my story.

This is a testimonial that I sent to people who attended Gary's spiritual retreat with me.

Dear advanced spiritual retreat group:

Below will be a testimonial of Gary helping to heal my mom, but before I get to that, I wanted to mention Paul Cardillo (a lawyer and close friend of Gary's). I met Paul about two years ago in Sedona, Arizona at a workshop. Paul was very instrumental in the process, as you will see.

Gary heals my mom:

Three or four days ago, I got a call from one of my sisters (I have six sisters, including me, making a total of seven). She told me that my mom was in the hospital for shortness of breath and dizziness and other things to do with her heart.

I packed my bag and got there as fast as I could. Tests were taken and not much found. The next day, she was released from the hospital around lunchtime. We headed over to my sister's house. At dinner time, we were all laughing about something and, just that quick, my mom was having a stroke.

911 was called. I put one of my hands on the mom's heart and the other on her back. I tried increasing my God light and connecting to hers so that I could help her in any way I could until the paramedics arrived. An ambulance took my mom to the hospital while my sister and I went in separate cars.

When we arrived at the hospital, the receptionist said that we could go back and be with my mom. My mom was slurring her words and tired; the doctor said the stroke affected the right side of her body. She was not able to lift her right arm and had difficulty with the right leg, also. It was difficult to comprehend all that was taking place. We were waiting for a room to open on the second floor in the hospital, so we just sat and waited with her. I had time to think. I knew there must be Demons here, but I am too close to the situation and too tired to get rid of them. I needed help and I knew, beyond a shadow of doubt that Gary was the answer. My only problem was I didn't have Gary's number with me. I called my sister in Chicago and ask her to get a hold of Paul in Florida because I knew he could get a hold of Gary. (This was all divinely guided.)

The next day, family flew in. My sisters were crying upon seeing my mother in this state. When she tried to eat, upon she could not hold anything with her right hand nor could she say anything clearly and yet I was a tower of strength. Usually, I am a blubbering idiot in emergencies.

I am an empath and have been since a child, yet I didn't realize this until a year ago. (This is what they call a person who feels someone else's energy.) The reason I tell you this is because, even though I was a tower of strength, I could feel something across my chest strangling me and I felt my God Cord was totally blocked. (For those of you who are reading Gary's book for the first time and don't know what your God Cord is, it is the cord of light that runs through all ten dimensions from the top of your head in the first dimension through all of the others, all the way up to heaven and God in the tenth dimension.) I was exhausted and knew that only Gary could help. It was a long day, yet I had a chance to call my sister in Chicago and ask her if she called Paul. She said, "Yes." And I knew something would change soon.

Everyone went home that day, but I decided to stay with my mom at the hospital overnight. We went to bed very early—around 6 p.m. Around 8 p.m. that night, I could feel that something was happening in the room. The room suddenly felt lighter and my chest was open and released from the stranglehold it had. My mom was snoring soundly; she was sleeping like a baby. I fell into a deep sleep, only to be woken up by a nurse checking my mom's vital signs. My mom fell back to sleep—it was already morning around 6:30 a.m. I thought, "I better lay here and meditate—going through the ten dimensions clearing the Demons away from Mom before all the family members started coming back." I knew I wouldn't get a chance later.

As I was meditating, I saw Gary all dressed in white with a white robe bowing before God humbly asking for my mom to be healed. At that moment, I knew that my mom was going to be healed. There was such peace in the room. Suddenly, the phone rang. It was my sister calling. It woke up my mom, who sat up and spoke clearly, moved her right hand and leg, got out of bed and went to the bathroom on her own.

I'm sitting there in shock, practically screaming to my sister, "She's healed. It's a miracle. She's walking! She's talking!" Like it was nothing, my mom walks over to the sink to wash her face and wants to put her contacts in her eyes. She says she's hungry and we ordered breakfast. All I wanted to do was call everyone in the family and say, "It's a miracle!"

Thank you ever so much to Paul for the divine connection to Gary.

And to Gary I want to say thank you for healing my mom. It's a miracle!

We Love You, Gary.
Love to all,
Carol O'Conner

I share this story with you because I'm not the one who healed Carol's mom; God was. All I did was use my spiritual gifts to clear the darkness and Demons that were creating the illness in her body and asked God to heal her. Carol had already cleared the Demons and darkness away from her mom the previous day by placing her hands on her back and allowing God light to flow through her into her mom which gave her mom the added strength to get through this. So, when I asked God to help, he just had to add a little of his healing light and a miracle happened. Anyone of you could have helped Carol's mom by helping clear the Demons and darkness and by asking God to help. That's why I want everyone on earth to understand all of the things I know, so everyone can help heal everyone else.

Carol was too emotionally close to the situation to fully help her mom, so I lent a helping hand; I hope that some day soon, everyone is able to heal each other with God light.

Testimonial by Deanna Garcia

Seeing a clear light

Several years ago, it was discovered that I had a rare form of cataracts. After numerous surgeries (13), including two sets of implants (a very rare operation), laser procedures and medications, the doctors said, "There is nothing left to try." I finally had to accept the limitations that would change my life: I have blurry, wavy, double and sometimes triple vision. Everyday when it becomes dusk I never leave my safe zone of home without assistance. UV lighting was like torture and sunlight was my enemy. Headaches, eye pain and depression were the daily schedule

A few months ago, I met Misty Jackson, whom I connected with immediately. One day, Misty called to tell me that her Angels (Misty had previously attended one of Gary's seminars where she learned how to communicate with her Angels) had been trying to tell her something and she finally figured it out. Misty took it upon herself to buy me a ticket to go see Gary; she made all the arrangements for transportation, since I cannot drive anymore. I am now legally blind. Misty and I felt that November 8, 2003 (the day I was going to see Gary) was the beginning of something good. We just felt positive.

On November 8, 2003, Misty took me to Gary's seminar. She walked with me, led me around and stayed until I was comfortable. While sitting there listening to Gary speak, I felt enlightened with the information he was presenting to all of us. I paid attention when he spoke to individuals with questions. I finally formed enough courage to ask Gary what he saw in the future for my eyesight. Gary asked me if I minded if his assistant, Dean, helped him in a healing on my eyes. He then transformed the invitation to the class to assist if they chose. I sat there with my eyes closed, praying. Gary then directed his assistant and the class to put their hands on me. When they put their hands on me, I started getting hotter and hotter inside my body. My thermostat was totally on overload. Gary then explained to me that he was getting rid of the Demons and dark energy's that were on my eyes. Afterward, I had tears running down my face and wasn't sure of anything at that moment. Gary then asked if I was all right. I just sat there looking around a dim-lit room and found myself actually making out a clear image of everything. I kept thinking, "Is this possible? Am I dreaming?"

I couldn't wait any longer. I quietly walked out into the corridor, down the elevator and walked out the front doors to see a dark night. I could see and read the signs. Cars passing by had two headlights instead of six and I clearly saw the faces of people walking by me. I went back to the seminar and felt like an explosion of peacefulness inside myself.

I remember saying, thanks to everyone and thinking, "No one will ever understand." I was so settled into the last several years of limitations that there was no reason to plan or explore much of a future. I had a lot more of a miracle than just clear sight. It was time to get busy with life again; with a purpose so strong that I haven't stopped bouncing.

I want to thank Gary for being that vessel of God, his assistant, Dean, for his strength and gifts and to the class who put their energies into giving to a stranger. God bless you all,

I never thought I was deserving of this special miracle, but I found out through the gifts that I received that day, that we all deserve miracles. We just need to ask.

Respectfully,
Deanna Garcia

This is another example of a healing.

I simply used my spiritual gifts to remove the microscopic Demons that were causing Deanna's eyesight problems. Demons come in all shapes and sizes. The healing of Deanna was a group effort. As I removed the Demons blocking Deanna's sight, my assistant, Dean worked in the higher dimensions keeping them clear so God's light would flow into Deanna allowing the healing to take place. The rest of the class also allowed God light to flow through them into Deanna. Thank God for everyone who helped Deanna to see again. And thank Deanna for wanting to be healed. Remember, God said that the person doing the healing and the person being healed both must truly want the healing to take place or it simply will not happen.

Demons affect us in many different ways. For Deanna it was eye problems. But it can also be in the form of cancer, aids or mental illnesses such as depression, panic attacks, bi-polar disorder and much more.

There are no boundaries for God's light. I believe that God's energy can and will heal all physical, mental and emotional problems. Simply learn to receive and use your spiritual gifts and remove the Demons causing the problems so that God's light can enter into you. It's actually a very simple process that I will teach to everyone. But first, I'd like to share with you a few more testimonials on healing.

Testimonial by Marilyn Frazier

On December 18, 2000, I had a complete mastectomy of my right breast. On January 4, 2001, I started an extensive regimen of chemotherapy and radiation treatments. I finished treatments October 2002. All through the horrific ordeal, my family and friends stuck by me. My very good and gracious friend, Gary Spivey did even more.

Eleven years ago, Gary and I met and my life from that point on has never been the same. He taught me about spirituality, how to truly get in touch with God and how to use the gifts he has for us. He taught me to use my gift of Clairvoyance to earn a living for my children. During the two years I lay losing my hair and in a deep depression, Gary would call me and help me meditate through the pain. I had a very difficult time with third-degree burns from radiation, until Gary showed me how to get to a higher level with my meditation. This kept me out of pain. It also heightened my closeness with God. Gary told me that God said I could live if I " wanted to."

At the end of October, I had been out of chemo for about two weeks. I had a reaction to some of the medications the doctors had given me. While I was in the hospital, they discovered two more tumors on my right chest wall. They told me they looked like they were stage five (which means get your affairs in order).

I went home and prayed about what had transpired. I knew I could not handle any more chemotherapy and the thought of more surgery was more than I can stand. I got a call from Gary and he wanted me to come out to California for a spiritual retreat. My son told me that if I could get out there, Gary could touch God and get me healed. I called the doctor to see if I could go and he said, "Yes, but you are scheduled to see the surgeon about those tumors when you get back." I agreed and hung up. I packed my duds and was off to California.

The trip was hard, but after being pushed in a wheelchair all over the airports and feeling like an invalid, I made it. Dean met me at the airport. He told me that God had given him some new gifts and he had been praying for me. I arrived at Gary's house and he showed me around. I could already feel the incredible energy in the house. I called home to see how everyone was doing, and my son said, "Mom, God told me if you could just get to Gary you could be healed." This is one of my miracle babies that Gary told me was so special. (That's another wonderful Gary story.)

The next day, we went to the church where Gary does his seminars. There were about 25 people at the seminar. Gary told me that he had handpicked them all because he wanted this to be very special. During the session, each one of us told why we were there. I told them all that I was there for a selfish reason; I had come to get a healing for my cancer. I have twins that are really special; I wasn't supposed to have any more children. I had my tubes tied twenty-four years ago. I have 12-year-old twins. I know that with all the difficulty I had bringing them into the world and because I'm 52 years old and all of my family members are too old to raise them, God had to give me a miracle.

We all received spiritual gifts and Gary took us to a lot of magical places in and around the Ojai Valley. It was the most beautiful and spiritual place I've ever seen. One of the most healing places I visited was the beach, where the dolphins were. With Dean's and Nil's (two very wonderful friends and spiritual people) help, I descended the hill. It seemed forever to get to the bottom—one of the side effects of chemotherapy left me with arthritis in every joint in my body. Once I was there and stood in the waters, there was no doubt why Gary had brought us there. We all shared our sorrows and joy and prayed for one another. Our kindred spirits melted together and we all knew each other on an intimate level that few people find in the real world.

Before lunch, we came back to the church and Gary helped God give everyone spiritual gifts. Mine was a chair. I looked at Bea—a terrific lady who is part of Gary's staff and my friend—and said, "A chair? What on earth?" After lunch, Gary started asking us what gifts we received. He spoke with a few people about their gifts then he looked around the room and said that God had told him to do something different. Gary said, "I want to put a chair in the corner and have Marilyn sit in it." He chose different people to lay their hands on me and pray. The energy was as thick as Jell-O. It was all pink, gold and brilliant white. I zoned out for what seemed to be forever. I heard Gary tell me to look up and get my healing from God. I knew I had it. I could feel all of the love from the special people who were around me— they were sending me their love and healing.

I thank God that Gary had taken a roomful of spiritual people and taught them how to see God so *they could assist in my healing.* It was an indescribable experience. When we all came to what seemed to be the *end, we were all crying—men and women alike— and filled with an unspeakable happiness. Everyone there knew something amazing had taken place. I told Gary that the gift God had given me before lunch was a chair and, of course, I had been bitching about what on earth could that mean. There I was sitting in my chair being healed. God truly does work in mysterious ways. I'm just glad he has a man like Gary who can discern what he wants done.*

When I got back to Tennessee, I was scheduled for a CAT scan, chest x-ray and to see the surgeon. When he came in to see me, he said, "Someone's been praying." I just looked at him and smiled. He read to me the report that the radiologists gave him before I went to see Gary. It said, "Needs biopsies, definite tumors on the right chest wall (maybe too large for surgery)." But the new report said there was nothing. I couldn't believe it.

My surgeon sent me to my oncologist who did not believe it. He scheduled me for the same test two more times before he said to me that the tumors weren't there. He, unlike my surgeon, didn't believe in miracles and dismissed the whole thing. I saw the tumors on the x-ray and the doctors had me preparing to leave this old world. Thanks to Gary's close walk with God, and the spiritual atmosphere I was consumed in for that weekend, I am healed.

Marilyn Frazier

In Marilyn's situation, she was physically sick with cancer, and I knew she could be healed if she just allowed God's energy into her. As everyone was projecting God's light into Marilyn, I was simply getting rid of the Demons that caused the cancer in Marilyn's chest. Once all of the Demons were gone, I heard God say, "That's it. The healing is done." You see, not only did everyone who was working with Marilyn want her to be healed, she, for the first time, truly wanted to be healed.

Many times when I'm working on people they, for some reason or another, don't believe they can be healed or they like the attention from being sick. Whatever the reason, the healing doesn't take place. From this point on, it was totally up to Marilyn to keep the God energy in her body so that the Demons could not make the cancer come back. Marilyn learned to use her spiritual gifts to keep away the Demons and keep the God energy in her body.

To this day, she is still cancer-free and the doctors still don't know what to believe. All I can say is that, with this simple process of using your spiritual gifts to get rid of the Demons and allow God's energy into your spiritual body, you can heal your physical body of all illnesses. All you have to do is want to be healed and believe it will happen.

The previous testimonials reflect but a few of the healings that I've seen take place where physical illnesses have been healed.

I would like to share with you one more story: This one is a little different because this shows how Demons can attack us mentally and start to ruin our lives. This story is about a very common and crippling disease—Depression. I have seen people from all walks of life and from all over the world with the same or similar problems. Now I'll share with you Betty's testimonial

Testimonial by Betty

Dear Gary,

First, I would like to explain the frame of mind that I was in prior to our session on May 3, 2004. For the last four years, I have been encountering a change within myself and my attitude toward my family and friends. I am normally a very positive and optimistic person, but I had become negative and angry toward almost everything in my life. I was very depressed mentally and physically. I was experiencing anxiety attacks; my body was cold continuously and I also lost interest in a sexual relationship with my husband. My family had become detached. My husband and I started to drift apart and our children started to become less interested in doing family things. We are normally a very close family.

I believe in God and the power of prayer. I also feel that I am a very spiritual person, but there was something very wrong here. I felt stuck, trapped, also confined by

something that I could not identify. This has all changed since May 3, 2004.

During our conversation, Gary, by your gift of healing and by the grace of God, you were able to detect that my spirit had been under extreme Demonic attack. Darkness was covering my thoughts, heart, lungs and, to my surprise, my desire to be sexually active. I had experienced several visions while going through this cleansing of my spirit. I saw the light that removed the Demons from my mind, lungs, back and heart. The most incredible healing was when you removed the Demons from my uterus. I cannot believe it, but from that moment, my feelings of love and desire toward my husband came back. My love for my family and friends came back to normal. This has not changed since that day. After just twenty minutes, I felt so unbelievably at peace. The warmth came back into my body. I felt love all over me. I was my true self once again. This has brought tears to my eyes, as it does now telling you my story. What was even more miraculous that evening was when my 18-year-old son, James, came home from work and took one look at me and said, "Mom, there is a glow on your face, like a light around you."

We started to discuss my experience that night and he was very happy for me. He also confirmed that I had not been myself and he told me how hard it was not being able to be as close as we were before. Again, this has all improved.

I'm sincerely thankful and will continue to share my experience with others in hopes of helping them realize this truly does happen. We live in a very spiritual world, yet some people find it hard to acknowledge. Gary, I hope that, through my testimony, people will believe there is a greater power out there and seek the healing power that God has given you in this life to help them heal their souls.

Best wishes and many thanks,
   Betty

This was a different kind of healing. This healing was getting rid of the Demons that were making her depressed and unhappy. By getting rid of these Demons, her happiness was able to shine through again, instantly. She was no longer depressed.

Demons can and will infect every part of our body and stop us from being who we truly are. After I removed Betty's Demons, she felt happy again, her sexual drive was back and she felt like her true self once again. As far as her son coming home and noticing the glow around her face, what he noticed was her natural God light/ energy (her Aura) that was now flowing into her, as it should flow into everyone.

Hearing these stories day in and day out and seeing these amazing changes in people's lives, I can only imagine what life would be like without Demons and dark energies. As I found myself imagining what it would be like, I felt this tremendous heat sensation in my body, and then I saw God. He told me, "That is my plan, to awaken everyone's spiritual body so we, as a society, can band together and get rid of the Demons and dark energies that plague mankind."

At that point, everything got really clear to me. Even though some of the things I see happen as I work with people on a daily basis can be considered miracles, I've realized that this indeed is normal. Miracles are normal. Being healed is normal. Living a blissful co-existing relationship with other people is normal. Being one with everyone on the planet and being one with God and the heavens at the same time is normal. Again, my only challenge is to show the rest of the world this process.

Remember, all healing—no matter what part of the body you're healing—must first take place in your spiritual body by getting rid of the Demons and dark negative energy in the spiritual dimensions around you.

Your Spiritual Body

Your spiritual body is made up of your spirit and soul. Both your spirit and soul lived in heaven before coming to live in your physical body.

As I mentioned before, healing is the process of getting rid of the Demons and dark energies that attack our spiritual body causing physical, mental and emotional illness in our physical body. I know it may seem a little complicated to understand but it's actually very easy and simple to understand, and I will teach you just how simple it is.

Throughout the rest of this book, I will use a few words such as Spiritual Body, Spirit, Soul, Higher Selves, God Cord, and Aura. Before I go any further, I need to explain to you what I'm talking about when I use these words.

Spiritual Body

Your spirit and your soul make up your spiritual body. The function of the spirit is to protect the soul. The easiest way to explain this is that the spirit part of your spiritual body is like the skin, muscles and bones of your physical body, and your soul part of your spiritual body is like the vital organs such as the heart and lungs to your physical body.

Both the spirit and soul live within your physical body.

Spirit

Your spirit is part of a heavenly life force that lives within you and which makes up your spiritual body. The spirit is the outer core of your spiritual body; the soul is the inner core, but they both live within your physical body.

The spirit lives in heaven until the time of conception. At the time of conception, when the female becomes pregnant, your spirit enters into your new physical body form, grows with you and is there at the time of your birth; waiting for your soul to enter your body.

Your spirit is put into your physical body to help protect your soul from the Demons and dark energies that try to destroy your soul.

Soul

Your soul is part of a heavenly life force that also lives within you.

The reason your spirit lives within you is to protect your soul because your soul has locked inside of it all of the spiritual knowledge of heaven. When your soul leaves heaven and enters into your physical body, God has to lock all of heaven's knowledge within your soul. If heaven's knowledge were not locked within your soul, your soul would glow so bright as it enters your body that it would alarm all of the Demons. They would attack your soul before it entered your physical body. They would rather have you dead than born with that knowledge already unlocked, knowing that one day you may be able to unleash heaven's knowledge unto the world.

There are many souls that slip through the cracks and make it into the physical body with heaven's knowledge already unlocked. These souls were sent to enlighten the world. Everyone's soul lives lifetime to lifetime waiting for you to unlock heaven's spiritual knowledge while still in your physical body. Your soul now waits within you for that moment when you unlock it and release your spiritual knowledge. I will reveal this spiritual secret as God did to me so everyone can unlock their souls. Your soul is the DNA of your spiritual body.

The DNA of your physical body is different from person to person, but the DNA of your soul is the same from soul to soul. So, as you see, everyone on earth is related, "spiritually speaking."

God explained to me that by unlocking the soul while still alive, we bring heaven closer to earth. The more people on earth who unlock their souls, means that we, as a society, will be that much closer in bringing heaven to earth. God also explained to me that this can be done in our lifetime if everyone learns to unlock their spiritual knowledge within.

As I see it through Gods eyes, if heaven was on earth, we would not have to return back to heaven. We would already be there living as one spiritually-related family.

Higher Selves

Higher selves are extensions of your spirit. We have hundreds of higher selves in the spiritual dimensions.

When you are born into the physical world, your soul enters your body. At that moment in time, your higher selves (which are extensions of your spirit) enter into the spiritual dimensions between heaven and earth. They are there to protect your soul from the Demons and dark energies that attack it.

Your higher selves look just like your physical body does. When you're looking into the spiritual dimensions with your spiritual eyes, you will see God, Angels, Demons and your higher selves. If you see someone that looks just like you, then you're looking at one of your higher selves. Your higher selves are on the front line of the battle between good and evil.

God Cord

Your God Cord is the connection between your spiritual body (your spirit and soul that resides within your physical body) and heaven. Your God Cord is a cord of gold energy that runs from heaven through all of the spiritual dimensions and connects to your spiritual body through the top of your head.

I will show you how to use your spiritual eyes to see your God Cord running from heaven and connecting to the top your head. I will show you how to have God energy flow from heaven down your God Cord and into your spiritual body. When this happens, you'll feel a warm sensation throughout your physical body.

Aura

Your aura is the glow around your physical body once your spiritual body is filled with God light/energy.

The next thing I must explain before I go any further is about the spiritual dimensions around us. This is where all healings takes place. If you keep these dimensions clear and allow God light in your spiritual body, you can eliminate all illness.

Spiritual Dimensions

Where are they? Why can't anyone see them? Are they being kept secret from us? Why doesn't my religion teach me about the spiritual dimensions? Do they really exist?

In the world where we live, people have been searching for many years for proof that other dimensions exist. Scientists now believe that they do exist, but they don't know how to see into them. Well I can tell you firsthand that they do exist. I work in them every day and I will teach everyone who is interested how to see them. It's very simple.

What does science have to say about dimensions?

For string theory to make sense, the universe should have nine space dimensions and one time dimension, for a total of ten dimensions.

If superstring theory turns out to be correct, the idea of a world consisting of more dimensions is one that we'll need to become comfortable with. But will there ever be an explanation or a visual representation of higher dimensions that will truly satisfy the human mind?

What do some spiritual texts say about spiritual dimensions?

In the book of Enoch from the *Dead Sea Scrolls*, he talks about the Angels who took him to visit the ten heavens.

The teaching of Kabbalah says, "Reality consists of ten dimensions. Nine of these dimensions are beyond time and space."

The one dimension where time and space exist, of course, is the physical dimension we all live in.

What does God have to say about dimensions?

When writing about the spiritual dimensions, I asked God, "How do you want me to explain the spiritual dimensions to everyone?"

He said, "There are many dimensions and most are beyond people's belief system. You have to teach the first ten dimensions, since it is in these dimensions where all healings take place."

The first ten dimensions are the dimensions I work in daily when I'm healing people. I will be teaching you about these ten dimensions. These are the dimensions that have a direct affect on your life. They can cause mental, physical or emotional illness within your physical body.

The first dimension is the Physical Dimension (Earth). Then there are eight spiritual dimensions between your spiritual/physical body and the tenth dimension, which is Heaven. Within the eight spiritual dimensions is where Demons and dark energies attack your spiritual body causing all illness.

I want you to look at the dimensions as a roadmap to heaven. Have you ever taken a road trip somewhere that you've never been? Before you left on your trip you probably looked at a roadmap and planned out your trip so you could arrive at your final destination. Along the way, you may have run into some obstacles, like taking a wrong turn, getting a flat tire, or even running out of gas. But once you got over the obstacles, you arrived at your final destination. Here, heaven is your destination, the spiritual dimensions are the roads and the Demons and dark energies causing physical, mental and emotional illness within your physical body, are the obstacles or blocks. I will teach you how to remove these obstacles from your life so that you can heal yourself through God's light which comes from heaven.

Before I teach you the dimensions, I want you to look at this picture.

When I was doing the research for this book, I was looking through books of artwork when I ran across this painting. This was painted hundreds of years ago. It depicts God explaining something to Adam and Eve. As soon as I saw this painting, I was in shock because someone painted exactly how I see the spiritual dimensions: they're layered one on top of the other. This meant that someone else could see the roadmap to heaven.

Now, because I can see in the spiritual dimensions and understand their layout, what I see in this painting is God explaining the spiritual dimensions (roadmap to heaven) to Adam and Eve. In the next few pages, everything will became clear to you and you will understand what I'm talking about.

When I saw this painting for the first time, I heard God say, "Stop, I want to explain something to you."

He then explained what this artist was trying to convey in his painting to the rest of the world. God said that the artist had a spiritual vision and was painting his vision; he was seeing what was really there. God then explained to me that many artists throughout history knew they could not really talk about their spiritual visions because of the severe consequences they would face, so they painted their visions and kept quiet. God told me that many of the spiritual texts were edited throughout history, but spiritual artwork was not and that's why spiritual artwork really holds the secrets to spirituality.

I believe the artists who were painting all of these great pieces of art knew that someday, somehow their secrets would be reveled to the world because God was speaking to them.

You can view this ancient religious painting and many more in full color with my spiritual interpretation of them at www.yourkeystoheaven.com.

The Spiritual Dimensions

The Creation of the World and the Expulsion from Paradise
Giovanni di Paolo (ca.1400, died 1482).
The Metropolitan Museum of Art, Robert Lehman Collection, 1975. (1075.1.31)

I've been using this dimension chart for many years in seminars and spiritual retreats all around the country when I teach about the dimensions. When God taught me how to see the dimensions, this is what I saw—dimensions layered one on top of the other.

The picture on the opposite page is the painting I discovered when I was writing this book. Do you see the similarities of the dimensions layered one on top of the other? So you can see why I think the painting represents God revealing to Adam and Eve the layout of the spiritual dimensions between heaven and earth.

First Dimension
Earth/Physical Dimension

This dimension is easy to understand. In this dimension, we live and experience life. We experience physical activities such as walking, talking, playing sports, singing or whatever else we do physically. We enjoy falling in love, friendships, and work. We experience positive emotions such as love, happiness and joy. We also experience negative emotions such as sadness, jealousy and anger. I will show you how these negative emotions are nothing more than Demons attacking you in the spiritual dimensions causing these feelings within you.

Also, this dimension is where your dreams take place: the perfect relationship, traveling to new places, having the perfect wedding, the perfect children, your dream job, house or car. Anything and everything you dream of takes place in this dimension. I will show you how Demons stand in the way of you achieving your dreams.

This dimension is where the spiritual cause and effect takes place. Cause is the Demons and dark energies that attack your higher selves in the spiritual dimensions, and the effect is what happens to your physical body because of the attacks on your higher selves. The effect can be in the form of mental, physical or emotional sickness such as depression, bi-polar disorder, attention deficit disorder, panic attacks, obsessive compulsive disorder, migraine headaches, cancer or aids. The list is long. All sickness, no matter if it's mental, emotional or physical is negative energy and negative energy is not part of God's plan. I will show you how to clear the spiritual dimensions and cure all illness.

I will say this again: You must believe you can be healed in order for any healing to take place. The Demons will always put negative thoughts in your head—making you think healing is not possible.

Second Dimension
Golden/First Buffer Dimension

This is the first dimension you have to use your spiritual eyes to see. This dimension surrounds Earth/Physical Dimension acting as a buffer to help keep out Demons and other dark energies that try to come into the physical dimension and attack your physical body. This dimension is also known as the Golden Dimension because when you see this dimension (with your spiritual eyes), it has a golden hue coming from it. In this dimension you will see many Angels helping to protect your higher selves that live in this dimension. You'll occasionally see Demons trying to break their way through this dimension—trying to get into the physical dimension so they can attack your physical body.

Third Dimension
Invisible/Second Buffer Dimension

The reason this dimension is called the Invisible Dimension is because the Demons and dark energies in this dimension have the ability to appear invisible to your spiritual eyes.

The first time I guide you through the clearing of the dimensions, I will have you stop in this dimension because God has a special spiritual gift for you that gives you spiritual sight to see the Demons and dark energies in this dimension. The spiritual gift will be presented to you in a small box. Inside the box, you will find a set of eyes. That set of eyes will give you vision into this dimension. When God presents the box to you, reach up with your physical hand and take it. You will envision a box in your physical hands. Once you can see the box in your hands, you will open it and take the eyes out of the box with your physical hands. Then, with your physical hands, touch your eyes. When you do this, your new spiritual eyes will be set in place.

(If you have been following along in this book, you should understand the process of receiving spiritual gifts. Receiving this special set of spiritual eyes is just another spiritual gift. On the CD I will guide you through the process of receiving your spiritual eyes so you can see in this dimension).

Once you gain vision in this dimension, you will see the Demons that attack your higher selves causing tremendous negative effects on your physical body such as physical, mental and emotional illness; as well as cause havoc in your life.

Note: If, by any chance, when you receive your spiritual eyes to see in this dimension you still cannot see, don't worry. You can still go through the process of clearing this dimension and healing yourself. Just remember, God said, "Everyone will see differently with their spiritual eyes. Some people will see everything as clear as looking at TV, some may see outlines and others may just sense or feel something in the beginning—then your vision will come to you."

So far in this book, you have read about how Demons and dark energies attack our higher selves affecting our spiritual/physical bodies in negative ways. I've talked about and explained Demons to you, but I never explained what a dark energy is. Now is the time for me to explain about dark energies.

We all live on this small planet called earth. If you look up into the sky at night you can see millions of stars and planets. As you're gazing up at those stars and planets, do you ever think or ask yourself are there any other life forms out there? If you think for one moment that we are the only beings that exist in the universe, you're wrong. These dark energies that I've been talking about are Aliens!

Aliens exist in many spiritual dimensions just like Demons.

Many people from all over the world ask me if I believe in aliens. My answer to them is always, "yes" because I see firsthand how destructive they are to our higher selves, causing illness (physically, mentally and emotionally) to our physical body. There's no doubt they exist and their mission is to keep us from using our roadmap to heaven.

Many people from all over the world believe in aliens in one form or another. Some people claim to have been abducted and many more have seen sightings of aliens or UFOs. The reason people can see aliens or UFOs in the physical dimension is because they can cross out of the spiritual and into the physical dimension. When they cross dimensions, this goes against the spiritual laws set up as a guideline to govern them. As crazy as this may sound to you it's true. When I first started talking about Demons, it probably sounded strange to you. Many of you may not have believed that Demons existed—even though Demons are recognized in almost every religious text and in religious artwork through out the world. Still you may or may not believe that Demons exist. Well, just like Demons, aliens do exist.

While growing up, I was always seeing Angels and Demons which made for interesting times. I would also see a dark energy that wasn't a Demon, but that would cause havoc in someone's life all the same. As I got older and my abilities grew stronger, I started understanding these dark energies and realizing that they were, in fact, aliens attacking our spiritual bodies in the spiritual dimensions. I would use my spiritual gifts to get rid of the aliens in the same manner I would get rid of the Demons. I would simply touch the aliens with my spiritual gift or just project God energy toward them and they would evaporate.

Back in the physical dimension, the person whom I removed the alien from would have the exact same feelings and reaction to their physical bodies that they have when I get rid of a Demon: A warm sensation would run through their body.

I know this is far out and very hard for some people to believe, but time and time again, as I would get rid of the aliens that were attacking peoples' spiritual bodies, they would feel the rush of warmth throughout their physical bodies. Then, whatever negative symptoms the aliens were causing in their physical body—whether it was physical, mental or emotional, would simply evaporate, reaffirming that what I was doing was really working. So I knew I wasn't crazy.

Testimonial by Jane

Imagine a world of bubble-headed aliens and grotesque Demons living inside of us and on our planet. Seems like a science fiction novel doesn't it? That's what I thought until I met Gary. I had a phone consultation with Gary; he immediately proceeded to do an energy clearing.

I'd been feeling pretty low energy and seemed to feel anxious at times, despite everything appearing fine. The fitness work, herbal supplements and medications weren't quite making me feel better. Then I went on quite an amazing mental, emotional and spiritual trip with Gary. Afterward, I felt so light and bright and was totally in my body and present. It was truly a wonderful feeling to have this much energy back.

Before the energy clearing, Gary taught me how to see with my spiritual eyes so I could see what was going on in the spiritual dimensions. During the energy clearing, there was a battle going on and, with one wave of Gary's light staff, the slimy little and big creatures were toast. I had a wide array of creatures on and in me like spiders, octopus things, and snakes—like the one on my spine. I had suits of wires running around me and down my spine to my tail bone. Geeez, no wonder I felt lethargic.

As he cleared these forms of negativity out of me, my hands started to feel warmer and my head became clear and lighter. I sure felt fantastic at this point. I had one last adjustment to go: a clearing of my headache. Gary taught me how to use my light wand (a spiritual gift). I pointed my light wand at my temple and pulled out a green slimy grub.

It was really helpful to learn how to visualize and see these critters and how to get rid of them. When our session was done, I felt like a load had been lifted, I felt light and bright and ready to dance the night away. The feeling of relief was peaceful and profound.

Much light and love to you,
Jane

I wanted to share with you Jane's testimonial because, not only was she being attacked by Demons in her spiritual dimensions, she was also being attacked by aliens in the alien dimension. I know this may sound a little strange, but, believe me, aliens do exist. You get rid of the alien that's attacking your higher selves the same way you get rid of a Demon—by using your spiritual gifts and God energy (light).

"Now as I looked at the living creatures, I saw a wheel upon the earth beside the living creatures one for each of the four of them. As for the appearance of the wheels and their construction... the four had the same likeness being as it were a wheel within a wheel. The four wheels had rims and they had spokes, and their rims were full of eyes round about. And when the living creatures went, the wheels went beside them and when the living creatures went, the wheels went with them, for the living creature was in the wheel."

Ezekiel I:16-20
Bible

Fourth Dimension
Dark Planet Aliens Dimension

When God was explaining the dimensions to me, he said to me in this dimension, "there are many dark planets." Dark planets are planets without God energy/light going to them from heaven. There are many different races of aliens that live on these planets. Their main objective is to try to keep God energy/light from reaching other planets so that planet will remain dark and the aliens will have another planet to occupy and add to this dimension.

The way God energy/light reaches a planet is when someone learns how to clear all of the dimensions between heaven and earth, allowing heaven's energy to flow freely from heaven to earth. The more spiritually enlightened the people on a planet are, the more God energy/light can reach that planet turning it into a light planet. The Angels are trying to enlighten as many spiritual bodies on earth as possible so earth can join God's ever-expanding universe of light planets.

Earth, according to what God has explained to me, is in the middle: It can either go light or dark depending on everyone's individual choice—if they want to be enlightened or not. This is why the aliens are trying to keep people from being enlightened and clearing their dimensions. The biggest challenge for the Angels to overcome is that there are more people on earth not enlightened than enlightened. Not only does an enlightened person bring God energy/light to the planet, they also have the power to help the Angels fight against the aliens and Demons that attack their higher selves and spiritual body causing physical, mental and emotional illness within them.

The enlightened people who are aware of the spiritual war going on, can help the Angels by using their spiritual gifts to clear the dimensions. One enlightened person has the ability to clear the spiritual dimension between heaven and earth. But if everyone on earth was enlightened and would clear the dimensions, we would be able to keep the aliens and Demons from attacking our spiritual bodies and higher selves and, at the same time, ending all illness, as we know it, on earth.

God said to me, "If everyone would put aside for a moment, all of the spiritual knowledge they previously learned from religion and stopped all of the arguing over who's religion is right or wrong and joined the fight against the Demons and aliens, then heaven can expand it's boundaries to include earth as a light planet."

"For our struggle is not against the flesh and blood, but against the rulers and the powers of this dark world, and against the forces of evil in the heavenly realms."

Ephesians 6:12
Bible

Fifth Dimension
Light Planets Aliens Dimension

In this dimension there are many light planets. The inhabitants of these planets obey the rules of the universe and are very willing to help lesser evolved planets who are trying to make their way through the darkness to enlightenment.

Light planets are planets that have energy coming from heaven to every living creature on the planet, and everyone lives in harmony with each other. There are planets in this dimension where good aliens live. Their main purpose is helping beings on planets that are in the middle of light and dark such as earth—so they can understand the importance of spiritual enlightenment and keeping God energy/light coming to their planet from heaven. These aliens are peaceful and helpful to all humans. When I'm teaching you to clear the spiritual dimensions, we're going to stop in this dimension for some help.

When I show you how to see in this dimension, you will see many different aliens and highly evolved spiritual beings all living together in harmony and peace. One being I see in this dimension all the time is Ganesh.

Ganesh is a Hindu god who has the head of an elephant and many arms; Ganesh is known as the Remover of Obstacles. Now, I'm not saying that Ganesh is an alien and I'm not saying he isn't, but he is always in this dimension hanging out with other spiritual beings. Another person I see here often is Buddha. Many times he has important information to share with whoever takes the time to talk to him. Many times I see God and Jesus here, also. God introduced me to someone called Ziatu, a tall, thin alien, neon blue in color and very intelligent. I also see a beautiful lady named Athena, with eyes all over her. She explained to me that she can see in omni vision—she can see in all dimensions and in every direction at the same time.

> *"The evil eye of the hostile-minded, (and) the evil-doer I have approached. Do thou, O thousand eyed one, watchfully destroy these!"*
>
> *Atharva Veda XIX, 35:3*

> *"Sanjaya had this unique 'Omnivision' or clairvoyance, by which he could see in his mind's eye and recount all events in real time on the battlefield happenings, while staying close to the blind king in safety and away from the battlefield. He was in effect the Seeing Eye of the blind king, with omnivision."*
>
> *- Bhagavadgita, BG Chapter 11*

In this dimension, I will guide you so you can see everyone yourself— so they can give you spiritual gifts to help you clear your energy and fight dark energies.

I don't want to confuse anyone with the information I've provided so far within this book. I know that many people may not believe in aliens. Some may not believe in Demons and still some people may not believe in Angels or even God.

God told me that it's important for me to share with you all of the knowledge he shared with me so you can learn what really does exist in the spiritual dimensions around us. It's up to you to do with this information whatever you want because, as God said, we all have free will to do whatever we want to do. I just hope that most of you can have an open mind and understand the concept that we are truly not alone in our universe. What you do with the information after that is really up to you.

Sixth Dimension
Demon Dimension

All of the Demons that I've talked about throughout this book come from this dimension.

All the Demon attacks on your spiritual/physical bodies originated from within this dimension. This is where all of those negative feelings come from such as: fear, worry, doubt, jealousy, anger, envy and so on. All of these negative feelings are just different Demons attacking your spiritual body or higher selves causing these feelings in you. All the Demons that have ever caused any terrible thing to mankind such as wars, diseases or plagues originated from here.

> *"Last of all I want to remind you that your strength must come from the Lord's mighty power within you. Put on all of God's armor so that you will be able to stand safe against all strategies and tricks of Satan. For we are not fighting against people made of flesh and blood, but against persons without bodies—the evil rulers of the unseen world, those mighty satanic beings and great evil princes of darkness who rule this world; and against huge numbers of wicked spirits in the spirit world."*
>
> *Ephesians 6:12*
> *Bible*

In my research to find written proof of my teachings, I ran across this saying from Ephesians so many times that I put one verse of it where I'm talking about the dark planet aliens dimension and one verse here when I'm talking about the Demon Dimension.

Both the aliens and Demons cause wars in the heavenly realms; they are who we are fighting against.

Seventh Dimension
Negative Projection Dimension

Higher selves, as you may recall, are extensions of your spirit.

In this dimension is where your higher selves are affected by negative thoughts or negative verbal words from other people and yourself. When you think negative or say something negative to other people or if they think or say something negative about you, that negativity sends a negative shock wave throughout this dimension. Any negative thought, whether it's yours or someone else's, is poison to your higher selves in this dimension. Either your higher selves are being affected by someone's negative thoughts or words or you are affecting someone else's higher selves with your thoughts or words.

Your higher selves help coordinate your life on earth by helping to bring to you your heart's desire, whatever it may be. Any negativity in this dimension makes it harder for your higher selves to help you accomplish your dreams on earth. Negativity in this dimension makes it harder for you to be happy, joyous, healthy and, above all, lucky. Continuous good luck—where everything always falls perfectly for you—is not just luck, but it's a result of your army of higher selves in this dimension not being affected by yours or anyone else's negative thoughts or words. The negativity in this dimension also directly affects your physical well being.

I will teach you how to clear all of the negative thoughts projected in this dimension by you and by others so that everyone's higher selves can exist happily. This is why you shouldn't think or say anything negative about anyone because you're hurting your higher selves as well as theirs.

Eighth Dimension
Positive Projection Dimension

In this dimension, people's positive thoughts affect your higher selves.

When people have thoughts such as love, kindness or anything that is positive, a vibration of love goes out into this dimension. This vibration makes you feel good deep inside of your physical body because your higher selves are extensions of your spirit and your spirit is part of your spiritual body. The vibration goes through your higher selves into your spiritual body and you feel it in your physical body. You also affect other people's higher selves in the same way when you think positive thoughts of them.

In this dimension, I will teach you how to keep your higher selves clean so that you can feel all of the positive thoughts of love and light from other people. You will also feel much happier with these higher selves clean and unblocked. Everyone should always think positive, loving thoughts of everyone—even strangers—because you're making them, as well as yourself, happy.

Ninth Dimension
The Bridge to Heaven—Receiving Your Keys to Heaven

To enter this dimension you must use your Keys to Heaven, a golden set of keys that God has placed within all of us. The keys are located in your spiritual body. Touch your chest and the keys will appear in your hand. Once you have your Keys to Heaven, you will look forward and notice a huge golden door. Your keys will unlock this door. Once the door is unlocked, the door will beam brilliant golden rays of light which will raise your vibration so that you may enter through the door. Most people feel a warm sensation of energy on the front part of their body as they face the door. Take your time. The door will open when it is ready. You'll start to see beaming white light as the door cracks open onto the golden bridge. This golden bridge is the bridge to heaven. It will look like a swinging bridge with golden white cables on each side. As you cross the bridge and get to the center, you may look ahead and see the tops of heaven's castle in the distance. Keep going until you get to the second golden door that looks exactly like the first one. You will use your Keys to Heaven to unlock the door to heaven. Once you cross through this door, you'll be in heaven. Heaven is the Tenth Dimension.

Testimonial by Gary Kaintz

I first discovered Gary Spivey on Jagger and Kristy's morning radio show here in San Diego. As I listened to Gary interact with a listener that had called in, I felt and saw to some small extent what was happening. Gary was giving this listener valuable information about a situation that had roots in a past life. He was careful not to give the listener information that she could not handle. I was very impressed in how Gary delicately handled this and thought, if I ever had another reading I would try him. He seemed to have more depth in his reading and dealing with spiritual aspects of life and not just the physical. Some time later I did make an appointment for a phone reading.

I felt strongly that this reading would be unusual in some unexpected way and that feeling was my main focus. Gary began describing what he was seeing and feeling and it was obvious to me that he was in a spiritual dimension. He asked if I was seeing or feeling any of this and, at first, I was not. As I focused in on his feedback, my spiritual eye began to open and I became aware from my own perspective what was going on. I realized he was taking me on a journey or that we were going on a journey and I tried to relax and be as aware as possible. Gary was leading the way.

I came to a door. Gary asked me to reach into my heart and take out a golden key. I did reach there and, to my surprise, I had a golden key in my hand. He asked me to insert the key into the lock and unlock the door. I did and then I pushed the door open. I was facing a bridge on the other side of which I saw another door.

Again, with Gary's prompting, I stepped onto the bridge to cross it. I looked down at my feet. They were bare. The bridge felt warm and alive with many colors vibrating in and out of it. The term rainbow bridge came to mind. I arrived at the second door and again, Gary asked me to use the golden key. Again, I turned the lock and the door swung open. I was facing a huge mansion surrounded by a beautiful garden in the middle of which was a swimming pool. There were people there looking beautiful and radiant. They expressed a silent welcome for me to come closer and Gary told me to go for a swim. And so I did. I felt warm, peaceful and harmonious and the swim seemed to cleanse me of all worry. I climbed out of the pool and, with Gary's instruction, walked back across the bridge. Gary told me that I could use the key anytime I wished—that I was welcome here.

My feelings validated what he was telling me. To prove the point, Gary instructed me to unlock the door and walk back across the bridge. I did and found myself back in the garden beside the pool. This time, Gary was there with me. Again I saw others—residents of this beautiful place.

As Gary was describing the scene to me and the people, I realized that I was seeing everything from my own perspective. Those that I saw had a human shape body or, more accurately, their energy system seemed much more refined than us humans. I think I was seeing a spirit shaped like us humans. They were all very attractive; smiles very radiant. The women were beautiful, yet I felt no sexual attraction. I knew this was where I wanted to live some day but the realization came that I would have to evolve to spirit-hood from my present human/animal state of consciousness. A person carrying energies of violence, lust, greed, intolerance, etc. could not live here as all these energies of animal nature would pollute this atmosphere. I felt the warmth and, for a moment, their love. That felt better than anything I had ever felt before.

Gary directed me to turn around and, as I did, I saw our present home, earth. Suddenly I felt very sad as I tuned into all the violence, destruction, lust, greed there. There was ugly smog-like energy surrounding our home. That changed almost immediately as beautiful radiant healing energies surrounded earth. The healing energies came from the spiritual beings we were with but seemed to be channeled through Gary. My mental question was immediately answered. These beautiful spiritual beings were constantly projecting these healing, life-saving energies toward us on earth, but needed people like Gary and me—people who had an earth energy frequency to serve as the channels. To say the least, this was all very enlightening. Gary mentioned that he saw a double helix surrounding the earth. I may have briefly seen that also, but what struck me was that I had been thinking of writing a book called The Spiral Staircase, the cover of which I envisioned a double helix. Somehow that dream had something to do with this experience.

Now I am writing this while reflecting on what happened. What I have written is my best description. I do not believe I completely understand all of this. As for Gary Spivey, I believe he has come to be a very clear channel of very powerful, healing energies. If we all could do that, what a great service for mankind—what great healing we could facilitate for our busted and broken way of life.

> *Gary Kainz*
> *Spring Valley, CA*

This testimonial was a little peek into what it's like to receive your Keys to Heaven. Like Gary Kainz, you, too, will receive your very own Keys to Heaven. While the experience is a little different for everyone, it always has the most healing effect on you.

Healing Continued...

People are always amazed when I do a healing on them—whether it is physical, mental or emotional—because they think it's some sort of a miracle. Well I guess it is a miracle, but I didn't do it. What I tell everyone is that I only removed the Demons: God did the healing.

All healings take place the same way. You must first use your imagination muscle (your spiritual eyes) and envision your body.

Secondly, once you can see your body, look at the part of your body that has the illness in it. You will always see a Demon attached to it. As soon as you see the Demon, take out your spiritual gift of a golden staff and touch the Demon: It will blow up as soon as you touch it and it will never return again.

Thirdly, you must fill your spiritual body with God energy; allow this energy to flow into your spiritual body removing all dark energy from within you.

Fourthly, you must fill all the spiritual dimensions with God energy/light, clearing all of the Demons and dark energies that are attacking your higher selves.

Fifthly, you must enter the Tenth Dimension (Heaven) and God will then complete your healing.

For example, if someone comes to me suffering from depression, I will first look at them with my spiritual eyes to see what's attacking them. I'll see a Demon standing behind them forcing dark energy into their head. I'll then use my spiritual gift of a gold staff and touch the Demon and watch it blow up in gold energy. Secondly, I'll use the same gold staff and insert it into the persons head causing the dark depression energy out of their head, which allows God energy to enter into their head. They instantly feel better and happier. Thirdly, I'll show them how to allow God energy into their spiritual/physical body, removing all dark energy from within them so the healing process can start. Fourthly, I'll look into the spiritual dimensions and I'll see Demons attacking their higher selves causing the depression in their head. I'll then show them how to clear the spiritual dimensions; getting rid of the Demons. Fifthly, I'll take them to heaven to meet God so he can finish the healing process.

If I'm working on healing someone with cancer, I will first look at their spiritual/physical body and see small microscopic Demons eating away at the cells of the body part that has the cancer. I will then use my golden staff and touch all of the Demons that are attacking that body part. They will blow apart when the gold energy touches them. Second, I will use the same gold staff and touch the part of that person's body that has cancer and I'll watch as all the dark energy leaves that body part. Then God energy rushes into the body part, starting the healing process. Thirdly, I'll show them how to allow God energy into their spiritual/physical body removing all dark energy from within them. This starts the healing process. Fourthly, I'll look into the spiritual dimensions and see thousands of microscopic Demons eating away on their higher selves; remember, what happens to your higher selves is what's happening to your spiritual body then affecting your physical body. I'll show them how to clear the spiritual dimensions, getting rid of the Demons attacking their higher selves. Fifthly, I take them to heaven to meet God so He can finish the healing process.

We all have darkness within us causing some sort of illness because of the Demons and aliens that attack our higher selves. In turn, our spiritual body gets sick which causes illness within our physical body. One of the biggest reasons why people are not healed is because of fear. Fear causes many people to block their healing by blocking their God energy from entering their body. Fear is nothing more than a Demon. The way this Demon works is by making you believe that being healed cannot happen that easily or making you doubt or believe you don't deserve to be healed. This Demon will make you believe that miracles can't happen in this day and age or that you don't deserve a miracle. This Demon will also infect people around you and make them tell you that you're crazy for believing you can be healed just by God's energy. They will tell you that a doctor is the only person who can heal you or that it's against your religion to believe you can heal yourself or others.

I have heard every excuse you can come up with, but the most important thing you need to know about healing is that you must believe without a doubt that you can and deserve to be healed. Then, and only then, will the healing take place.

By clearing the spiritual dimensions, you will remove the Demons causing fear and doubt within you, allowing your natural healing process to begin. This healing process works the same for all illnesses, no matter if it's physical, mental or emotional. I know that some people will say this sounds too easy and others may say this sounds too complicated, but as God said to me, "It's complex until you learn— but very simple once you do."

Now let's begin your healing process.

Note: First I want you to read the process of how healing works then I will ask you to stop and play the CD so that I can walk you step-by-step through the process of healing yourself from physical, mental and emotional illness.

Preparing for the Healing

After reading the steps to being healed, you will need to find a quiet place without any distractions from anyone or anything. You must have quiet alone time. If you are serious about being healed, you must absolutely make time and take time to heal yourself. Please don't have anyone around you who will not support your decision about healing yourself. They will only bring negativity into the healing process and make it harder for your healing to take place.

Remember, Demons are very tricky and infect all of us in many different ways. They will try to make you think this will not work, you don't have time to heal yourself, your spouse will be home soon, the children need you at that very moment or there's something at work you forgot to do. Believe me, you will run into many obstacles, but if you look at all of the obstacles as Demons, you will not let them stand in the way of healing yourself. The last thing the Demons want is for you to be healthy and enlightened. Please do yourself a favor; make time and take time.

In the chapter Seeing and Hearing Spiritually, I taught you a four-step meditation, with the last step being there is no step four. You learned to allow God's healing energy to enter your body. You learned to receive spiritual gifts and to see, hear and talk to God and your Angels.

The next meditation I'm going to teach you is much the same. Except this time, as you allow God's energy to enter your body, I'll teach you how to allow God's energy to heal your physical, mental and emotional problems/illness by eliminating the darkness in a specific area. I will show you how to clear all ten dimensions making it possible for your healing to come to you directly from God in Heaven (tenth dimension). God has the ability to be in all ten dimensions and so do you. For your spiritual healing to occur, all ten dimensions have to be clear of all darkness.

I can't express to you how important it is to be able to receive and use your spiritual gifts. Receiving spiritual gifts is the most important step in being able to heal yourself and others.

Step One:
Using Your Spiritual Gifts

The first step in healing is getting rid of the Demons attacking your physical and spiritual body.

Before you start your healing process, find a comfortable place to sit. Don't lie down because you may fall asleep. Once you are comfortable and relaxed, close your eyes. I want you to relax your body and get comfortable. I want you to shut off your brain by not thinking about anything. If you are an over-thinker, then just keep telling yourself, there is no place I need to be at this moment except right where I'm at.

Once you shut down your brain, I want you to visualize with your imagination soft white feathers surrounding your entire body. Once you are surrounded by all of these feathers, you will feel the tension within your physical body leave you as it is absorbed by the feathers. Just release all of the tension and allow it to flow out of you and into the feathers. You're becoming as light and comfortable as the feathers that surround you.

Now, tilt your head back a little so that your face is pointing upward, but not so far back as to make you uncomfortable or hurt your neck. With the same imagination you used to visualize the feathers, think of a beautiful ocean: see the blue ocean with waves coming onto the pristine white sandy beach. Now see yourself standing on the beach with the sand between your toes, just feel the warmth of the sand on your feet. Look up and see a beautiful blue sky with white fluffy clouds floating past you. I want you to just relax and enjoy the ocean, sand and blue sky.

Change the blue sky to a pure golden sky. Now imagine the gold sky opening up and you can see a bright gold energy/light shining through the sky. Imagine this bright light shining down through the sky and surrounding your whole body. Let it surround your head, neck, shoulders, arms, chest, back, stomach, legs and feet. Just relax and allow this bright light to surround your whole body.

Once this is done, look back up at that bright light shining through the golden sky, and then imagine yourself floating up through the golden clouds and sky, entering into the light.

Now that you're in the light, look down and imagine that you're standing on a golden floor. Look around and you'll see you're in a room with a golden floor and walls.

Now, using your spiritual eyes, envision yourself standing in front of your physical body; you are looking at yourself. While looking at yourself, scan over your body looking for any dark energy within you that is causing physical, mental or emotional illness. Your physical illness will have dark energy in the form of a serpent or snake within that body part.

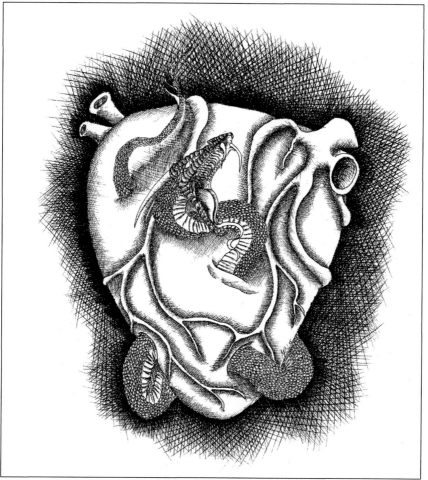

If you have a mental illness, your head will have a dark energy (Demon) within it. If you have emotional problems/illness, your stomach will have dark energy (Demon) in it. If you don't see a serpent/snake or Demon around your illness, you are probably over-thinking it and trying too hard to see. Just relax and allow the vision to come to you. Demons come in many shapes and sizes. Whatever Demon you see is the Demon causing the illness. When you see the Demon, take your physical hand and touch your chest. Take out your spiritual gift of a golden staff (just envision your staff in your hand) and touch the Demon, watching it blow up in gold energy.

Now, while looking at yourself, take the golden staff and touch the body part that has the illness within it. Watch as the darkness evaporates when the staff touches that body part. If you have a physical illness, touch the body part that is sick; if it's a mental illness, you will touch your head and, if it's an emotional illness, you will touch your stomach because all emotions come from your stomach. Once you have used your golden staff and removed the darkness from within the body part that was sick, it's time to fill your spiritual/physical body with God energy/light eliminating all darkness within you. Remember, where there is light, darkness can't exist.

Step Two:
Connecting Your God Cord
Remember, your God Cord is the invisible cord of energy that flows from heaven through all of the spiritual dimensions and connects to the top of your head in the physical dimension. It connects the spiritual body that's inside of your physical body with heaven. It's very important to have God energy flowing from heaven to your spiritual/physical body at all times for the healing process to take place. Having God energy in your body will keep all darkness out so you can heal and prevent any physical, mental or emotional illness.

The first thing you must do is to locate your God Cord; you will do this by using your imagination muscle (third eye). At this moment, you are in a golden room. While in this golden room, look up and imagine the golden ceiling turning into a beautiful blue sky. Once you see the blue sky, imagine that the blue sky turns into a golden sky. Once you see the sky turn gold, imagine a stream of gold energy flowing from the golden sky connecting into the top of your head.

Step Three:
Clearing Your Spiritual and Physical Body
Now that your God Cord is connected to your head, just imagine gold energy flowing from the golden sky down your God Cord into the top of your head. You may feel physical warmth on the top of your head.

You must allow this energy to flow into your spiritual/physical body. Envision the gold energy entering through the top of your head and entering into your body, filling it up with gold energy from your feet to the top of your head. Envision this energy penetrating all the cells of your body and, when this energy penetrates the cells of your body, allow this energy to remove all of the darkness from within your body. Using your spiritual eyes, look at your body. You will see dark energy leaving your body as the gold energy fills up your body. Envision the sick body part glowing with God energy. There can only be dark or light within your body and now you're replacing all the darkness with light. While this gold energy, or God energy, is flowing into you, just relax and allow the energy to do its healing work. You will know when the inside of your body is clear of all darkness by the bright glowing energy inside of you. You will see this with your spiritual eyes, and you will feel the physical sensations of heat and a feeling of lightness inside your body. The next step in your healing process is to clear the spiritual dimension—getting rid of the Demons and dark energies that attack your higher selves causing illness within you.

Step Four:
Clearing the Dimensions
Now that your spiritual/physical body has God energy flowing into it, you will now begin to clear the ten spiritual dimensions starting from the First, earth, working your way all the way to heaven, the Tenth. The dimensions can be cleared easily when your spiritual/physical body has God energy flowing into it. That's why you always clear your spiritual body first. To clear the dimensions, you're going to allow your God energy, that's flowing from the golden sky down your God Cord and into your spiritual/physical body, to flow out of you into the dimensions. You need to envision yourself looking like a giant light bulb of gold energy.
First Dimension
Earth/Physical Dimension
At this moment, you are standing in a room with a gold floor and walls. The ceiling is a gold sky with a stream of gold energy/light coming down and attaching to the top of your head—filling up every cell of your body. Now envision the gold floor turning into the earth.

Envision earth as a globe and you're standing on top of earth. When you can see yourself standing on the earth, look up and see the God energy flowing from the golden sky through your God Cord into your spiritual/physical body lighting you up like a light bulb from the inside out. Then envision this energy flowing out through every pore of your skin and surrounding the earth. This energy is clearing all of the darkness from around the earth and your higher selves. Now look up and you will see the golden sky. The golden sky is what separates the Earth Dimension from the Buffer/Golden Dimension. Now envision the earth surrounded with gold energy all the way to the sky. Just envision this dimension filling up with gold energy like water filling a bathtub. Once the energy reaches the golden sky, envision yourself floating up from earth through the sky. Once you go through the sky, envision yourself standing on top of the sky. You are now in the Second Dimension.

Second Dimension
Golden/First Buffer Dimension

You will do the same process in this dimension as you did in the Earth Dimension. Envision God's golden energy flowing down your God Cord filling up every cell in your body and then flowing out of your body filling up this dimension with gold energy. Just allow God's golden energy to fill this dimension—clearing everything from the ground all the way to the sky. But this time, when you look at the sky, you will notice that the sky is dark.

In this dimension, you will see your higher selves. They will look just like you, physically, but they may look beat up—like they were in a horrible fight. Just envision your God energy flowing from you and surrounding them and you will see them heal instantly. In this dimension, you may see Angels flying around or you may see little dark Demons. There is nothing to fear because your God energy will protect you. If anything of a dark nature comes around you, they will be annihilated by the God energy coming from you.

Your God energy will not have an affect on any Angels—you cannot harm them because they are made of God energy. Now envision God energy flowing into and through you then into this dimension and filling it up. When the God energy reaches the dark sky, the sky will turn gold. Once the sky turns gold, envision yourself floating through the golden sky and standing on top of it.

You're now in the Third Dimension.

Third Dimension
Invisible/Second Buffer Dimension
Now that you're standing on the golden sky, ask God for the spiritual gift to see in this dimension.

The reason this dimension is called the Invisible Dimension is because the Demons and aliens in this dimension have the ability to be invisible to your spiritual eyes

Now that you're standing on the golden sky, ask God for the spiritual gift to see in this dimension. You will see God hand you a golden box. Reach up and take it from him. Open the box. In the box you will see a new set of spiritual eyes; reach inside and remove the set of eyes. With your physical hands, touch your eyes and the spiritual eyes will be set in place. Now, with your new spiritual eyes, look around and you may see Angels and Demons battling. The Angels are fighting to protect your higher selves. The Angels know that if the Demons cause damage to your higher selves, this, in turn, causes damage to your spiritual body and you will become sick in your physical body. By allowing God energy to fill this dimension, you're helping the Angels by killing the Demons and healing your higher selves.

Clearing the dimensions isn't only helping to heal your higher selves, it's helping to heal the higher selves of everyone on earth because the spiritual dimensions connect everyone on earth. The Demons that you kill will not come back, but there are always more Demons waiting to take their place. If everyone on earth understood how to allow God energy to fill the dimensions—getting rid of all the Demons—then, before long, everyone on earth would be happier and healthier. God told me, "By doing this one thing, that we're all capable of, this would help to unite everyone in the world—bringing us closer to world peace."

Now let us continue.

You will do the same process in this dimension as you did in the previous dimension. Envision God's golden energy flowing down your God Cord filling up every cell in your body and then flowing out of your body filling up this dimension with gold energy. Just allow God's golden energy to fill this dimension, clearing everything from the floor all the way to the sky and turning the dark sky gold.

Once this dimension is full of gold energy, look up and envision yourself floating through the sky into the Fourth Dimension where dark planet aliens exist. But, just before you go through the sky, ask God for a spiritual gift of a cloak. The cloak will automatically surround your body making you invisible to the aliens in the Fourth Dimension

Fourth Dimension
Dark Planet Aliens Dimension

Now that you're standing on top of the sky, allow your God energy to flow through you filling this dimension quickly all the way to the sky and turning it gold. Remember, the aliens in this dimension don't want anyone on earth to become enlightened; these aliens infect everyone on earth with darkness.

In this dimension, you will see spaceships that look like submarines or round saucers with lights all around them. You'll see little bubble-headed aliens, tall skinny weird aliens, lizard-looking aliens, and many more. These aliens do not want you to become enlightened. Always remember that.

Allow your God energy to flow through you then into and around everything you see. You will see everything that God's energy touches explode and be swept away in a windstorm of light You will also notice a silence in your physical ears.

There is a spiritual war going on and these aliens are not on our side, so allow your God energy to fill this dimension, clearing out all of the alien projections and dark energy. Once you've turned this dimension gold, envision yourself floating through the sky and standing on top of the sky in the Fifth Dimension

Fifth Dimension
Light Planet Alien Dimension

These aliens want everyone on earth to become enlightened.

Allow God energy to flow through you and into this dimension the same way you did in the other dimensions. God energy does not hurt these aliens because they already have God energy (light) inside them. You may see aliens greeting you and giving you gifts because, when you project God energy into their dimension, they can feel it and it feels good to them.

Once you're in this dimension, look down and you will see yourself standing on a silver platform. Walk forward and you will be greeted by Ganesh (The Hindu God: He looks like an elephant that stands on two feet and has four arms). He has a gift for everyone who enters this dimension. Take the gift, thank him and place the gift in your chest. Everyone's gift will be different. I'm not saying Ganesh is an alien, but he does greet you. Many times you'll see God, Angels, Mother Mary and Buddha, also.

(Note: I will go into much more detail on the CD as I'm walking you through this dimension.)

You can spend as much time here as you would like talking to these spiritual beings. When you're finished, envision your God energy flowing through you all the way to the sky. When your God energy touches the sky, envision yourself floating up and through the sky into the Sixth Dimension.

Sixth Dimension
Demon Dimension

This dimension, as I said before, is where all negative emotions come from, emotions such as fear, worry, anger, jealousy, envy and many more. Remember, when you're feeling any of these negative emotions in your physical body, its always a Demon infecting your higher selves which, in turn, affects your spiritual body making you feel these emotions in your physical body.

Filling this dimension with God energy, whenever you're feeling any of these negative feelings, will make the feeling go away instantly. Demons also attack our higher selves in this dimension causing many physical, mental and emotional illnesses within us. Keep this dimension clear and your higher selves healthy by making sure your spiritual body has God energy flowing into it and you can cure yourself as well as prevent all illnesses.

Just allow your God energy to flow through you filling this dimension. Once you have filled this dimension with God energy, look up and envision the dark sky turning Gold. Then envision yourself floating up through the sky into the Seventh Dimension.

Seventh Dimension
Negative Thought Projection Dimension
This is where other people's negative thoughts affect your higher selves. In this dimension, you'll see many higher selves. Just allow your God energy to engulf all of your higher selves—clearing everything away from them. Once this is done, envision a force field of gold energy around all of your higher selves; surrounding them and protecting them.

Now you must clear everyone's negative thought projections from this dimension.

First, look up and envision a golden sky. Secondly, envision the sky falling slowly down to the ground. Envision the sky as it falls being a sticky gold energy. What this energy is doing is taking away all of the negative thought projections that are around your higher selves and that are caused by people thinking negative of you. Thirdly, envision this sticky energy rolling up into a ball and just disappearing—taking with it all of the negative projections. Follow these three steps three to four times and it will remove all the negative projections in this dimension. Once you allow the sticky energy to come down from the sky and remove all negativity, you must allow your God energy to fill this dimension and surround all of your higher selves to protect them.

When this is done, envision yourself floating through the gold sky into the Eighth Dimension.

Eighth Dimension
Positive Thought Projection Dimension
In this dimension, people's positive thoughts affect your higher selves—thoughts such as love, happiness and joy. In this dimension, you do not project gold energy. You envision blue energy and you do this the same way as you did when you allowed the gold energy to flow through you but, instead, envision blue energy flowing through you. Fill this dimension with blue energy engulfing all of your higher selves. This is clearing away anything that may be blocking the positive feelings of love, happiness and joy that these higher selves should be feeling. When these higher selves feel love, joy and happiness, you will also feel these emotions in your physical body. So allow this blue energy to engulf and fill this entire dimension.

Once you're finished, envision the blue energy touching the sky and then envision yourself floating through the sky into the Ninth Dimension.

Ninth Dimension
The Bridge to Heaven—Receiving Your Keys to Heaven

When you see yourself standing on top of the blue sky, stop here for a moment and ask God for your Keys to Heaven.

Everyone has keys to heaven. You were born with them. You just need someone to show you where they're located and how to access them. Now is the time. Ask God to release your Keys to Heaven. Once you ask him, you may feel a warm sensation in your chest. In the spiritual dimension, just put your hand to your chest and your keys will appear in your hand. You will see two keys on a necklace; one smaller than the other. Now that you have your keys, look forward and you will see in front of you a huge golden door. Walk toward this door. When you get to it, you will see a keyhole. You must use your keys to unlock the door and enter through it. Place the smaller key into the keyhole and turn the key. The door will open. Walk through, make sure you close the door behind you and place your keys on your neck for safe keeping. You will see a beautiful city glowing with gold energy and Angels flying over the city. There will be a bright gold energy shining from the city and glorious music that's soothing to the soul. If you look toward the city, you'll see a huge wall surrounding the whole city. Walk closer to the city and you will see a bridge leading to another huge golden door. This bridge is made of gold and is suspended by gold ropes crossing over a huge moat that goes all the way around the wall. In the moat you will see gold energy running like lava from a volcano. Cross the bridge. Once you cross the bridge, you will be standing in front of the Door to Heaven (The Tenth Dimension).

I would like to share with you a testimonial of Jeff's experience when he crossed the bridge to heaven and entered into the Tenth Dimension (Heaven) and was healed.

Testimonial by Jeff

I was listening to a radio show in San Francisco when I heard Gary. After the show, I called and made the earliest possible appointment to talk to him. I knew he had some answers for me. We spoke of spiritual matters, and Gary cleared my body of sixteen Demons. As each was removed, I felt warmth in my body.

After that, Gary showed me how to see in the spiritual dimensions, then he said to hold out my hand, as if I were to receive something. He showed me where I was receiving a golden key and he said to grab it. After I received the key, I saw a golden door. Gary said to use the key to open the door. As I put the key into the keyhole, I felt warm healing sensations on my face, chest and the whole front part of my body. In the spiritual dimension, I saw beams of gold and white light coming from the door.

Gary explained to me that the warmth I was feeling was the energy of the door itself blowing out and getting rid of all the dark energies so that the door may open and that I may step into heaven. The door then started to open and I saw beams of bright white light coming through the door. I walked through the door onto a bridge. It was cloudy, but I could see a city and buildings in the distance. I then proceeded across the bridge; it looked to be a swinging bridge much like the Golden Gate Bridge with lots of cables holding it in place. Each cable was beaming with brilliant white light.

I then came upon another door. Gary said this was the Door to Heaven. I used my key to open the second door and entered into heaven. There was an image in front of me. I couldn't look directly at him.

Gary said, "Don't be afraid: This is Jesus." Jesus took my hand and we walked toward these two large pillars. Beyond the pillars was water and there Jesus baptized me. Afterward, he directed me to a figure who was reading scriptures. Gary said, "This is God."

God placed scriptures on my heart and said, "He belongs to us." When God put the scriptures on my heart, I felt bright and warmth inside of me. God told me, not to worry. "Your Demons are gone."

When this was finished, Gary said take the key and go back out through the door, down the bridge and through the golden doors.

Gary said, "God has a message for you: Stop doing what you are doing."

At that moment I knew exactly what Gary meant and I knew what God meant by saying my Demons were gone. I'm a drug user; I was using crystal meth every day for about four years. That day, I took what I had—about $200 worth of drugs—and flushed it down the toilet. I felt liberated and ecstatic at the same time. To this day I haven't had the urge to use drugs ever again. Six months later, I'm still visiting heaven daily and hanging out with God. This is much better than using drugs.

Gary, I can't thank you enough,
  Jeff

Jeff was a drug user and needed help to kick the habit. The Keys to Heaven allowed him to enter heaven and, once he made it to heaven, God worked on his spiritual body, removing the drug Demons from him. In the physical dimension, he had the strength to flush his drugs down the toilet and stop using them. So you see, even a drug addict is worthy of meeting God and receiving a healing.

"Have courage, Enoch, do not fear and they showed me the Lord from afar, sitting on his very high throne. For what is there on the tenth heaven, since the Lord dwells here? On the tenth Heaven is God in the Hebrew tongue he is called Avavat."
  The Book of Enoch from the Dead Sea Scrolls
  XX: 3

Tenth Dimension
Heaven—Being Healed by God

Now back to the Ninth Dimension for a moment: You've just crossed the bridge to heaven and now you're standing in front of a huge golden door. This door is the Door to Heaven. To enter heaven, you must use your Keys to Heaven. These are the keys which are on the necklace around your neck. Remove the necklace and use the larger of the keys to unlock this door. You will have rays of light and gold energy shining through the cracks and from under the door. When the door opens, you will be engulfed with gold energy. This energy will remove any darkness you may have in your spiritual body. Once this energy engulfs you, you must then enter into heaven closing the door behind you, placing the key around your neck.

Once you close the door behind you, you will be standing in heaven.

You will be greeted by Angels. They will wrap you with a gold drape, and then they will bring you to see God. The Angels will lead you down a golden path through the most beautiful gardens that you have ever seen. You will see roses, trees and many other flowers, all of them of a very vibrant golden color. You will pass alongside a huge pool that runs through the center of heaven right up to God's castle. There are dolphins swimming in the pool. As you are walking alongside this pool, you will see many Angels walking along with other people guiding them and showing them around heaven. If you look around, you will also see many beautiful houses, all of them made of gold.

The Angels will then guide you up a golden staircase through the front door of a huge castle. You will turn right and walk down a long hallway made of marble and then you will come to a tall door. It looks about twenty feet tall and it's made of pure silver. The Angels will bring you through the door. Once you go through the door, directly ahead of you will be God's throne. The Angels will take you to the foot of the stairs leading up to the throne and, at this point, the Angels will leave you. Then you will see God come down the stairs and meet you.

You will be face to face with God.

He will look at your energy and see if there are Demons or any negative energy left within your spiritual body causing illness to your physical body. If there is, then this is where God will get rid of the Demons or negative energy causing your illness. He will place his hand on your forehead and take the Demon or dark energy out of you. You will see it explode in light. When God gets rid of the Demon or negative energy, he will fill your spiritual and physical body with his green healing energy.

Once he's filled your spiritual and physical body with his healing energy, you should thank him. Your healing is now complete.

Now it's up to you to keep the Demons and dark energy away by clearing your spiritual dimensions and return to heaven daily so your illness in the physical dimension can also go away. When God is finished healing you, give him thanks. You can give him a hug, shake his hand or just tell him, thank you. Once you give him thanks, the Angels will come to guide you back into the gardens of heaven where you can just hang out with Angels or loved ones that have passed away. You can also hang out with pets that have passed away. You can stay there for as long as you want. Angels will approach you and give you messages and show you around. Just realize that you are in heaven and, while in heaven, make sure you take time to feel the vibration of heaven. You'll feel happy and peaceful; all of your problems will simply go away. There is no prejudice, hate, envy, jealousy or any other negative vibration. The energy and vibration of Heaven is what God wants on earth.

Remember, when you're ready to leave, you will see the Door to Heaven. Use your key to open the door, making sure you shut it behind you, locking it. Start walking back across the bridge. As you're walking across the bridge, it's time to enter back into your physical body. As you're walking, I want you to imagine your physical body is standing on the other side of the bridge. As you approach yourself, stop and join your spiritual and physical bodies together.

At this point in the guided meditation, I will awaken you.

You now have access into heaven any time. One very important thing to remember, now that you have access to heaven, is that you must keep your God Cord, spiritual/physical body, and all of your spiritual dimensions clear of the Demons and aliens that attack you because this is how you heal yourself of any physical, mental or emotional illness.

I can show you the way, but I can't make you continue to clear yourself daily. If you do clear yourself daily, then miracles will not only happen, but will become normal and a way of life for you.

Note: I've included a few more important testimonials of people being healed through the power of God's energy. You can read them now or you can go to the section on the CD entitled, Healing, and I will walk you through your very own healing. If you proceed with your healing now, I recommend that you come back and read these testimonials.

At this time, I would like to share with you another testimonial from Linda who was suffering from severe migraine headaches. I helped remove the Demons making her feel better, but the Demons came back after a short period of time. This is why you must learn to keep the Demons away so your healing can be permanent and not temporary.

Testimonial of Linda Stewert

For more than twenty years, I have suffered with acute migraine attacks, sometimes for days at a time, several times a month. I have gone to numerous doctors, specialists and neurologists. I have taken tension headache medicine daily—up to six a day, I also have tried migraine prevention medicines along with Imitrex and Replax, but nothing worked well.

My husband has taken me to the emergency room numerous times with migraines so severe that I couldn't walk from the car. There has not been a morning, for as long as I can remember, that I woke up without a headache. Many times, I have laid on the bathroom floor and dried my hair because my head throbbed too badly to sit up. Most nights I don't sleep due to headaches and, when I do sleep, I have night terrors, so I prefer the nights I can't sleep. Due to lack of sleep and constant pain, I suffer from depression. Doctors have me on high blood pressure medication because I have had high blood pressure most of my life, two different anti-depressants, muscle spasms medication, and sleeping pills, along with all the medication for my headaches.

Years ago I was told that I had thirteen lesions on my brain, but no one knew why. Last year, my MRI showed fifty-three lesions and I was told I had MS, no doubts. I was sent home with a bag of videos and information about MS to discuss with my husband which type of injections I wanted to start. My husband and I decided that I was on so much medication as it was that I did not want to be tied down to shots three to four times a week that have flu like symptoms?

I spoke to my family doctor and he suggested I ask for a spinal tap. The spinal tap came back inconclusive and I asked to be sent to an MS specialty clinic. That neurologist ran a series of tests and stated one-hundred percent that I did not have MS—that the lesions were caused by uncontrolled high blood pressure and severe migraines attacks. So all my medication was changed again!

I was back to square one.

Also, in 1999, my eye doctor informed me that I had a small cataract in my left eye. In 2003, it was still there but had not gotten any larger so he decided not to do anything about it until it began to get larger.

A few months before I got to know Gary, he came into our furniture store to buy furniture for a bed and breakfast he was remodeling in North Carolina for his sister, Joyce. Gary and my husband became friends right away. I stayed in the office; I had spoken to Gary in passing, but I really didn't know him. Anyway, I came into work one morning after being up all night with a headache. Tony, (my husband) knew Gary was in town and had heard him on the radio. He knew about his abilities to help people as a spiritual healer. Tony asked me if he could call Gary for help. I thought, well, I've tried everything else; I was willing to try anything.

What I'm about to tell you may be hard for some of you to believe, but it is completely true and nothing has been fabricated, so here it goes.

Over the phone, Gary was able to see things about me—things I hadn't told him. Gary had me close my eyes to block out any distraction. He was able to see Demons trying their best to wear me down. After they had done all they could do to me physically, they had started working on me during my sleep. He told me that my insides looked like barbwire.

First, we worked on my pain; I felt different areas of my head get warm and, as a different area began to get warm, the pain left until there was no pain at all. Next, we cleansed my body of all Demons. As my feet began to get hot, then my legs and arms, I felt like a heavy load was being lifted off me—a load I didn't even know I was carrying. My spirit felt lighter and freer than it ever had.

Gary took me through the clouds into heaven where I was able to receive spiritual gifts to fight off the Demons when they tried to return. We continued to talk about personal things in my life and I felt this amazing peace and freedom throughout my whole body. I have never felt such total happiness and peace in my entire adult life

Once I emerged from my office, my husband noticed a difference immediately. My eyes had a sparkle to them. As the day went on, problems occurred as they always do when you own your own business. I normally freak out, and can't handle problems without getting upset. Instead, on this day, the problems weren't really problems. It's almost like I had this wonderful change in me and nothing could touch me. No matter what, I couldn't be brought down off this spiritual high.

A couple of weeks later, my husband and I were scheduled to go on a vacation. This was the first vacation we had been on in more than thirteen years that I didn't get sick. I didn't need sleeping pills and I felt great the entire time.

The week we returned from vacation, I had my routine eye exam. My doctor could not find my cataract. He scheduled me for a follow up check up the very next week so he could have more time, because he stated cataracts don't just disappear. A week later I had my second eye exam. Once again, no cataract. He was totally astounded.

Weeks went by without even a minor headache, until a hectic Saturday at work. As the day went on, I began to feel a little more pressure in my head and by the time I got home, I had a full-blown migraine and was extremely nauseated. Gary was doing a seminar out of state and I was unable to reach him. Finally, in desperation I took an Imitrex and went to bed in total darkness, because light and sound were unbearable. The Imitrex wasn't working, so I took a prescription sleeping pill trying to achieve some measure of relief. Right before I was ready to go to the emergency room, Gary called Tony. I hurt so bad that I didn't want to talk, but Tony put the phone to my ear. My husband sat at the foot of the bed in tears and witnessed what I'm about to tell you next.

Within seconds, Gary had me sitting up in bed and he was talking me through my migraine. He was able to help me achieve a place, mentally, where the pain was not able to touch, where Demons aren't strong enough to hold on. There were Angels placed at each corner of my bedroom to watch over me during the night. Remember that I had taken a sleeping pill. Well I felt so good that I got out of bed, went downstairs to the den with my husband and realized I had not been able to eat all day because I was queasy. So I fixed myself a sandwich and stayed up till 11:00 before I went to bed and slept peacefully. That was five weeks ago, and I have not needed any pain medication or sleep aid until a week later.

Gary said he could teach me how to heal myself. I am a true believer that Gary has been blessed with the ability to help others, I am so thankful and honored that I can call him my friend. The amazing powers we have to heal are beyond anything any pill can do.

The day I was going to e-mail this article to Gary, it was nowhere to be found on my computer. I searched every program and this article had completely disappeared. Of course, I was frustrated to say the least.

But the article missing was only the beginning of a terrible day. This was six weeks since my last headache.

It was my birthday and a birthday dinner was planned for me with my family. My headache started that morning. As the day went on, it increased in intensity. I had some errands to run and barely made it through the grocery store without passing out. I came home, took a migraine pill, turned out all the lights and tried to go to sleep. My husband came home around 6:00 and I didn't want to let everyone down so I touched up my makeup and off we went to meet our daughter and son at a local restaurant. Once we arrived, I knew I was in trouble. Still I was going to fight my headache with everything I had. Before the waitress could bring water, I looked at my husband and he knew that I needed to get to the hospital. On a migraine scale, I was a ten plus in pain.

At the emergency room, the lights were intensely bright, children were running wild, the TV was playing, the sliding doors kept opening and then a helicopter took off from the roof. After waiting for an hour, throwing up, holding my head in my lap, crying, my husband finally got fed up and relented to my pleading to just take me home. On the way home, which is approximately a fifteen-minute drive, he had to pull over seven times for me to throw up. Once home, I took two prescription migraine pills and a 30mg RX sleeping pill.

NOTHING HELPED!

I then took another migraine pill and half of a sleeping pill, still no relief. This was the first time I have ever begged GOD to take me home. The pain was indescribable. Finally, I took the other half of the sleeping pill and drifted off to a fitful sleep.

Within an hour, I was back awake and hurting just as bad. My husband had fallen asleep with his hand on my chest because he was afraid I was going to stop breathing. I managed to climb out of bed and make it to the bathroom where I got sick again. I then took another migraine pill and another sleeping pill. At this time, I had taken 90mg of RX sleeping medication and three migraine pills. I would have done anything to relieve my pain. It felt like knives were constantly being stabbed into my head. I honestly believed that I was going to have a stroke or die before morning.

Finally morning came and my husband called my regular doctor, who is also a blood and cancer specialist. Tony was told to get me there immediately. My blood pressure was 214 over 110. The doctor gave me a shot for nausea, gave me a strong blood pressure pill and started an IV because I was dehydrated. He put an oxygen mask on me and gave me a shot of Demerol. I don't know the exact dosage because I was in and out of consciousness. They had me in the private room with blankets over the windows and they were working with flashlights because of the extreme pain I was in. I have been with this doctor for more than twenty-five years and I truly believe everyone in the office was scared. At some point, I was given a second bag of glucose, another shot for nausea and more Demerol.

After five hours in the doctor's office, my migraine had subsided on the scale to a two. My bottom number of my blood pressure was down to 102. I actually felt halfway human again. After begging, I was released to be taken home and was given medicine to put me to sleep. I did doze off and on for the rest of the day with my husband by my side. The next morning, I still had a nagging headache, but I was able to function. I knew that I had to go to work: My employees needed their paychecks and I'm the only one who can do payroll. At my office, I couldn't read the time card—they were all blurred. I have 20/20 vision and don't wear glasses, but I couldn't see, so I sent my son to the local drug store to buy a pair of reading glasses and I was able to get through writing the checks. I still felt awful, couldn't eat yet and was extremely tired.

Shortly after lunch, Tony was able to reach Gary. Tony explained a little of my situation to Gary and Gary *was able to channel through Tony to see what was going on with me. Gary told Tony that I was being attacked by Demons on top of Demons and that the Demons were trying to kill me. They almost succeeded.*

I was put on the phone with Gary and he worked with me. Within minutes, Gary targeted areas of my body and I began to feel heat in my head and feet. While he was fighting to rid my body of the Demons, my hand that was holding the phone began to shake uncontrollably. I felt healing light going through my body. I actually felt the Demons being exiled from my body and I felt Angels taking their places. The most amazing thing was that I no longer had any pain at all!! I took off the reading glasses because I no longer needed them and my energy level was as if I had just woken from a good night's sleep.

I've been so excited about the amazing experiences I have had that I've told everyone I know. All of my friends have witnessed me having a migraine at some point and they are all astonished by how great I feel and look after Gary has helped me. I've been told by numerous people that I have a glow about me and I'm sure it's my Angels watching over me. Also, with the meditations Gary taught me—and not the medications the doctors gave me—my blood pressure is normal for the first time in a very long time.

Linda Stewart
Troy, NC

I taught Linda how to receive spiritual gifts from God so she would have her very own protection from the Demons and darkness. I showed her how to keep the spiritual dimensions clear and how to use her new spiritual gifts to get rid of the Demons that were attacking her, causing the severe headaches.

By learning how to get rid of the Demons, she can keep the headaches away. I explained to her that I can only show her, but she must keep them away. I continue to monitor Linda because of the severity of her headaches. But once I showed her how to get rid of the Demons, she no longer needs me to clear her Demons. She does it herself.

Testimonial by Sophia & Tom McKinnon

I wanted to write you and let you know of the miracle that happened to us. My 3-year-old son was right in the middle of medical testing. The doctors could not figure why his liver and spleen were larger than normal. They were at least twice the normal size for a three-year-old. We spent months in and out of hospitals; he had every blood test possible. They even did a live liver biopsy while he was awake at San Francisco General Hospital. This was the hardest thing I believe my husband and I had ever gone through...not knowing what was wrong with our son.

Well, one day I was driving down the road in a daze because of my own fears regarding our son's health. I turned on the radio to listen to the radio program I always listen to (The Doghouse in the Morning). You were on the radio doing readings for callers. I was amazed at how accurate you were caller after caller. I remember you were talking to a young man about his grandmother who had passed away. You stated that you could smell chili cooking; it was a very strong smell. The young man said that his grandmother was always cooking chili when she was alive. This phone call caught my ear because it just so happened that I prepared homemade chili before I left the house. After listening to your accuracy, phone call after phone call, I called your office to arrange a reading hoping you could help give my husband and I some answers about our son's health problem. We wereable to see you that afternoon in San Francisco. My husband and I were desperate for answers. My husband was a bit of a skeptic. As soon as we walked in, you looked at my son and said that his spleen and liver were three times the normal size. We almost fell over because there was no way for you to have known this. You put your hands on his head and said that he would be fine now. About a week later, we were at a scheduled ultra sound and the doctor could not believe that his organs had gone down to normal. The doctor had no answers but was very surprised. My son will be 6 years old this December and is growing and going strong. Thank you for your help with this miracle. I would have never believed it had I not lived it!

Always,
Sophia

With Sophia and Tom's son, all I did was use my spiritual eyes to look at his body. Once I did, I noticed his organs to be abnormally large. I then cleared the Demons and dark energies from his physical and spiritual body allowing his God energy/light to enter his body, healing his organs.

Remember, once Demons and dark energies are removed from your body, healings can and will happen.

Testimonial by Jessica

Gary,

Thank you so much for all the great guidance and healing you have blessed us with. My husband and I made our first appointment with you in August 2004 as I was facing some huge choices with work and a possible relocation; you gave me great advice which I took. You spent most of the call with my husband, Steve, helping him with his serious health issues.

Steve has been a type 1 brittle diabetic since age 13 and has never had the diabetes under control. He has had his fair share of ICU hospital stays and his doctor says he has one of the worst cases of diabetes he has treated in someone so young (28 years old). A few years ago, he was treated for brain damage due to seizures from his blood sugar crashing so low and so often. During this appointment, you focused in on all of his health problems including his depression—you said his health aura looked like "Pig Pen" and he had three large depression Demons around him. You removed the Demons and, that day, his depression was gone. He physically felt great and could run up and down stairs with no effort; normally he would be out of breath halfway up. In April, we made a second appointment with you, as his depression was back. You again removed the Demons. You then worked with him specifically on the diabetes—removing the dark energy. You said that God gave him a new pancreas. Immediately after this appointment, his blood sugars dropped from between 300-400 to under 200 consistently. In June 2005, we attended your Spiritual Retreat in Ojai, California. He experienced a group healing and, again, saw his blood sugars drop in half. His doctor is thrilled that, for the first time in his life, his sugars are under control. He says there should be damage in his internal organs, pancreas, liver—but they test healthy. His doctor is also pleased when we are able to decline the depression medication (it goes back Be forth).

My 7 yr. old son, Jake, had to write a friendly letter as an assignment at school to anyone he chose. He chose you, Gary, thanking you for helping his dad feel better. I think this is the greatest compliment we could give you, as I know it comes from a child's heart and ours as well. The meditations we learned at your retreat have really enhanced our lives and we try to pass them on to others. We are grateful for our experiences with you and really love you!

Gratefully, Jessica and Steve

In Steve's case, I removed all the Demons and dark energies in his physical and spiritual body allowing his God energy/light to enter him so his healing could begin.

When working with Steve, one of the first things I saw was the depression Demons around his head. I removed the Demons and his depression was gone. When I said that God gave Steve a new pancreas, I saw God in the spiritual dimension with a spiritual gift of a new pancreas for him. Once the Demons and dark energies were removed, God placed Steve's new pancreas in his body. According to Jessica, Steve's blood sugar immediately dropped by half When he attended my spiritual retreat, I noticed that some of the Demons and dark energies had returned, so I had everyone gather together to do a group healing on him. A group healing is when everyone clears the Demons and dark energies from someone, allowing God energy/light to enter their body. After the group healing, Steve's blood sugars went to normal levels for the first time in his life. His depression comes and goes because the depression Demons come and go, but now he is aware of it and can use his spiritual gifts to get rid of the Demons causing his depression.

Always remember, we have the power to heal ourselves and others. You just need to have faith and believe it can really happen.

The next testimonial I would like to share with you is about a woman who has Alzheimer's. I'm sharing this testimonial with you, not because she was healed, but because I believe that, if we keep enough God energy/light in our physical and spiritual bodies, we can prevent Alzheimer's or any illness from happening to us.

This is what happens to someone's spiritual body when they get Alzheimer's.

Testimonial by Cheryl about her Mom

Hi Gary,

I came to you because I wanted to know if my mom, who has Alzheimer's, is okay. I wanted to share with you my thoughts on our visit.

When our session first began I asked you if you could tell me if she was doing okay. You looked at her and could see her spirit sitting outside of her body. She told you that she was so excited that you had come. She said she was bored; she couldn't do anything, not even her crossword puzzles. My mother loved her crossword puzzles. You then said that she pointed to her used up physical body and said, "What am I supposed to do with that?" We all laughed. That is totally something my mom would say. She thought you were an Angel and asked if you had come to get her. She thought she was dead and she was ready to go. After you explained to her that her physical body was still alive and that her spiritual body would slip in and out of her physical body, she asked if you could put a pillow over her body's head. You said, "She really means it." That is the kind of life she lived, very matter of fact. She told you that she knows it is time to go and she does not want to live this way. She told you that if Cheryl were here, she would do it for her. She kept asking if you were an Angel. My mom and I were able to talk for a while through you; she wanted to know where I was. I told her, in California. She said she wanted an orange, or some fruit. That fruit seemed to be the only taste that came through from her spent body. Then you chuckled and said, "I get it now; California oranges." My mom said, "You're not a very smart Angel."   Again, we all laughed. You said, "Your mom has a great sense of humor." My mom has a great sense of humor and I miss it horribly. She said that if anyone could find a way to talk to her, she knew it would be me who would figure it out. At that time, you saw Jesus come into the room and pull down the shade and she was gone. It gives me great peace to know he will take good care of her now. Thanks for helping me get to speak to her.

Thank you so much for being you.
Cheryl

I know this testimonial was not about Cheryl's mom being healed, but I wanted to share it with you anyway because, as I said before, I believe that, by having enough God energy/light in your body, you can prevent any illness from happening to you.

Testimonial by Dr. Ira Shandles

My name is Dr. Ira Shandles and I am a physician and surgeon practicing in the Tampa Florida area for twenty-one years. I've known Mr. Gary Spivey for fourteen years. In that time, I've had the opportunity to confer with him on three personal health matters concerning my spouse, myself and a good friend's father. In the first case, my wife had a frightening episode of driving along an expressway at high speed when she suddenly went blind for no explicable reason. Mr. Spivey explained to me that this was due to a swelling around a cranial blood vessel and that it was a totally reversible matter. This was confirmed when a local neurologist corroborated that she had suffered an optical migraine secondary to a birth control medication.

I, myself, had a routine physical accompanied by an EKG. The EKG, for the first time in my life, was interpreted as abnormal by the computer-based EKG software. This was famous and well-regarded equipment. I immediately contacted a cardiologist for consultation. Prior to the visit, however, I called Mr. Spivey and asked him, when he had told me that I had one of the strongest hearts he had ever seen, how could this be? He answered that there was nothing wrong with my heart and not to worry. Two hours later, I received a call from the center where the EKG had been performed and was told that, after a number of such abnormal readings had occurred in a row, the equipment was checked and found to be improperly calibrated and that my EKG was normal! All the same, a specialist later did corroborate this.

And last, a dear friend, like family to me, her father was stricken with cancer and lying in the hospital. She begged me to call Gary because they were planning some vast, heroic measures to help him, but she did not want to put him through any hopeless, painful endeavor. Gary told me to tell her to tell the attending physicians to check his brain. The cancer had attacked his brain and it would be fruitless. She later convinced the doctor to order a brain scan. The brain was riddled with cancer.

He died peacefully thereafter.

I'd like to think that, as a physician I am also a scientist. I therefore, try to keep an open mind. These events occurred as described. As a scientist, I would say simply that they speak for themselves.

Dr. Ira D Shandles

This is an example where seeing spiritually was very important to everyone concerned. I was happy that Ira's friend's father did not have to go through needless torture as he was already terminal because of the cancer being in his brain. They were ever so grateful that they got to spend some very special time with their father without torturing him with chemo and radiation therapy.

I would love to be able to teach doctors how to see with their spiritual eyes as I can, so they could diagnose patients spiritually and medically. It would be very beneficial to all doctors to be able to see what's going on in the spiritual dimensions. If presented properly to an open minded physician, it can save everyone involved a lot of time, trouble, pain, suffering and even lives.

The Complete Woodcuts of
Albrecht Durer c.1498
Dover Publications, Inc.

SPIRIT REPLACEMENT
HOW TO REPLACE YOUR WORN OUT SPIRIT

"For I will take you from the nations, gather you out of all countries, and bring you into your own land. Then I will sprinkle clean water on you, and you shall be clean; I will cleanse you from all your filthiness and from all your idols. I will give you a new heart and put a new spirit within you; I will take your heart of stone out of your flesh and give you a heart of flesh. I will put my spirit within you and cause you to walk in my statutes, and you will keep my judgments and do them. Then you shall dwell in the land that I gave to your fathers; you shall be my people, and I will be your God."

Ezekiel 11: 17,18,19,20
Bible

Everything you've read so far in this book is knowledge I've gained from listening to what God has been teaching me. I know it works because of my direct hands-on experience of working with people—showing them how to repair their spiritual and physical bodies.

One of the most harmful things that happens to you in the spiritual world when you get attacked by Demons and aliens is that your spirit becomes severely damaged. I've seen, time and time again, what I refer to as Swiss-cheese spirit; this is what I call someone's spirit that has holes in it because of the spiritual attacks on them. Every person I've ever worked on has holes in their spirit, because we all get attacked in the spiritual dimensions. No one is exempt from spiritual attacks—I mean no one: from kids to the elderly in every nation and race. Demons are not prejudiced; they attack everyone.

When I first started noticing holes in peoples spirits, I would always try to fill their spirit with God energy, but the energy never stayed in for very long because of the holes. I just thought this is what happens to a spirit and there's nothing I can do to fix it. Then one day, before I started working on someone's spirit, I heard God say, "Let me show you the process of replacing someone's old spirit with a new one, so they don't have holes in their spirit anymore."

God then said, "As you know, your spirit is part of the heavenly life force that makes up your spiritual body. At conception, the spirit comes from heaven and enters into your physical body. Its purpose is to grow with you and, when the soul arrives at birth, to protect your soul from the Demons and dark energies that will try to keep your soul from enlightenment. Your higher selves, which are the extensions of your spirit, live in the spiritual dimensions. They are on the front lines of spiritual attacks and, every time one of your higher selves is attacked, your spirit within you is damaged: This is what causes the holes you see in everyone's spirit. This is why everyone must receive a new spirit."

God then explained to me that everyone's spirit keeps a memory of heaven within it. When your spirit first enters your body, it's not affected by Demons, dark energies or people's negative thoughts because the soul hasn't entered yet. (Remember, the soul doesn't enter the body until birth, the spirit, at conception.)

He further explained to me that your spirit enters your body with all of heavens attributes within it such as: love, non-judgment, caring, non-prejudice, oneness, happiness, joy, humor, fun and all other positive attributes. Now, from the time your soul enters your body (at birth) your higher selves begin to be attacked within the spiritual dimensions causing damage to your spirit. Remember, the reason higher selves get attacked when the soul enters the body is because the Demons and dark energies don't want the soul to reach enlightenment and the spirit protects the soul.

Your spirit also gets holes in it by people's negative thoughts. Every one of us has Demons that affect us in some way and, since we have Demons, you can bet they will cause us to think negative thoughts toward someone else causing damage to their spirit.

You can really cause damage to a newborn child's spirit. The newborn child has this perfect spirit inside of them—a spirit that came straight from heaven. But the parents, guardians, siblings and friends who are around the newborn are not aware of the damage they can cause to the new little spirit. Since Demons affect everyone on earth, the Demons will affect the people around the newborn, making them get angry and have negative thoughts toward the newborn for no reason. Not only are you causing damage to the child's spirit, you may be causing mental, physical and emotional damage to that child. The child's precious spirit within already has to deal with Demons attacking them, so lets make it a little easier on them by learning to get rid of our Demons so we don't attack them, also. Remember, our negative thoughts toward others cause damage to their higher selves which cause damage to their spirit.

I know that many people will say you have to discipline your children, but do you? Well I guess that as long as everyone on earth stays darkened down to God's spiritual secrets and continue to let the Demons and dark energies rule earth, we will have to continue to damage the newborn child's spirit. I know, because of my discussions with God, that we, as a society, must change and welcome the new spiritual awakening we are about to witness.

Adults and children alike have some negative characteristics. These negative characteristics are because you have holes in your spirit. Demons and people's negative thoughts attack your higher selves causing holes in your spirit which allows dark energy into your spiritual body. And anything you have wrong with your spiritual body, directly affects your physical body. You might be a control freak, selfish, greedy, envious or jealous—the list can go on forever. Keep your higher selves clear within the spiritual dimensions and replace your spirit often and you can actually get rid of all negative feelings within yourself.

When you change your spirit, you will replace the beat up one with a new one. When the beat up spirit leaves, so does the negative attributes and the positive attributes from heaven return into you because your new spirit comes straight from heaven.

With the new spirit in you, the new Godly attributes will cross over into your physical body because, what happens to the spiritual body happens to the physical body. There is one catch: You must want to retain these new attributes and, to do so, you must mentally change your negative thinking and adopt a new positive way of thinking. Even though the Demons causing the negative feelings are gone and you have a new spirit within you, the old mental knowledge of the negative feelings you had are still within you. However, without the Demons attacking you and with a new spirit within you, then changing your mental habits will be a breeze.

Don't forget, everyone has a spirit inside their body; your spirit lived in heaven before entering into you. Before the spirit came to live in you it was living in total oneness with all spirits in heaven. Because every man, woman and child has a spirit within them, this makes us all related spiritually. Everyone belongs to the same family; God's.

Spirits take such a beating while in our physical body that they must be protected and make sure they heal properly while in heaven. When it's time for a spirit to return to earth and wait on an incoming soul, a spirit must leave the protection of heaven and venture out and live all alone within someone's physical body vulnerable to all the Demon and human attacks that take place. This is why God has me sharing these spiritual secrets with you so you can understand what's going on around us spiritually; so you can protect yourself and your loved ones.

I want you to look at the picture of a woodcutting I used on the title page of this chapter. Look at God's hand with the stars around it. When you see God put your new spirit into your body, you will see a bright light in his hand with stars around it.

Testimony by Jeff Linnartz

Gary, I just wanted to get back to you and say, once again, what an experience I had with you last Friday. To start off with, when you released the Demon from around my head, chest, stomach and legs, those areas got really light and tingly. It really makes a big difference when the dark energy is taken away. (I haven't coughed at night since then, which I usually do every night.)

Also, what an amazing experience when you showed me how to replace my worn out spirit! You told me that one of your gifts was to be able to show people how to replace their spirit. When it was complete, you told me that my new spirit was green, and when I opened my eyes all I could see was green. It was amazing! After that, I felt different. It's hard to explain, but I felt different ... stronger. You also said I would be tired as my new spirit and body were getting used to each other and boy was that the truth. I had a hard time staying awake at work that night and have been pretty tired these last few days, since.

The biggest thing that happened, which I realized once we were off the phone, is that I got to see God's face. He looked over his left shoulder at me. I grew up religious and tried to picture God many times, and I guess that he looked somewhat like I had imagined.

Your friend,
Jeff Linnartz

(Note: First read the process of replacing your spirit. After you read it please stop and play the CD so I can walk you step-by-step through the spirit replacement process that has been performed on many thousands of people throughout the world.)

In the process of spirit replacement you will repeat the same steps that are in the healing chapter by first filling your spiritual and physical body with God energy/light, then clearing the spiritual dimensions from earth to heaven. I can't emphasize enough the importance of filling your spiritual and physical body with God energy/light and clearing the spiritual dimensions. The more you go through these steps, the easier and quicker it will become. In Chapter Eight, I will repeat the steps once again for clearing your spiritual dimensions. This may sound or feel repetitious to you, but you must get used to doing this method of clearing your spiritual dimensions because this is where all the spiritual attacks happen to your spiritual body, and, in my opinion, causing all of the physical problems you have.

Same as preparing for a healing: Make sure you have uninterrupted time for yourself. Remember, you are very important in God's world, so make time and take time to replace your tattered spirit.

Step One:
Connecting to your God Cord

Remember, your God Cord is the invisible cord of energy that flows from heaven through all of the spiritual dimensions and connects to the top of your head in the physical dimension. It connects your spiritual body, that's inside of your physical body, with heaven. It's very important to have God energy flowing from heaven to your spiritual/ physical body at all times. Having God energy in your body will keep all darkness out so you can prevent any physical, mental or emotional illness.

Before you start your spirit replacement process, find a comfortable place to sit. Don't lie down because you may fall asleep. Once you are comfortable and relaxed, close your eyes. I want you to relax your body and get comfortable. I want you to shut off your brain by not thinking about anything. If you are an over-thinker, then just keep telling yourself there is no place I need to be at this moment except right where I am.

Once you shut down your brain, I want you to visualize with your imagination soft white feathers surrounding your entire body. Once you are surrounded by feathers, you will feel all the tension within your physical body leave you as it is absorbed by the feathers. Just release all the tension and allow it to flow out of you and into the feathers. You're becoming as light and comfortable as the feathers you're surrounded by.

Now, tilt your head back a little so that your face is pointing upward, but not so far back as to make you uncomfortable or hurt your neck. With the same imagination you used to visualize the feathers, think of a beautiful ocean: see the blue ocean with waves coming onto the pristine white sandy beach. Now see yourself standing on the beach with the sand between your toes, just feel the warmth of the sand on your feet. Look up and see a beautiful blue sky with white fluffy clouds floating past you. I want you to just relax and enjoy the ocean, sand and blue sky.

Change the blue sky to a pure golden sky. Now imagine the gold sky opening up and you can see a bright gold energy/light shining through the sky and connecting to the top of your head. That stream of gold energy is your God Cord.

Step Two:
Clearing Your Spiritual and Physical Body

Now that your God Cord is connected to your head, just imagine gold energy flowing from the golden sky down your God Cord into the top of your head. You may feel physical warmth on the top of your head. Just allow this energy to flow into your spiritual/ physical body.

Envision the gold energy entering through the top of your head and entering into your body, filling it up with gold energy from your feet to the top of your head. Envision this energy penetrating all the cells of your body. When this energy penetrates the cells of your body, allow this energy to remove all of the darkness from within your body. Using your spiritual eyes, look at your body you will see dark energy leaving your body as the gold energy fills up your body. There can only be dark or light within your body and now you're replacing all the darkness. While this gold energy or God energy is flowing into you, just relax and allow the energy to fill your body. You will know when the inside of your body is clear of all darkness by the bright glowing energy inside of you. You will see this with your spiritual eyes, and you will feel physical sensations of heat and a feeling of lightness inside your body.

Step Three:
Clearing the Dimensions

Now that your spiritual/physical body has God energy flowing into it, you will begin to clear the spiritual dimensions starting from earth and working your way all the way to heaven. The dimensions can be cleared easily when your spiritual/physical body has God energy flowing into it. That's why you always clear your spiritual body first. To clear the dimensions, you're going to allow your God energy, that's flowing from the golden sky down your God Cord and into your spiritual/physical body, to flow out of you into the dimensions. You need to envision yourself looking like a giant light bulb of gold energy.

First Dimension
Earth/Physical Dimension

At this moment, you're standing on a sandy beach under the golden sky with God energy flowing into your spiritual body. Now change the vision of the sandy beach into the earth. Envision earth as a globe and you're standing on top of the earth. When you can see yourself standing on the earth, look up and see the God energy flowing from the golden sky through your God Cord into your spiritual/physical body and lighting you up like a light bulb from the inside out. Then envision this energy flowing out through every pore of your skin and surrounding the earth. This energy is clearing all the darkness from around the earth and your higher selves. Now look up and you will see the golden sky. The golden sky is what separates the Earth Dimension from the Buffer/Golden Dimension. Now envision the earth surrounded with gold energy all the way to the sky. Just envision this dimension filling up with gold energy like water filling a bathtub. Once the energy reaches the golden sky, envision yourself floating up from earth through the sky. Once you go through the sky, envision yourself standing on top of the sky. You are now in the Second Dimension.

Second Dimension
Golden/First Buffer Dimension

You will do the same process in this dimension as you did in the Earth Dimension. Envision God's golden energy flowing down your God Cord filling up every cell in your body then flowing out of your body filling up this dimension with gold energy. Just allow this gold energy to fill this dimension clearing everything from the ground all the way to the sky. But this time when you look at the sky you will notice the sky is dark.

In this dimension, you will see your higher selves. They will look just like you physically, but they may look beat up, like they were in a horrible fight. Just envision your God energy flowing from you and surrounding them. You will see them heal instantly. In this dimension you may see Angels flying around or you may see little dark Demons. There is nothing to fear because your God energy will protect you. If anything of a dark nature comes around you, they will be annihilated by the God energy coming from you.

Your God energy will not have an affect on any Angels—you cannot harm them because they are made of God energy. Now envision God energy flowing into and through you then into this dimension and filling it up. When the God energy reaches the dark sky, the sky will turn gold. Once the sky turns gold, envision yourself floating through the golden sky and then standing on top of the sky.

You're now in the Third Dimension.

Third Dimension
Invisible/Second Buffer Dimension

Remember the Demons and aliens in this dimension had the ability to be invisible to you, but with your new spiritual eyes that you received in the healing meditation, they will never be invisible to you again.

Now, with your spiritual eyes, look around and you may see Angels and Demons battling. The Angels are fighting to protect your higher selves. The Angels know that if the Demons cause damage to your higher selves, this, in turn, causes damage to your spiritual body and you will become sick in your physical body. By allowing God energy to fill this dimension, you're helping the Angels by killing the Demons and healing your higher selves.

Clearing the dimensions isn't only helping to heal your higher selves, it's helping to heal everyone on earth's higher selves because the spiritual dimensions connect everyone on earth. The Demons you kill will not come back, but there are always more Demons waiting to take their places. If everyone on earth understood how to allow God energy to fill the dimensions, getting rid of all the Demons, then before long everyone on earth would be happier and healthier. God told me, "By doing this one thing, that we're all capable of, this would help to unite everyone in the world, bringing us closer to world peace."

Now let us continue.

You will do the same process in this dimension as you did in the previous dimensions. Envision God's golden energy flowing down your God Cord filling up every cell in your body then flowing out of your body filling up this dimension with gold energy. Just allow God's golden energy to fill this dimension, clearing everything from the ground all the way to the sky turning the dark sky gold.

Once this dimension is full of gold energy, look up and envision yourself floating through the sky into the Fourth Dimension where dark planet aliens exist. But just before you go through the sky, remember to use your spiritual gift of a cloak. It will make you invisible to the aliens in the Fourth Dimension

Fourth Dimension
Dark Planet Aliens Dimension

Now that you're standing on top of the sky, allow your God energy to flow through you filling this dimension quickly all the way to the sky, turning it gold. Remember, the aliens in this dimension don't want anyone on earth to become enlightened; these aliens infect everyone on earth with darkness.

Allow your God energy to flow into and around everything you see. You will see everything that your energy touches explode and be swept away in a windstorm of light. You will also notice a silence in your physical ears.

There is a spiritual war going on and these aliens are not on our side, so allow your God energy to fill this dimension, clearing out all the alien projections and dark energy. Once you've turned this dimension gold, envision yourself floating through the sky standing on top of the sky in the Fifth Dimension

Fifth Dimension
Light Planet Alien Dimension

These aliens want everyone on earth to become enlightened.

Allow God energy to flow through you and into this dimension the same way you did in the other dimensions. God energy does not hurt these aliens because they already have God energy (light) inside of them. When you're finished filling this dimension with God's energy, envision yourself floating through the sky into the Sixth Dimension.

Sixth Dimension
Demon Dimension

This dimension, as I said before, is where all negative emotions come from such as fear, worried, anger, jealousy, envy and many others. Remember, when you're feeling any of these negative emotions in your physical body its always a Demon infecting your higher selves which in turn affect your spiritual body making you feel these emotions in your physical body.

Filling this dimension with God energy whenever you're feeling any of these negative feelings will make the feeling go away instantly. Demons also attack our higher selves in this dimension causing many physical, mental and emotional illnesses within us. Keep this dimension clear and your higher selves healthy by making sure your spiritual body has God energy flowing into it, and you can cure yourself as well as prevent all illness.

Just allow your God energy to flow through you filling this dimension very quickly destroying everything in it. Once you have filled this dimension with God energy, look up and envision the dark sky turning gold. Then envision yourself floating up through the sky into the Seventh Dimension.

Seventh Dimension
Negative Thought Projection Dimension

This is where other people's negative thoughts affect your higher selves. In this dimension you'll see many higher selves. Just allow your God energy to engulf all your higher selves, clearing everything away from them. Once this is done, envision a force field of gold energy around all of your higher selves surrounding them and protecting them.

Now you must clear everyone's negative thought projections out from this dimension.

First, look up and envision a golden sky. Secondly, envision the sky falling slowly down to the ground. Envision the sky as it falls being a sticky gold energy. What this energy is doing is taking away all of the negative thought projections that are around your higher selves by people thinking negative of you. Thirdly, envision this sticky energy rolling up into a ball and just disappearing—taking with it all the negative projections. Follow these three steps three to four times and it will remove all of the negative projections in this dimension. Once you allow the sticky energy to come down from the sky removing all negativity, you must allow your God energy to fill this dimension surrounding all of your higher selves to protect them.

When this is done, envision yourself floating through the gold sky into the Eighth, Dimension.

Eighth Dimension
Positive Thought Projection Dimension

In this dimension, other people's positive thoughts, such as love, happiness and joy, affect your higher selves. In this dimension, you do not project gold energy. You envision blue energy. You do this the same way as allowing the gold energy to flow through you but, instead, envision blue energy flowing through you. Fill this dimension with blue energy engulfing all of your higher selves. This is clearing away anything that may be blocking the positive feelings of love, happiness and joy that these higher selves should be feeling. When these higher selves feel love, joy and happiness, you will also feel these emotions in your physical body. So allow this blue energy to engulf and fill this entire dimension.

Once you're done, envision floating through the sky into the Ninth Dimension.

Ninth Dimension
The Bridge to Heaven—Receiving Your Keys to Heaven

Note: This dimension is where you receive your Keys to Heaven. If you have been following along in this book, you have already received your Keys to Heaven. Once you have your keys, you don't have to go through the process again. They are always with you and easy to access.

Now put your hand to your chest and your keys will appear in your hand. You will see two keys on a necklace—one smaller than the other. Now that you have your keys, look forward and you will see in front of you a huge golden door. Walk toward this door. When you get to it, you will see a keyhole. Use your keys to unlock the door and enter through it. Use the smaller key, put it in the keyhole and turn the key; the door will open. Walk through and make sure you close the door behind you, and place your keys on your neck for safe keeping. You will see a beautiful city glowing with gold energy and Angels flying over the city. There will be a bright gold energy shining from the city, and glorious music that's soothing to the soul. If you look toward the city, you'll see a huge wall surrounding the whole city. Walk closer to the city and you will see a bridge leading to another huge golden door. This bridge is made of gold and is suspended by gold ropes crossing over a huge moat that goes all around the wall. In the moat, you will see gold energy running like lava from a volcano. Cross the bridge. Once you cross the bridge, you will be standing in front of the Door to Heaven (The Tenth Dimension).

Tenth Dimension
Heaven—Receiving Your New Spirit

You've just crossed the bridge to heaven. Now you're standing in front of a huge golden door: This door is the Door to Heaven.

To enter heaven, you must use your Keys to Heaven, which are on the necklace around your neck. Remove the necklace and use the larger of the keys to unlock the door: This door will have rays of light and gold energy shining through the cracks and from under the door. Behind this door is heaven. When the door opens, you will be engulfed with gold energy: This energy will remove any darkness you may have in your spiritual body. Once this energy engulfs you, you must then enter into heaven closing the door behind you, placing the key around your neck.

Once you close the door behind you, you will be standing in heaven.

An Angel will meet you. Tell the Angel you are here to change your spirit. The Angel will walk with you through the gardens bringing you to God. You will see heavens pool with dolphins swimming in it. After passing the pool, you will see God sitting on a golden bench. The Angel will then leave you with God. You must ask God to please give you your new spirit with all of heaven's attributes: love, compassion, non-judgment, caring, non-prejudice, oneness, happiness, joy, humor, fun and all the other positive attributes you want. God will then place your new spirit in your spiritual body. In that moment, when God gives you your new spirit, if you look with your spiritual eyes you will see God touch you on the head. When he touches your head in heaven, he's putting your new spirit in you. At that moment when he touches your head, your spirit is floating down your God Cord entering into your physical body. Your spirit will enter your body through the top of your head and settle into your chest. Once it's in your chest, you will see (with your spiritual eyes) a bright swirling light in the middle of your chest and feel warmth (in your physical body) as your new spirit penetrates into every cell of your body. As this is taking place, you'll notice your old spirit leaving your body by floating up your God Cord and entering back into heaven where it will go through the healing process that repairs the damage that occurred to it while on earth protecting your soul. If you see your old spirit leave, you will notice that it has holes and black spots on it. While your new spirit is settling into your body, you may notice a feeling of lightness, warmth or a tingling sensation throughout your body. Each time you replace your spirit, you may feel the same sensations because you're removing your old spirit and the negativity that was attached to it and replacing it with pure untainted God energy.

Synchronizing the Body, Mind and Spirit

Once your new spirit is in your body, you will have to synchronize the body and mind with the spirit so that your body and mind can recognize your new spirit.

The first thing you will synchronize is your mind with your spirit. You do this by asking God to synchronize your mind with your spirit. You will see God touch your head. When he does, his green healing energy will enter into your head. This energy will synchronize your mind and spirit together as one. You will see (spiritually), as the green energy flows from heaven down your God Cord and into your head, the healing energy going in through the top of your head and enter into your mind (brain) so they can operate together. Once the green healing energy enters into your brain, you must relax and allow it to do its job. It's your job to get the healing energy into the brain, and then you must allow the energy to do its work. You'll notice the green healing energy in your head swirling around. Some of the green energy will leave your head and enter into your body blending with white swirling energy inside your body. This is your new spirit synchronizing with the mind.

Next you have to synchronize your physical body and your spirit together. You do this by asking God for his blue energy to synchronize your body and spirit together as one.

You will see (spiritually), as the blue energy flows from heaven down your God Cord and enters through the top of your head, that it enters into all the muscles, nerves, bones, organs and cells of your body. Everything in your physical body will have blue energy flowing into it. This blue energy will synchronize with your new spirit. You will see your spirit (a bright white light) blending with the blue energy—becoming one, synchronizing together the body and the spirit.

Next you will synchronize the body, mind and spirit together as one unit. You do this by asking God for his gold energy. You will see gold energy flowing from heaven down your God Cord entering into your body through the top of your head. This energy will enter into your mind (brain) first blending with the green healing energy that's already in your head. Just allow the gold energy to blend into your mind. Then the gold energy will flow into your whole body blending together the body, mind and spirit so everything can work together as one. You will notice the green energy of the mind and the blue energy of the body and the white energy of the spirit turning gold when the blending takes place.

When the body, mind and spirit work together as one, it is connected to heaven and earth. This is when the physical and spiritual bodies live together as one in harmony and bliss. When you change your spirit, you'll notice an immediate change in your energy. You will feel more peaceful and relaxed.

Always remember, when changing your spirit that you must also change your mental approach to life, so that your new spirit and your mental awareness can be one. Remember, heaven is on earth; it's inside of you.

As you go through life, you may change your spirit many times, but there's one thing you need to know; you, and only you, can change your spirit. If you know someone who should or who wants to change their spirit, there is no shortcut. They'll have to learn the process on their own. You can introduce them to the process as I did with you, but it's up to them to make the change.

Once your spirit replacement is complete, give God thanks for replacing your spirit. You can give him a hug, shake his hand or just say thank you. When you're finished giving God thanks, the Angels will guide you through the gardens of heaven back to the door that leads out of heaven. At this point, you can tell the Angels you would like to stay in heaven for a little while longer or you can leave. If you stay, you can hang out with the Angels or loved ones who have passed away. You can also hang out with your pets that have passed away. Remember, when you do leave, use your key to open the door, making sure you shut it behind you, locking it. Start walking back across the bridge. As you're walking across the bridge, it's time to enter back into your physical body. As you're walking, I want you to imagine that your physical body is standing on the other side of the bridge. As you approach yourself, stop and join your spiritual and physical bodies together.

At this point in the guided meditation, I will awaken you.

Note: Stop now and play the Spirit Replacement section of the CD. I will walk you step-by-step through the process of replacing your spirit the same way God did with me. This process has been performed on many thousands of people throughout the world with amazing results.

SOUL UNLOCKING
HOW TO UNLOCK HEAVENS
KNOWLEDGE HIDDEN WITHIN YOU.

Once God taught me the process of spirit replacement, he then told me to teach other people how to replace their spirits, so I went out and started teaching others. I taught in large seminars, my spiritual retreats and also in my private consultations with people. Everything was going well; I was doing as God told me to do. Then, one day as I was changing my spirit, God said he had something new for me to learn. God said, "It is time to unlock the spiritual secrets that are locked within you."

Of course, my first question was, "What do you mean: spiritual secrets locked within me?"

God explained to me that a person's soul is the spiritual DNA of their spiritual body, and the soul holds all of the spiritual secrets of heaven locked within it. As the DNA of the physical body is different from person-to-person, the DNA of the soul is the same in everyone. Everyone's soul is made up of the same spiritual DNA. Everyone's soul comes from the same spiritual family and holds the same spiritual secrets of heaven locked inside of it. So you see, everyone on earth is related, "Spiritually speaking."

God said, "Everyone's soul lived in heaven before it was sent to earth to live within a human body, and the soul has all the knowledge of heaven." The soul cannot survive on earth without a human body because there is not enough God energy (light) on earth for it to survive. The human body helps to protect the soul from Demons and other dark energies. Your soul comes back to earth lifetime after lifetime in an attempt to bring enough God energy (light) to earth so that, eventually, one day it does not have to return within a human body. The spirit, along with the human body, protects the soul from the Demons and other dark energies that are trying to ensure that enough God energy (light) will never come to earth.

God said, "If there is enough God energy on earth, then one day your soul would be able to come and go between heaven and earth, as it was meant to be."

When your soul left heaven and entered your physical body, your soul's heavenly knowledge and secrets had to be locked within it to protect it from the Demons and other dark energies that would certainly try to kill it. This is why Demons and dark energies are always trying to keep you darkened down spiritually, mentally, emotionally and physically—so that you don't unlock the God knowledge that is within you.

Sometimes, when a soul is put in a human body, it has more of its spiritual knowledge and secrets unlocked than other souls. This is why you have healers, psychics and other spiritually gifted people on earth. The more the soul knows, the more gifted the human body is. Everyone is spiritually gifted and, once you unlock your knowledge and secrets, your gifts will start to expand.

The soul's DNA holds the Keys to Heaven. This is why, when you approach heaven's door and you are asked for the Keys to Heaven, you find that they were already inside of you. You just had to touch your hand to your chest to receive your keys.

God then asked me, "Remember when you were a child and you would go into trances and, in the trance, you would see a vision of a darkness surrounding and engulfing the earth? Then the Angels would hand you a set of keys. One of the golden keys would unlock the earth and it would start to glow with a radiant gold energy."

I said, "Yes."

He then said, "The true meaning of your ongoing vision as a child, represents people on earth unlocking their spiritual knowledge and all joining together as one family to defeat the Demons and dark energies that attack everyone. On earth, if someone was attacking one of your family members, you would defend them. Everyone on earth is your spiritual brother and sister and they are being attacked by Demons and dark energies, so let's all unite together and fight against the Demons and dark energies that are attacking us. If this happens, then earth will become a light planet. No one would ever have to worry about Demons and other dark energies attacking them ever again because heaven would be on earth."

I started getting excited about learning the secrets that were inside of me. I was thinking that, once the knowledge was released, I would know everything about spirituality. God explained to me that, once the knowledge is unlocked, it is not as if you know all the spiritual secrets at once, because the human mind would not be able to comprehend all of the secrets at one time. All of that knowledge being downloaded into your brain would simply drive you crazy. When you're ready for the knowledge, it will be released little by little to you. The more you understand, the more you will learn. Your soul knows what's best for you.

In the process of soul unlocking, you will repeat the same steps that are in the healing and spirit replacement chapters. I can't emphasize enough the importance of filling your physical/spiritual body with God energy/light, clearing the spiritual dimensions and replacing your spirit. The more often you go through these steps, the easier and quicker it will become. This may sound or feel repetitious to you, but the more you get used to doing this method, the easier and quicker it gets.

Same as preparing for a healing or spirit replacement: Make sure that you have uninterrupted time for yourself. Remember, you are very important in God's world, so make time and take time to unlock your soul.

Step One:
Connecting to your God Cord

Remember, your God Cord is the invisible cord of energy that flows from heaven through all of the spiritual dimensions and connects to the top of your head in the physical dimension. It connects your spiritual body that's inside of your physical body with heaven. It's very important to have God energy flowing from heaven to your spiritual/physical body at all times. Having God energy in your body will keep all darkness out so you can prevent any physical, mental or emotional illness.

Before you start your soul unlocking process, find a comfortable place to sit. Don't lie down because you may fall asleep. Once you are comfortable and relaxed, close your eyes. I want you to relax your body and get comfortable. I want you to shut off your brain by not thinking about anything. If you are an over-thinker, then just keep telling yourself there is no place I need to be at this moment except right where I'm at.

Once you shut down your brain, I want you to visualize with your imagination, soft white feathers surrounding your entire body. Once you are surrounded by all these feathers, you will feel all of the tension within your physical body leave you as it is absorbed by the feathers. Just release all the tension and allow it to flow out of you and into the feathers. You're becoming as light and comfortable as the feathers you're surrounded by.

Now, tilt your head back a little so that your face is pointing upward, but not so far back as to make you uncomfortable or hurt your neck. With the same imagination you used to visualize the feathers, think of a beautiful ocean: See the blue ocean with waves coming onto the pristine white sandy beach. Now, see yourself standing on the beach with the sand between your toes, just feeling the warmth of the sand on your feet. Look up and see a beautiful blue sky with white fluffy clouds floating past you. I want you to just relax and enjoy the ocean, sand and blue sky.

Change the blue sky to a pure golden sky. Now, imagine the gold sky opening up and you can see a bright gold energy/light shining through the sky connecting to the top of your head. That stream of gold energy is your God Cord.

Step Two:
Clearing Your Spiritual and Physical Body

Now that your God Cord is connected to your head, just imagine gold energy flowing from the golden sky down your God Cord into the top of your head. You may feel physical warmth on the top of your head. Just allow this energy to flow into your spiritual/physical body.

Envision the gold energy entering through the top of your head and entering into your body, filling it up with gold energy from your feet to the top of your head. Envision this energy penetrating all the cells of your body and, when this energy penetrates the cells of your body, allow this energy to remove all of the darkness from within your body. Using your spiritual eyes, look at your body and you will see dark energy leaving your body as the gold energy fills up your body. There can only be dark or light within your body and now you're replacing all of the darkness with light. While this gold energy or God energy is flowing into you, just relax and allow the energy to fill your body. You will know when the inside of your body is clear of all darkness by the bright glowing energy inside of you. You will see this with your spiritual eyes, and you will feel physical sensations of heat and a feeling of lightness inside your body.

Step Three:
Clearing the Dimensions

Now that your spiritual/physical body has God energy flowing into it, you will begin to clear the ten spiritual dimensions starting from the first, Earth, and working your way all the way to Heaven, the tenth. The dimensions can be cleared easily when your spiritual/physical body has God energy flowing into it. That's why you always clear your spiritual body first. To clear the dimensions, you're going to allow your God energy, that's flowing from the golden sky down your God Cord and into your spiritual/physical body, to flow out of you into the dimensions. You need to envision yourself looking like a giant light bulb of gold energy.

First Dimension
Earth/Physical Dimension

At this moment you're standing on a sandy beach under the golden sky with God energy flowing into your spiritual body. Now, change the vision of the sandy beach into the earth. Envision earth as a globe and you're standing on top of earth. When you can see yourself standing on the earth, look up and see the God energy flowing from the golden sky through your God Cord into your spiritual/physical body, lighting you up like a light bulb from the inside out. Then envision this energy flowing out through every pore of your skin and surrounding the earth. This energy is clearing all of the darkness from around the earth and your higher selves. Now look up and you will see the golden sky. The golden sky is what separates the Earth Dimension from the Buffer/ Golden Dimension. Now envision the earth surrounded with gold energy all the way to the sky. Just envision this dimension filling up with gold energy like water filling a bathtub. Once the energy reaches the golden sky, envision yourself floating up from earth through the sky. Once you go through the sky, envision yourself standing on top of the sky. You are now in the Second Dimension.

Second Dimension
Golden/First Buffer Dimension

You will do the same process in this dimension as you did in the Earth Dimension. Envision God's golden energy flowing down your God Cord filling up every cell in your body then flowing out of your body filling up this dimension with gold energy. Just allow this gold energy to fill this dimension, clearing everything from the ground all the way to the sky. But this time when you look at the sky, you will notice that the sky is dark.

In this dimension, you will see your higher selves. They will look just like you physically, but they may look beat up, like they were in a horrible fight. Just envision your God energy flowing from you and surrounding them. You will see them heal instantly. In this dimension, you may see Angels flying around or you may see little dark Demons. There is nothing to fear because your God energy will protect you. If anything of a dark nature comes around you, they will be annihilated by the God energy coming from you.

Your God energy will not have an affect on any Angels—you cannot harm them because they are made of God energy. Now envision God energy flowing into and through you, then into this dimension and filling it up. When the God energy reaches the dark sky, the sky will turn gold. Once the sky turns gold, envision yourself floating through the golden sky and then standing on top of the sky.
You're now in the Third Dimension.

Third Dimension
Invisible/Second Buffer Dimension

Remember, the Demons and aliens in this dimension had the ability to be invisible to you. But with your new spiritual eyes, which you received in the healing meditation, they will never be invisible to you again.

Now, with your spiritual eyes, look around and you may see Angels and Demons battling. The Angels are fighting to protect your higher selves. The Angels know that if the Demons cause damage to your higher selves, this, in turn, causes damage to your spiritual body and you will become sick in your physical body. By allowing God energy to fill this dimension, you're helping the Angels by killing the Demons and healing your higher selves.

Clearing the dimensions isn't only helping to heal your higher selves, it's helping to heal the higher selves of everyone on earth because the spiritual dimensions connect everyone on earth. The Demons you kill will not come back, but there are always more Demons waiting to take their places. If everyone on earth understood how to allow God energy to fill the dimensions, getting rid of all the Demons, then, before long, everyone on earth would be happier and healthier. God told me, "By doing this one thing, that we're all capable of, this would help to unite everyone in the world, bringing us closer to world peace."

Now let us continue.

You will do the same process in this dimension as you did in the previous dimensions. Envision God's golden energy flowing down your God Cord filling up every cell in your body, then flowing out of your body filling up this dimension with gold energy. Just allow God's golden energy to fill this dimension, clearing everything from the ground all the way to the sky and turning the dark sky gold.

Once this dimension is full of gold energy, look up and envision yourself floating through the sky into the Fourth Dimension where dark planet aliens exist. But, just before you go through the sky, remember to use your spiritual gift of a cloak. It will make you invisible to the aliens in the Fourth Dimension

Fourth Dimension
Dark Planet Aliens Dimension

Now that you're standing on top of the sky, allow your God energy to flow through you filling this dimension quickly all the way to the sky, turning it gold. Remember, the aliens in this dimension don't want anyone on earth to become enlightened; these aliens infect everyone on earth with darkness.

Allow your God energy to flow into and around everything you see. You will see everything that your energy touches explode and be swept away in a windstorm of light. You will also notice a silence in your physical ears.

There is a spiritual war going on and these aliens are not on our side, so allow your God energy to fill this dimension, clearing out all of the alien projections and dark energy. Once you've turned this dimension gold, envision yourself floating through the sky, then standing on top of the sky in the Fifth Dimension

Fifth Dimension
Light Planet Alien Dimension

These aliens want everyone on earth to become enlightened.

Allow God energy to flow through you and into this dimension the same way you did in the other dimensions. God energy does not hurt these aliens because they already have God energy (light) inside of them. When you're finished filling this dimension with God's energy, envision yourself floating through the sky and into the Sixth Dimension.

Sixth Dimension
Demon Dimension

This dimension, as I said before, is where all negative emotions come from such as fear, worry, anger, jealousy, envy and many others. Remember, when you're feeling any of these negative emotions in your physical body, it's always a Demon infecting your higher selves which, in turn, affects your spiritual body making you feel these emotions in your physical body.

Filling this dimension with God energy whenever you're feeling any of these negative feelings, will make the feeling go away instantly. Demons also attack our higher selves in this dimension causing many physical, mental and emotional illnesses within us. Keep this dimension clear and your higher selves healthy by making sure your spiritual body has God energy flowing into it, and you can cure yourself as well as prevent all illness.

Just allow your God energy to flow through you filling this dimension very quickly, destroying everything in it. Once you have filled this dimension with God energy, look up and envision the dark sky turning gold. Then envision yourself floating up through the sky into the Seventh Dimension.

Seventh Dimension
Negative Thought Projection Dimension

This is where other people's negative thoughts affect your higher selves. In this dimension, you'll see many higher selves. Just allow your God energy to engulf all of your higher selves, clearing everything away from them. Once this is done, envision a force field of gold energy around all of your higher selves surrounding them and protecting them.

Now you must clear everyone's negative thought projections out from this dimension.

First, look up and envision a golden sky. Secondly, envision the sky falling slowly down to the ground. Envision the sky, as it falls, being a sticky gold energy. What this energy is doing is taking away all of the negative thought projections that are around your higher selves resulting from people thinking negative of you. Thirdly, envision this sticky energy rolling up into a ball and just disappearing—taking with it all of the negative projections. Follow these three steps three to four times and you will remove all of the negative projections in this dimension. Once you allow the sticky energy to come down from the sky and remove all negativity, you must allow your God energy to fill this dimension surrounding all of your higher selves to protect them.

When this is done, envision yourself floating through the gold sky into the Eighth Dimension.

Eighth Dimension
Positive Thought Projection Dimension

In this dimension, people's positive thoughts, such as love, happiness and joy, affect your higher selves. In this dimension, you do not project gold energy. You envision blue energy. You do this the same way as allowing the gold energy to flow through you, but, instead, envision blue energy flowing through you. Fill this dimension with blue energy engulfing all of your higher selves. This is clearing away anything that may be blocking the positive feelings of love, happiness and joy that these higher selves should be feeling. When these higher selves feel love, joy and happiness, you will also feel these emotions in your physical body. So allow this blue energy to engulf and fill this entire dimension.

Once you're done, envision floating through the sky into the Ninth Dimension.

Ninth Dimension
The Bridge to Heaven—Receiving Your Keys to Heaven

Note: In this dimension is where you receive your Keys to Heaven. If you have been following along in this book, you have already received your Keys to Heaven. Once you have your keys, you don't have to go through the process again. They are always with you and easy to access.

Now, put your hand to your chest and your keys will appear in your hand. You will see two keys on a necklace—one smaller than the other. Now that you have your keys, look forward and you will see in front of you a huge golden door. Walk toward this door. When you get to it, you will see a keyhole. You must use your keys to unlock the door and enter through it. Use the smaller key; put it in the keyhole and turn the key. The door will open. Walk through and make sure you close the door behind you and place your keys on your neck for safe keeping. You will see a beautiful city glowing with gold energy and Angels flying over the city. There will be a bright gold energy shining from the city, and glorious music that's soothing to the soul. If you look toward the city, you'll see a huge wall surrounding the whole city. Walk closer to the city and you will see a bridge leading to another huge golden door. This bridge is made of gold and is suspended by gold ropes crossing over a huge moat that goes all around the wall. In the moat, you will see gold energy running like lava from a volcano. Cross the bridge. Once you cross the bridge, you will be standing in front of the Door to Heaven (The Tenth Dimension).

Tenth Dimension
Heaven—Receiving Your New Spirit

You've just crossed the bridge to heaven. Now you're standing in front of a huge golden door: This door is the Door to Heaven.

To enter heaven, you must use your Keys to Heaven, which are on the necklace around your neck. Remove the necklace and use the larger of the keys to unlock the door: This door will have rays of light and gold energy shining through the cracks and from under the door. Behind this door is heaven. When the door opens, you will be engulfed with gold energy: This energy will remove any darkness you may have in your spiritual body. Once this energy engulfs you, you must then enter into heaven, closing the door behind you, placing the key around your neck.

Once you close the door behind you, you will be standing in heaven.

An Angel will meet you. Tell the Angel you are here to change your spirit. The Angel will walk with you through the gardens, bringing you to God. You will see heaven's pool with dolphins swimming in it. After passing the pool, you will see God sitting on a golden bench. The Angel will then leave you with God. You must ask God to please give you your new spirit with all of heavens attributes: Love, compassion, non-judgment, caring, non-prejudice, oneness, happiness, joy, humor, fun and all of the other positive attributes you want. God will then place your new spirit in your spiritual body. In that moment, when God gives you your new spirit, if you look with your spiritual eyes, you will see God touch you on the head. When he touches your head in heaven, he's putting your new spirit in you. At that moment, when he touches your head, your spirit is floating down your God Cord entering into your physical body. Your spirit will enter your body through the top of your head and settle into your chest. Once it's in your chest, you will see (with your spiritual eyes) a bright swirling light in the middle of your chest and feel warmth (in your physical body) as your new spirit penetrates into every cell of your body. As this is taking place, you'll notice your old spirit leaving your body by floating up your God Cord and entering back into heaven where it will go through the healing process that repairs the damage that occurred to it while on earth protecting your soul. If you see your old spirit leave, you will notice that it has holes and black spots on it. While your new spirit is settling into your body, you may notice a feeling of lightness, warmth or a tingling sensation throughout your body. Each time you replace your spirit, you may feel the same sensations because you're removing your old spirit and the negativity that was attached to it and replacing it with pure untainted God energy.

Synchronizing the Body, Mind and Spirit

Once your new spirit is in your body, you will have to synchronize the body and mind with the spirit so that your body and mind can recognize your new spirit.

The first thing you will synchronize is your mind with your spirit. You do this by asking God to synchronize your mind with your spirit. You will see God touch your head. When he does, his green healing energy will enter into your head. This energy will synchronize your mind and spirit together as one. You will see (spiritually) as the green energy flows from heaven down your God Cord and into your head. The healing energy will go in through the top of your head and enter into your mind (brain) so they can operate together. Once the green healing energy enters into your brain, you must relax and allow it to do its job. It's your job to get the healing energy into the brain, and then you must allow the energy to do its work. You'll notice the green healing energy in your head swirling around. Some of the green energy will leave your head and enter into your body—blending with white swirling energy inside your body. This is your new spirit synchronizing with the mind.

Next, you have to synchronize your physical body and your spirit together. You do this by asking God for his blue energy to synchronize your body and spirit together as one.

You will see (spiritually) as the blue energy flows from heaven down your God Cord and enters through the top of your head, then enters into all the muscles, nerves, bones, organs and cells of your body. Everything in your physical body will have blue energy flowing into it. This blue energy will synchronize with your new spirit. You will see your spirit (a bright white light) blending with the blue energy, becoming one—synchronizing together the body and spirit.

Next, you will synchronize the body, mind and spirit together as one unit. You do this by asking God for his gold energy. You will see gold energy flowing from heaven down your God Cord entering into your body through the top of your head. This energy will enter into your mind (brain), first blending with the green healing energy that's already in your head. Just allow the gold energy to blend into your mind. Then the gold energy will flow into your whole body—blending together the body, mind and spirit so everything can work together as one. You will notice the green energy of the mind and the blue energy of the body and the white energy of the spirit turning gold when the blending takes place.

When the body, mind and spirit work together as one, it is connected to heaven and earth. This is when the physical and spiritual bodies live together as one in harmony and bliss. When you change your spirit, you'll notice an immediate change in your energy. You will feel more peaceful and relaxed.

Always remember when changing your spirit, that you must also change your mental approach to life, so that your new spirit and your mental awareness can be one. Remember, heaven is on earth; it's inside of you.

As you go through life, you may change your spirit many times. But there's one thing you need to know; you and only you can change your spirit. If you know someone who should or who wants to change their spirit, there is no shortcut. They'll have to learn the process on their own. You can introduce them to the process as I did with you, but it's up to them to make the change.

Step Five:
Soul Unlocking

Now that you have cleared your spiritual dimensions of all Demons and dark energies and your spirit replacement is complete, it is time for your soul unlocking. If you have just replaced your spirit and are still with God, you then have to ask God for a soul unlocking.

If you had a spirit replacement earlier and are doing just a soul unlocking, you must enter through the Door to Heaven where you will meet an Angel. Tell the Angel that you are here to unlock your soul and the Angel will guide you through the gardens alongside heaven's pool where the dolphins swim. You will see God sitting on a golden bench. Tell him you are here for your soul unlocking.

When you ask God for a soul unlocking, you'll see (with your spiritual eyes) God place a bright white light inside your chest. This light will descend down your God Cord and enter into your spiritual body that resides in your physical body. It will settle in the middle of your chest the same way your spirit did. Once God's energy is in your chest, you will see it with your spiritual eyes and feel the warmth in your physical body. This light will now spread throughout your spiritual body revealing to you a golden key located in your forehead or third eye. This is a very important key for your soul unlocking.

When you see the key, reach up and touch your physical hand to your forehead and take your glowing key out of your head. Now, using your spiritual eyes, look at your hand. You will see your soul-unlocking key in your hand. Most people see it as a shimmering, glowing golden key. But sometimes people may see their key as multiple colors or even rainbow colors. With your spiritual eyes, look at your heart: You'll see a keyhole in your heart. Place the key into the keyhole and turn it to the right. You will notice little rainbow-looking double helix DNA symbols being released inside of your body.

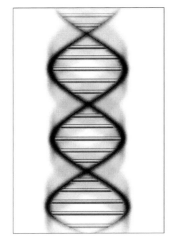

Design by Nils Lawernce

This represents the unlocking of your soul's spiritual knowledge and secrets.

When this happens, it is releasing the soul's DNA so that your spiritual knowledge can be unlocked. Relax and allow the process to take place. You'll see (with your spiritual eyes) gold energy filling every cell of your body. Your body will feel alive as the spiritual knowledge is released. You'll feel healthier, happier and rejuvenated; allow this energy to fill up the inside of your body. There is no time limit on how long it takes—you must simply allow it to happen. You'll have a sense of when the process of soul unlocking is complete because you'll feel larger-than-life and extremely happy.

If you look at yourself with your spiritual eyes, you will see a golden glow everywhere and tiny DNA symbols throughout your spiritual body.

Once this step is finished, envision the earth in front of you. Look at the earth as if you were out in space looking back at the earth—so you can see it in its entirety. Now, envision a keyhole in the center of earth.

Take your key out of the keyhole in your heart and place it into the keyhole in the earth, turning it to the right.

With your spiritual eyes you will see a gold energy spinning around the whole planet.

Design by Nils Lawernc

What this gold energy represents is earth's very own spiritual DNA. God explained to me that God planets have a spiritual DNA of their own and earth is becoming a God planet. God said, "The more people who unlock their spiritual DNA and the DNA of earth, the sooner heaven can be on earth." My mission is to get everyone on earth to unlock their spiritual DNA and earth's spiritual DNA. Thus heaven, one day very soon, will be on earth.

Our Father, who art in heaven,
Hallowed be thy Name.
Thy kingdom come,
Thy will be done,
On earth as it is in heaven.

- Matthew 6: 9-10

Once your soul unlocking is complete, give God thanks for releasing your spiritual DNA. You can give him a hug, shake his hand or just say, thank you. When you're finished giving God thanks, the Angels will guide you through the gardens of heaven back to the door that leads out of heaven. At this point, you can tell the Angels that you would like to stay in heaven for a little while longer or you can leave. If you stay, you can hang out with the Angels or loved ones who have passed away. You can also hang out with your pets that have passed away. Remember, when you do leave, use your key to open the door, making sure you shut it behind you; locking it. Start walking back across the bridge. As you're walking across the bridge, it's time to enter back into your physical body. As you're walking, I want you to imagine that your physical body is standing on the other side of the bridge. As you approach yourself, stop and join your spiritual and physical bodies together.

At this point in the guided meditation, I will awaken you.

Soul unlocking is different from a spirit replacement. Spirit replacement can be done as often as needed. Soul unlocking takes place only once in your lifetime. Once the soul unlocking is complete, you will start to notice the difference in your physical body because now your spiritual DNA is unlocked.

As I said earlier, you will not have all of the answers to spirituality immediately. That knowledge will come to you as you ask and when your soul feels it is time.

In the coming times, you will see more and more gifted children and adults on earth because of all the God energy starting to come to earth. The more God energy on earth and the more people who learn to release earth's spiritual DNA by doing a soul unlocking, the more spiritually gifted and at peace everyone will become. Their souls will be able to release more of its spiritual knowledge without the fear of being possessed by the Demons and dark energies that plague mankind.

The next chapter in this book is about gifted children and how and why their lives are very different from others, and what precious spiritual knowledge adults can learn from them.

"And it shall come to pass in the last days, saith God, I will pour out of my Spirit upon all flesh: and your sons and your daughters shall prophesy, and your young men shall see visions, and your old men shall dream dreams."

- Acts 2:17

(Note: Stop now. Go to the Soul Unlocking section of the CD and you will be walked through the process of soul unlocking.)

GIFTED CHILDREN
UNDERSTANDING EARTHS PRECIOUS CARGO

Everyone is born spiritually gifted, but our society has taught many kids to block their spiritual gifts because it's not always socially acceptable to be able to see God, Angels and Demons or receive spiritual gifts.

Some children are made to feel ashamed or scared of their natural God-given abilities simply because the parent or guardian doesn't believe or understand what's going on. The children are told that it is just their imagination, or their gifts came from the devil. Many times, parents just don't want to or don't have time to hear their children's stories about what they are seeing and hearing spiritually. There are many reasons why children suppress their spiritual abilities and one of the biggest reasons is that society doesn't accept this as mainstream, normal or cool. The result is that these children are made to feel ashamed of who they are and the gifts they possess.

At one time in history, many people didn't believe that the earth was round. They could not see it, so they didn't believe it. But there were a few people who believed that the earth was round and they set out to prove it. Once the earth was discovered to be round, people started accepting that fact. Well, just like the people who didn't believe the earth was round, there are many people in our present time who don't believe that communicating with God and Angels is real or possible. These are the same people who suppress their natural spiritual abilities and their children's natural spiritual abilities.

One thing I'm sure about is that the children are our future. I know that many of them have natural spiritual abilities far beyond my abilities, so let us not make them feel ashamed of their gifts, but rather make them feel proud. Let us tell them how special they are. We, as a society, need to awaken to the next generation of spirituality and realize that our children are the next great spiritual generation. Don't suppress their abilities, you may stop your child from becoming a great healer, teacher, spiritual leader or just happy.

One of the messages God gave me was that in the next ten years, our planet will experience the largest spiritual awakening in our world's history. During these ten years, all of the people who live on earth will become aware of their spiritual abilities by becoming aware of their God energy. I think that people will come to understand, in a universal stance, what it means to be spiritually gifted and how important it is. I think that we will understand innately that we are all connected with a higher power. We are connected with our Angels, Heavenly Hierarchy and God. We have many beings of light that are able to bestow amazing gifts to us that will help us live in total bliss and peace with our neighbors. I see us living as one with our neighbors, ourselves and everyone around the world—the same way it is in heaven.

To help us with this transition, there are many children being born with their souls already unlocked and with access to all of heaven's secrets. There are adults who are already here with huge arsenals of spiritual gifts and spiritual knowledge that they are not yet fully aware of because they have not yet experienced their soul unlocking. These children and adults were sent here to help us win all of our battles against the Demons and dark energies. These gifted children and adults will have an innate sense of what their spiritual abilities are in this lifetime. They may seem aloof in some traditional areas of learning, while they are spiritually brilliant in others.

Many of the children being born today and for the last thirty years, have an amazing God energy that they are born with. Many of these children are far more gifted at 3 or 5 old than I am today. The biggest problem is that these children were not born with an owner's manual and parents were never told how to properly develop these children. Because previous generations of children were not born with these special abilities already unlocked, many adults have no clue as to what's really going on with their children. This is why it is so imperative that everyone on earth learns about their spiritual abilities.

In many cases, these children are more spiritually gifted than any spiritual leader or teacher I have ever met or heard of. However, it is unfortunate that, in our somewhat spiritually archaic society that we call our physical dimension, we, as a society, usually do not understand these kids. We try to stuff these children into a mold of teaching that is out-of-date and doesn't work anymore. By trying to satisfy the system, the school, the teacher or the parent, many times it is doing horrible damage to these children. I see it daily. Because these kids are far more spiritually advanced, they may not be aware of some things going on around them in the physical dimension which makes it hard to pay attention in class, or they may not understand school lessons the same way as other kids do because they are on a different vibration and are able to naturally see in all of the ten spiritual dimensions. Most of society doesn't understand these children. Doctors are quick to diagnose these children with many different disorders.

Most of these kids are natural empaths.

An empath can feel the physical pain or emotional pain of whomever they're around. For example, this phenomenon happens frequently with identical twins: They can feel each other's pain from even long distances. Many times, these gifted kids will do this with everyone around them as if their identical twin is everyone alive. They're noticing the dark energies and Demons that are plaguing their classmates. They may pick up on a drug vibration from a classmate who has a parent who abuses drugs, or a gifted boy may notice the little girl sitting next to him in class as she suddenly looses a baby tooth. This may create a dilemma for the girl, as she may think she is now ugly and the boy feels exactly what she does.

These gifted children will always feel a need to help the other person. They will want to get rid of the darkness or mend the pain. I don't know if that would be considered attention deficit disorder or maybe not a disorder at all. Maybe it should be called Spiritual Heightened Awareness (Non-Disorder). Maybe we should diagnose everyone who is not aware of their spiritual abilities as having Spiritual Suppression Disorder. Well, that would be just about everyone on the planet.

Sometimes the darkness will be a little overwhelming for the gifted child. It can manifest itself in many different ways. Many children may see monsters or Demons in their bedrooms. This may cause the child to be scared, upset, angry, rebellious, loud or even withdrawn. As these children have so much going on in their little spiritually gifted heads, it becomes difficult for them to keep track of it all. The only guidance they have is God, Angels and other spiritual beings. Parents, peers and teachers may not understand what's going on with them.

With no guidance and, sometimes, even with wrongfully prescribed psychiatric medications, they lose their abilities to protect themselves from dark energies and Demons as they lose their ability to stay connected with God, Angels and higher spiritual beings. This is why I'm bringing this spiritual awareness to everyone.

For example, if your child was a star athlete, a gifted singer or academically brilliant, you would encourage this child to flourish and be the best they can with their gift. You would not stop him from using his gift. So why are so many spiritually gifted children being robbed of their gifts? It's not the parents', teachers', doctors' or societies' fault for being unaware of their gifts, but it is now time for us to try to understand and embrace these children, for it is the children who may lead us forward with God's plan to unite heaven and earth. The star athlete, singer and academically brilliant child all have role models to look up to and are accepted socially. Unfortunately, not many people understand that the spiritually gifted child possesses a natural talent, also.

In the same way as you would not stop your child from using his or her talent, you would not stop their coach from coaching them. The main coaches that the gifted child has are God and his Angels. I know that there aren't many assistant coaches in the physical world to serve as guides for the spiritually gifted child, and that's why I'm trying to teach everyone on earth the importance of learning how to communicate with God and Angels. You may have to be an assistant coach for a spiritually gifted child.

God assigns their Angels (coaches) to them as they come into this physical life at birth. They are here to help guide and teach them. You may have a child who is very talented in many parts of his or her life. Why not help them in the spiritual part of their life? The best way to teach you child is to learn yourself, so that you can be an assistant coach.

Unfortunately, dark energies can attack and overcome the spirit of the gifted child the same way that they can attack your spirit and overcome you. The child may then become covered in layers of darkness so that the Angels have a difficult time seeing and attaching directly to the child's energy. This seems to occur when these children are forcefully brought back into the physical dimension by different medications such as attention deficit disorder drugs or any of the other psychiatric drugs that are so popular in our society today. In the physical dimension, these children may learn more from the lesson of the day given by their teacher, however, in the spiritual dimensions, they may not be able to hear a message from their Angels or receive a spiritual gift from God.

Nevertheless, before being born into their physical bodies, these beautiful beings of light were told that they were going to be incredibly special They were told that they were coming here to help us save our planet and create more light. Now, these sensitive young children are being told that they have disorders or that something is wrong with the way their brains work. This is just another obstacle of darkness and another Demon trick they must endure. I hope and pray that they will get through this somewhat spiritually intact.

Imagine your mother and grandmothers or your father and grandfathers who have passed away and are now in heaven, choosing the souls of your children. Sometimes these children have souls with the vibration of an Angel, along with the spiritual gifts of an Angel. Many children who are being born today, will emit a radiant heat that is tremendously noticeable when they are held. This radiant heat may make you feel as if you are getting a suntan from the inside out. It may make you feel flush or give you a head rush. You may also notice, in a dimly lit room, a slight glimmer of light around the top of your child's head. This is what was interpreted in Biblical times as a halo or bright aura. If you notice these somewhat subtle, but very telltale signs of spiritual energy around your child, or any child around you, you may want to be aware that the child is in for a "less than ordinary" life, and so are you. If you sense this from a child that is not your own, you may want to be a good assistant coach and inform the parents. It will better prepare all parties involved for what lies ahead.

As parents try to deal with the glowing prodigy of a child, with all of the unusual idiosyncrasies that someone able to tap into universal knowledge may have, they may realize that it's not so much Uncle Joe that they take after, but the child takes after God, Jesus, the Archangel Michael or some amazing saint. Many parents have recognized that their children are different because the child is able to see a grandmother or family member who died before the child was ever born. Not only do they see them, but they also have ongoing conversations with them.

Many doctors and experts misunderstand the situation of gifted children. Many of you may have been one of these children until you were forced to fit into society and become "normal." What is normal?

Doctors really don't know how to explain what's wrong with their patients. Many doctors diagnose these spiritually gifted children and adults with mental disorders or learning disabilities such as attention deficit disorder (ADD), because they don't have any spiritual training as to what's really going on. However, when I look at these children and adults with my spiritual eyes, many of them have strong bright white auras (energies). Some children may have blue auras. These children may be known as Indigo children. When I look at one of these children, I see lustrous glows and many Angels, and they have powerful spiritual gifts.

Most of the children I work with have innate abilities and spiritual gifts that they brought into this lifetime to help enlighten their families as well as the entire planet. These children have an astonishing ability to see Angels and darkness. They are able to project their light to get rid of darkness and heal, not only themselves and their families, but also everyone on earth.

One of the most enlightening things that I have encountered, that gives me validation and makes me understand more of the truth, is when I have the pleasure of working with gifted children.

I have had many parents call me in frustration; not knowing what to do. They love their child and they only want the best for their child in every way. At the same time, they simply do not know what to do when their child's startling spiritual abilities/talents start popping out.

One day, as 1 was teaching a group of people, 1 was explaining how gifted children are able to see energy such as God, Angels, Demons (monsters), loved ones who have passed and earthbound spirits or "ghosts" that are around them. Earthbound spirits are usually someone who has committed suicide. The reason their spirit is earthbound is because, by killing yourself, you are cutting your physical life short by dying before your time. When you kill yourself, your spirit is not ready to die and does not go back to heaven. Suicide is totally against God's number one rule (don't kill yourself).

A spirit may also be earthbound when a person dies a tragic death. The spirit may not know the physical body is dead yet, so it gets confused and remains stuck earthbound without a body. These spirits are very disruptive to whomever they're around, especially to gifted children. Because of the child's God energy and glowing bright light, the lost spirit is naturally drawn to him or her. Gifted children are able to see auras around people as well as people's Demons. They can see all of these things. With being able to see all of this, it's a wonder how the gifted child mentally holds together without anyone explaining to them what they are seeing. When they come screaming into their parents' room at night saying, "I'm not going back in there, there's a monster hanging over my bed," many times they really are seeing something. It could be a Demon, earthbound spirit or, sometimes, children see Angels and they panic because they don't understand what they are seeing. Even an Angel can scare a child. It's a wonder that these children do as well as they do with little or no guidance. And the parents usually have no clue about what their children are seeing, hearing or feeling.

Now back to the group I was teaching.

I was talking about seeing auras and, as 1 was making my aura brighter, I was explaining to people what to look for. There was this one young man, about 20 years old, who raised his hands and said, "I can't believe it. My whole life 1 thought that 1 had some malfunction with my eyes. My eyes sometimes blur, as if 1 am seeing the air. It sometimes looks like the heat coming off of a hot road-almost like a mirage." For the first time in his life, he realized that what he had been seeing was energy. There was nothing wrong with his physical eyes. On the same note, there was another man in the crowd who raised his hand to share what finally made sense to him about his 6-year-old son who was always asking him if he could see the air. That same child spoke of having a dream where an Angel gave him a purple crystal necklace that gave him super powers to protect his father and himself from any darkness. This made no sense to the father until he heard me explaining about spiritual gifts and darkness.

As I talked to the crowd of people, it was interesting to see their reactions on different spiritual truths because they almost always went through something that previously made no sense to them, like the 6-year-old boy seeing the air and asking his father why he couldn't see it. The father would not have had an answer for his son because he was not born with his spiritual eyes nor had he learned yet how to ask God for the spiritual gift of sight in the spiritual dimensions. In this millennium, we have people with supernatural spiritual abilities. There are all of these gifted children as well as adults with spiritual gifts.

As I said before, when you receive spiritual gifts, or when you use your spiritual gifts to clear your dimensions, you will feel warm sensations within your body. Many times, a mother has taken her child to the doctor because her child has so much heat radiating from him at night, that the mother thought something was wrong. This heat simply means that their Angels have moved around the child to keep them warm and to give them light so that no darkness will attack them while they sleep. If you have a child who kicks off the covers at night because they are hot to the touch and they don't have a fever, it's a spiritual heat that is present and that is normal.

They best way that I can help you understand what it's like to be a spiritually gifted child is to explain a couple of sessions where parents have brought their gifted child in to see me. After taking the child to every category of doctor or specialist under the sun, most of the time, after jumping through all of the medical and psychiatric hoops with their child, they still have no explanation or a bad, nonconclusive, conflicting or even insulting explanation, such as ADD, ADHD, autism, or any number of other medically made-up tags with the word "disorder" attached to the end.

When I'm working with children and adults with any physical, mental or emotional illness, I always teach them an alternative cure to their illness or problems. That cure is to learn how to get rid of the Demons or dark energies in the spiritual dimensions causing the illness within your physical body then allow God's energy/light to enter your physical body healing the illness. I have a saying I always tell people to remember "Meditation instead of Medication."

The following is the story of a client who had a problematic child. He was at the end of his rope and feeling hopeless as, unbeknownst to him, the Demons and dark energies were attacking his gifted child. This story is not that uncommon. I have heard these types of stories over and over again. This is how I know what I know. I am able to tap into and describe exactly what the child sees and feels. Remember, I was a gifted child and born with my soul already unlocked, so I understand exactly what traumas they are going through. This is Tom's Testimonial.

This is a long testimonial, but it's important for you to realize what the child, as well as the parent, goes through. All gifted children are the same, but different. Some will get attacked by Demons and dark energies more severely than others, depending on their spiritual abilities.

Testimonial by Tom

Dear Gary,

My wife and I were happily married for seventeen years before deciding to have a child. We were both very hard and dedicated workers; maybe some might even consider us being workaholics. We were exceptionally close, as we even seemed to think alike. For seventeen years, we not only worked together at the same engineering firm where we met, but we had breakfast together, carpooled to and from work and ate lunch and dinner together every single day. Everyday, we even held hands when driving to and from work. My wife and I experienced closeness all the time, which few couples experience.

Working hard was our life. As dedicated professionals, we were fortunate to be blessed, as our work was appreciated. Our lives did not go through widely fluctuating cycles of good times, great times and bad times as it does for most people. Our lives seemed to be uniformly good almost all of the time. But from the moment our son was born, our lives instantly changed, unfortunately, not for the better. Instead of experiencing joy and tighter family bond, only the opposite prevailed. We were continually faced with stress, torment and headache. We are professional department managers, proficient in handling high stress conditions and demanding schedules everyday, but that was nothing compared to what we began experiencing the moment our son was born.

Joshua was born through a C-section due to complications during a lengthy labor. From the moment he was born, he was crying. He needed to be held continually, day and night. The nurses were very glad when we left the hospital after two days, as they now could get back to their normal routines. Not only did Joshua need to be held all of the time, he was very particular as to who could hold him. For the majority of nights throughout his life, he would only accept his father.

This issue only intensified as he got older. Most of the time, with his intense crying, we came to believe that this was just a matter of having the colic. He only slept a total of about six hours per twenty-four hour period. This meant that his ten to twenty minute naps during the day were no more restful than those followed with walking the floors for two to five hours prior to another short sleep period. Unlike most babies, who may be happy just to be held, Joshua demanded that you stand up at all times with him. One could not sit down or lay down while holding him. This meant that I typically had to exist on a total of three to four hours of sleep in a twenty-four hour period. Again, my sleep was usually limited to twenty-minute intervals. To magnify this experience, the process repeated itself everyday, seven days a week, month after month for the first fourteen months! At the age fifteen months, his sleep marginally improved.

We continually felt that something was severely wrong and changed pediatricians five-times over the first year, as all of our concerns seemed to be falling on deaf ears. Even though we were first time parents, we felt intelligent enough and logical enough to know that unrelenting intense crying and throwing up three to four times every single day was very abnormal. We requested that the mother's milk be tested and asked for any other tests to be performed to find out why he was in such pain all of the time and experiencing great difficulty sleeping. Our first two pediatricians provided no assistance or suggestions. Not until we were on our fifth pediatrician did we find a doctor who was concerned and proactive in having tests performed.

Blood tests revealed that Joshua was violently allergic to soy, wheat, peanuts, dairy, eggs and corn. His reactions were so rapid and volatile, that a single piece of cheese, the size of a pinhead, could cause him to turn red and throw up in fifteen seconds. At 15 months, when his prevailing medical condition was diagnosed, we were issued Epi-pens in case a food reaction caused an epileptic fit. Aside from these food allergies, he is also allergic to airborne components and has severe asthma; asthma so severe that he was hospitalized five times during the first year. He has swollen, itchy eyes and nose almost twenty-four hours a day. With the numerous medications he is on now, including steroids, he has partial relief to some of his discomforts.

Up to this point, some might say, "What is the big deal? So he has a few medical issues which are slowly being corrected." In conjunction with these medical ailments are the attitude and psychological issues that I will now lightly summarize. These other non-health issues were so unmerciful on our nerves that it made the health issues look very minor in contrast.

Day and night, Joshua was always a "high need" baby. He needed continuous attention. He was never able to just sit or lay by himself for any given time. Healthy or sick, Joshua needed someone to attend to his every need. As he turned 1 year old, the doctors said that he will want to do things for himself and will not want help any longer. Well, that was not the case. Up to 3 and a half years old, Joshua would not even want to feed himself.

My wife and I both continued to work, as we could not financially afford for one of us to stay home and raise Joshua. With the high cost of fulltime nannies, that option was also out for us. This left us with the option of leaving Joshua during the day with the best full-service daycare that we could find. But, being around dozens of babies and children every day, he easily became sick due to his weak immune system. With Joshua's constant illnesses and asthma, my wife and I needed to take off from one to two days every single week to tend to him. Since he was sick most of the time and in the twenty percentile weight category for his age, we certainly could not afford to wait for him to feed himself, hence we continued to feed him and do everything possible to assist his sleeping so that his health could marginally improve.

If this were an average child, one would certainly say that we were spoiling him. According to the consensus, we should just let him cry rather than giving in to all of his needs, and let him eat when he was good and hungry. As if we hadn't heard this from dozens of friends, family, teachers and every pediatrician we saw. But we always knew that our situation was very different. First of all, when Joshua cried, it was not a little anemic cry, but a violent penetrating one that was totally unrelenting. We once let him cry for two hours. At the end of that time, he was angrier than ever, resulting in more intensified crying. From such hard crying, his body became very weak and he would vomit mucus and suffer from an asthma attack. Now, with his asthmatic condition, it would take treatments and about six hours to get his body physically straightened out. His physical health condition held us hostage to his emotional demands.

Joshua demanded things all of the time and was extremely impatient. Stressing patience with him definitely fell on deaf ears. If we did not instantly give in, we had hell to pay, as his crying would cause asthma and sickness, which took hours to treat. Our giving in to his demands was done for two reasons, permitting us a brief moment without crying and trying to keep him healthy.

As Joshua grew older and could talk more proficiently, between the ages of 1 to 2 years old, we tried to reason with him. Joshua always lacked focus and was also hard to teach and talk to. He couldn't sit for more than thirty seconds while you tried to read him a book, yet you had to be with him every waking moment, as he did not want to be alone. Again, everything was always done his way. On top of his high needs and stuttering, we felt he also probably had attention deficit disorder (ADD).

During this age when Joshua was starting to speak, he would tell his teachers at school that he had a sister and she was dead. He never directly told us this, but we confirmed to his teachers that he never had a sister. Numerous odd issues such as this kept mounting, for which we had no explanation. It would not be until two years later, when I met you (Gary), that all of these questions were answered.

At 3 and a half years old, he still refused to feed himself and refused to go potty on the toilet—something that most children do by 2.5 years. He always went to the bathroom in his pants, which meant changing his underwear about six times a day. He routinely said that he wanted to cry and that he did not want to be a big boy. He wanted to be a baby.

I've always felt that our problems were so unique that there were probably no more than one out of ten million parents that could even understand what life was like with Joshua. Joshua had extremely rapid mood swings, which occurred frequently. He could be a happy, fun-loving, sparkly-eyed boy one moment and, the next second, he was intensely angry with fierce and highly focused penetrating eyes. As in repeatedly flicking a light switch on and off, such mood swings could vacillate practically instantaneously and occur dozens of times in a short overall period of time. Nothing was simple with him. There were no yes and no answers to simple questions, just initiations of major confrontations. As an example, getting out of the car and getting into the car are two typical and routine everyday events which, for us, was a source of an impending lengthy conflict.

At the age of 3, he was able to get more sleep at night, although he was up an average of six to eight times every night. Each time that Joshua woke up, he always cried. He could just sit up with his eyes still closed and cry. Why can't he, just for once, wake up nicely without crying? We knew that something was wrong, but couldn't imagine what it could be.

With the physically and emotionally difficult times we had with Joshua as a baby, things were only marginally getting better as he got older. By the time Joshua turned

3 years old, my patience was worn very thin. I used to be extremely patient, but now I was angry at the world all of the time. Just looking at other parents with happy, content babies used to make me furious, as I knew we never had any moments of blissful peace and happiness since our child was born. While my patience, in general, was depleted toward anyone else, I always seemed to reach down inside to offer Joshua what little I had left. Inside, I knew that Joshua was killing me and had sucked out all of the life in me. I felt over the last two years, as if there was something like a cancer just eating away at the core of me. This deep feeling totally consumed my will to live. I hated each and every day as I, like a robot, mechanically performed the functions I had done the day before, as I knew I would do the day after. With the way that Joshua was developing, there appeared to be no future for him. I knew that my life would continue downward in its death spiral because of Joshua. My only hope in ending this daily misery was to end my life. The last four years with Joshua was beginning to feel like an eternity to me. It was hard to fathom how I could possibly endure twenty more years with him.

I was finalizing plans to have an automobile "accident," getting papers in order and completing a few final chores in order to minimize the burden and stress on my family after I was gone. It was during this period that I heard you on the radio. One morning Joshua, in a routinely bad mood, slammed the car door shut, locking the keys in the car as his mom was dropping him off at school. As with most mornings, Lynda was understandably flustered because of Joshua and, rather than calling AAA, she called me at work asking for me to open the car door. My first unmentioned thought was why didn't she call a locksmith, as I work forty-five miles away from her? Since work was slow, I thought to myself that this might save a $50 charge, so I agreed to come down to open the door. As I pulled out of the parking lot, already angry, I needed little reason to honk at a car *that was blocking my way out of the driveway. I knew I was a walking time bomb-ready to go off with little provocation. While driving down to Joshua's school, I heard you, Gary, for the first time on the radio. As you began talking, you mentioned a golden baby. I knew at that moment the real reason I was in the car at that time was to hear you. I was not only compelled, but also driven to see you. When I got back to the office, I immediately made an appointment with you. That was the beginning of the restoration of our family.*

The first time I met you, Gary, you apologized for taking so long to decipher the problem. Normally, you said that you could see the problem within a few seconds, but in Joshua's case it took you about ten minutes to determine that Joshua had three souls. Joshua, besides having his own soul, also had the souls of a little girl and that of an angry Demon. These three souls were all using Joshua's body somewhat like a game of musical chairs. The little girl was actually Joshua's aborted sister from fifteen years earlier. Her soul was confused and had been with us for all of these years until Joshua was born. Gary, you told me that you led her to the light, so I certainly hope that she is in heaven now. As far as the Demon is concerned, we don't know where it came from or why, but thank you for getting rid of it. You advised that it would take about two months for things to clear up completely and that two additional visits would be required.

I started to see a difference that very night as I watched Joshua playing. There was this look of peace and tranquility on his face, which I had never seen before. The very next day, when I picked him up from school, he was in a tremendously wonderful mood. His eyes sparkled and he exhibited an unbridled joy as he played. I was actually giddy with delight that night as I played with him. For the first time in four years, I saw only Joshua and all of Joshua-for the first time ever. He is a wonderful gift of life and now, for the first time, I am able to feel joy about having a son. Additionally, that same day I noticed that, while driving to work, I no longer felt angry. For the previous few years, I just stewed in anger as I drove to and from work and mentally reviewed any and every past incident that could help fuel ones anger. I was now able to shed this anger which I developed since Joshua was born. For some reason, the anger in Joshua's Demon also radiated into me and was consuming me. That internal drain, which I experienced over the last two or more years, is now gone and has not come back.

Gary, I'm an engineer who thinks and analyzes quantitative issues daily. Over the last four years with Joshua, my wife and I have had hundreds of unanswered questions about Joshua of which the most important was; why doesn't Joshua like his mother? Now, I am not a religious person, do not go to church and do not normally even think about unproven concepts such as heaven or hell. But upon hearing your answer to our outstanding problems, all of a sudden all of the pieces in the puzzle came together. I knew definitely that this was the answer. It was as if a jigsaw puzzle with one thousand pieces fell on the floor and one instantly knew where all of the pieces go. As hard as it was for me to even repeat it to my wife (our son had a Demon inside of him), I knew that it was the Demon that created all of the turmoil in our lives. At this time, we still do not know why and where the Demon came from, but it certainly explained why a baby and young child would hate his mother-because that hate came from something else and not from Joshua himself.

About three months ago, I didn't even think that there was anything that could make me happy again. I imagined winning the lottery, but even that couldn't provide me with relief, as Joshua's Demon made life seem so eternally unpleasant. But now I can feel normal again and can fully gain pleasure from being with my son.

I just wanted to thank you once again for saving my life and possibly that of my son and my wife. I know that, without your help, we would have never figured out the real source of Joshua's problems.

Sincerely,

Tom

P. S. Gary, I just wanted to let you know that Joshua's teacher at daycare called two days after we had seen you. She wanted to know what we had done to this child. When we asked, "What do you mean?" She said, "I can't believe he doesn't act out anymore. He's happy and plays with all the other children. He's social and behaves well. He's a joy to be around. Whatever you are doing, keep it up." I smiled and told her, we will.

Gary, Here is a brief summary of some of Joshua's traits before and after I first consulted you:

BEFORE OUR FIRST VISIT:

- *Never at peace when awake or asleep*
- *Slept very lightly (pin dropping would wake him, yet thunder wouldn't)*
- *When sleeping, always looked in pain or tormented*
- *Always woke up crying from a nap*
- *Since birth, cried so hard that every muscle in his body would flex*
- *Would change moods after nap*
- *Zero patience to wait for anything*
- *Anger frequently arose to tantrum magnitude levels for no reason*
- *Highly moody—rage to laughing could flip-flop repeatedly within seconds*
- *Showed no fear to anything.*
- *Couldn't read him even one page from a book*

- *Seemed to hate his mother since birth—especially at night*
- *Never wanted Mom—said that we don't need her (wouldn't miss her when on trips for eight days)*
- *Always wanted Daddy to hold him all of the time— even at 3.5 years old*
- *Would not respond to normal discipline—only responded if Dad went berserk*
- *At school, mood always changed—good morning/ bad afternoon or vice versa*
- *Told teachers about his dead sister, said he talked to her every day (would not talk to Mom and Dad about sister)*
- *Confrontational about everything*
- *Said he wanted to be a baby—wanted to cry and did not want to be a big boy*
- *Wanted us to be mad at him—asked for spankings*
- *Poor concept of time*
- *Nothing was simple—everyday getting out of the car was a fifteen minute ordeal*
- *Went berserk when going to see Gary for the first time*

AFTER OUR FIRST VISIT:

- *Joshua was happy—teachers noted difference the very first day*
- *Could wake up from naps without crying*
- *Could play by himself without needing constant attention*
- *Wanted to be self-sufficient and do things by himself*
- *Wanted to be good and be a big boy*
- *Had patience and would accept the word, "no"*
- *When crying, would now sound like an average child—intensity gone*
- *Crying would only last a few seconds and he could be easily consoled*

- *Accepted his mother as an equal—not hesitant to go to her*
- *Now asked for his mother and missed her when away*
- *Now was afraid of dark clouds and thunder storms*
- *Began talking of things he saw like ghosts, bad guys (Demons)*
- *Woke up crying one night—said there was a ghost in his bed*
- *Woke up crying the next night—said there was a ghost trying to open the door*
- *When Joshua was by himself, he would talk to the bad guys—he would see a lot of them in our house*
- *Bad guys (Demons) would tell him to "shut up" or say "damn it"*
- **Always asking where the sun is during the daytime**

Sometimes I get people that have such complex spiritual disorders and problems that it takes me a little while to figure out and identify what's going on within them.

In Joshua's case, I had to find his true soul and then see what was attacking it. Then I had to separate each individual soul problem that was causing the complex disorder within his soul. As I started working on Joshua, it took me a little time to figure out the complexity of what was going on. Once I understood one aspect of Joshua's problem, I was able to see the next problem, and then something else, and then something else. As I finally got all of the pieces of the puzzle, I was able to put the puzzle together.

With Joshua, I was able to first see that he had an earthbound spirit with him. This earthbound spirit had been with him since birth. I was able to identify the earthbound spirit as a confused and lost female spirit. She said she was Joshua's sister. I then traced the spirit back and found that she, indeed, was Joshua's sister. I looked up at Tom and asked, "Was there an abortion earlier on?" With his eyes wide open, he said, "Yes, there was an abortion early in our relationship." Looking a little concerned, I said, "Give me a minute; at least I figured out one piece of the puzzle."

Many times as a spirit is coming into the physical dimension, if there is some sort of interruption such as an abortion, the spirit will stay in earthbound hovering mode not knowing where it should be and not really understanding what it should do next. Usually, these particular spirits can be disruptive and they will always gravitate toward the individual who has the brightest light: In this case, it was Joshua.

I then asked the Angels to bring the light to take this spirit back to heaven. The light is a beautiful beam of white light energy that you're able to ask for. Two or three very special Angels will bring the light down and around the earthbound spirit. The spirit will then ascend upward (to heaven with the Angels) engulfed in a bright elevator of light. The spirit is now back where it came from—not lost and causing havoc anymore in an in-between dimension of darkness and confusion. This usually gives enormous relief to whomever the earthbound spirit is around. Earthbound spirits can be huge problems, not only for the person that is earthbound, but also for everybody around. Many unexplained poltergeists, ghosts and haunted houses can simply be explained as an earthbound spirit.

The one thing I figured out is that sometimes, when people's natural life span is unexpectedly or accidentally interrupted, their spirit can be earthbound and very tormented. Suicides almost always fall into this category.

Once I sent the spirit to the light, I could tap into Joshua's energy and see that it was now brighter and that his life-force was now supporting him, not him and the spirit that called herself his little sister. I realize that this is probably very strange for some people to understand, but these types of soul disorders are common with gifted children.

Once the spirit was gone, I looked at Joshua's energy again and realized there was a very dark Demon face over his face, which meant that there was a Demon attached to his true soul. I then saw that the dark Demon was not only attached to Joshua's soul, but it would also attach and attack anyone who was around him. This is the reason why, when Joshua would scream and cry, it would be as if a screeching pain would go to the core of your soul—because, indeed, it did! I knew I had to get rid of it very quickly. With one of my spiritual gifts, I projected light into the Demon as it slipped out of Joshua and blew up in God energy (light).

I was working with Joshua's energy through his father. Joshua was not in the room. I'm always very sensitive not to traumatize children who are already traumatized enough with what is going on. Usually, the sensations they feel when alleviated from a dark spirit will simply be that of lightness and a warm feeling as healing God energy rushes back into their body. I do not add light; I only get rid of the dark. The God energy already belongs to them.

As I removed all the darkness, my vision was that of Joshua glowing. As a matter of fact, he looked like a huge spotlight. He was one of the brightest lights I had ever seen. His bright aura of white light let me know that, of course, this is a gifted child and the Demons were doing everything in their power to keep him dark so he could never find out about his true spiritual abilities. Joshua is now 9 years old and an honor role student.

These children, who are being born everyday and have been since the mid-seventies, are indeed the most amazing light beings this planet has ever seen. Unfortunately, they're also the most attacked by the Demons.

In one of my private sessions, I was reading a lady named Jennifer who asked me about her children. As I looked at her children, I saw that their energy was glowing with this amazing blue, gold and white energy. I knew that they were very spiritually gifted. Jennifer explained to me that, throughout their whole life, they had visions of Angels and Demons which, on one hand was comforting and on the other a little scary. According to what I was able to see and what Jennifer was able to tell me, I realized that they were confused and had many questions that needed to be answered. I informed her that I would be glad to talk to them and help them sort it out.

Testimonial by Jennifer

Dear Gary,

I am writing this letter in regard to my reading with you this past Saturday evening. You expressed a desire to work with my sons, Scott and Tony. I want you to know that I appreciate your compassion for your gift. I hope that by working with them, they will be able to reach their full spiritual potential, as well. As I told you, their experiences have, at times, caused them some anxieties. I am hoping that by working with you, whatever level of abilities they might have, they learn to respect it and not fear it.

I wanted to write about some moments I have experienced with them over the years. I hope this will help you to some degree.

When Scott and Tony were 3 and 2 years old, we moved to Texas. A few years later, my husband's brother (Jake) was killed in an auto accident. A couple of days after the accident, his spirit came to visit Scott. The night it happened, I was restless and kept checking the children. I was hearing someone in their bedroom and, when I would check on them, they would be sound asleep, but the toys in their room had been moved around and, two times, the overhead light came on all by itself.

The next day after school, Scott told me that a spirit friend had come to visit. He said that he looked a lot like Daddy and wore a blue uniform shirt and pants (Jake had worked for an automotive service where the men wore blue uniform pants and shirts. He and my husband looked so much alike that they were often mistaken for each other). Scott had not seen Jake since he was a baby and had no knowledge of these things. Scott was about 6 now. He told me that his "Angel friend" came and took him flying (he would go flying often) and took him up to see heaven. I asked him to describe heaven and he said it was beautiful and there was music everywhere. He said that he got to play with two other little boys. One, he said, was there because he had had a bad heart and the other little boy was not born yet. He said that, after a while, his spirit friend told him it was time to go back home and he came home and went back to sleep. Scott, we have been told, has attention deficit disorder, as discussed with you. He has always felt like an outcast and always feels he isn't like all the other kids. He struggles with that. After our reading, you explained how you are in your "read" mode (the dazed-like state that you're in when you're doing a psychic reading). I asked Scott about his problems focusing in class and he practically explained it the same way to me, word for word. He said that he drifts off to where he wants to be, but that when he comes back, he gets scared because he does not know where he is. He says that he stays confused for a while before figuring it out.

Tony has just really started seeing spirits more recently. He is very assured of himself and he knows where he is going. He has seen spirits in their physical form as well as their dark form. Scott says he sees them in their dark forms as well as hearing them sometimes. They both say that the spirits usually dart around so quickly that they can barely catch a glimpse of them, but they know they are there. Tony says they try to sneak up on them. Scott has just lately started to anticipate things happening right before they happen. Tony has had those moments, too. Tony told me that his great grandmother came to see him at school. He could not hear her, but he could smell her perfume while he was at his locker. He said that sometimes, when he closes his locker door, something knocks on the door from the inside. He says that he just ignores it.

Peace be with you always,
  Jennifer

As I began to work with Tony over the phone, I was amazed by the amount of God light and Heavenly Hierarchy that appeared in the room.

Now, throughout the book, I have mentioned Heavenly Hierarchy and I'm sure that many of you are wondering who I am talking about when I mention Heavenly Hierarchy. I'm talking about Jesus, Mother Mary, Buddha, Ganesh, the ArchAngels and, what I call, the Royal Council, which is made up of the highest spiritual beings in the universe.

Tony received several spiritual gifts. One gift was a staff and another was an amulet. The staff was for healing and the amulet was for strength. I, then, had a vision of Jesus entering the room with the brightest white light healing energy radiating from his hands, and he touched Tony's head. I never know exactly what to expect when I'm working on someone's energy; clearing their spiritual dimensions and connecting their spiritual body within their physical body. God explained to Tony that he will be a healer and be able to help people. God told Tony that he will have clarity now. Just then, as quickly as everything had come, I heard the words, "This is finished."

When working with someone, I never know how much that person understands about what just happened. Knowing that Tony is a gifted child, I knew he would understand it more quickly because he could see everything I saw in the spiritual dimensions, many times, with even more clarity. Tony can now see in the spiritual dimensions and is aware of his healing abilities.

I remember thinking what a gifted child Tony is, and how lucky Scott is to have a brother with so many spiritual gifts. Then later, when I talked to Scott, I saw an even brighter light, amazing knowledge and tremendous spiritual talent and insight. I cannot remember if I have ever seen brothers who were so spiritually gifted in every way. As I talked to Scott, I saw Heavenly Hierarchy and God himself. It seemed as though God was having a conversation with Scott and he was able to understand everything God was saying.

I managed to get rid of a little darkness and some Demons that were around the boys. I explained to them how to project light so they would be able to get rid of darkness themselves. I didn't have to tell them twice. They understood every words I said. They saw everything I saw.

I was very happy to get Jennifer's letters saying that events had settled down for them. They were now just two normal boys playing ball and doing what boys do. In addition to that, they now had a total sense of being divinely led with an awareness of their spiritual gifts, heaven, God and their Angels, and that they were specially put here to help people like I do. Their gifts were no longer strange to them; they were normal. I only wish that, when I was their age, I could have had someone explain all of this to me. It would have saved me a lot of time and confusion trying to figure it out. I was ecstatic that I could be there for them. I was happy that I could explain exactly what was going on and the beautiful plans that God had in store for them.

This is a follow up letter from Jennifer.

Dear Gary,

Tomorrow you will be having your session with my son, Scott. I had spoken to your assistant after your session with Tony and told him some of the things you should keep in your file.

After you spoke with Tony, you spoke with me and told me that Tony had a vision of God. Tony was very elated about his session and was on a physical and mental high for some time. Tony came back downstairs and told his father and uncle about the session. He told them that God had held his face in his hands. Well, as he was speaking of this, you could start to see the outline of fingers appear on his cheeks and face!!! Honest to God. We were all in awe. It happened right in front of us. Then he said that he still had the warmth in his hands and, when he touched his father's chest, his father said that you could feel the warmth through his shirt radiating through his chest. He then touched his uncle's chest and his uncle was shocked that he could feel it through, not only his shirt, but his sweatshirt, as well. His uncle touched the area on his sweatshirt where Tony had put his hand, and his sweatshirt was still very warm there.

Now Gary, I am not sure what any of this means. All I know is that something tried really hard to interfere with our initial reading. I truly feel that you are a part of this picture. I feel that you are an instrument here.

Thanks again for all you have done,
   Jennifer

This is an update from Jennifer

Dear Gary,

Hi ... from far away ... I hope all is well with you and your crew. I am writing to give you some sort of update on how things are going with Scott and Tony.

Like I told you in my last letter, they are both very preoccupied at the moment playing ball and such. Both Scott and Tony seem to feel that they are starting to realize what they will be doing with their gifts. Scott feels that he is meant to help people get rid of their Demons. He says he feels like he can sort of sense if someone is troubled by one. He feels that he will be able to bring peace to someone who is troubled emotionally and physically. He said God told him that he is special, that there are only a few people in the world right now who can see him and speak to him as freely as Scott can. Scott says that he can hear God without seeing him. Gary, Scott seems to be more at peace with himself now and our relationship is getting closer. The wall that was there is coming down some. He is so very private about his gift; I have to wait for him to convey what he wants me to know. He says there are things that only he and God can know for now. Interestingly enough, my mother reminded me the other night about something that I had forgotten from Scott's childhood. When Scott was very small, he used to tell us that he saw and spoke with a "ghost" friend named Mary. Well, I feel now that the Virgin Mary has been appearing to Scott for a long time. I feel that this is the same "Mary."
Incidentally, when Scott relays something to me about his visits with God, what he tells me always seems to come true.

I hope we can help one another mutually. I know that you are writing a book. I hope that these things will be of some help to you.

Take care,
Jennifer

In the case of both of these gifted children, they were born with their souls unlocked. They were seeing spiritually, but not able to understand on their own what was going on with them. They would tell their parents and the people around them about the incidents that were occurring, such as being visited by a figure that resembled their father. Luckily enough for them, their mother was understanding and open enough to connect the dots. She realized that there was a lot more going on than just a child's vivid imagination.

It can be traumatizing for a child when they see Angels or Demons around them so, when they tell their parents or other adults about their experiences, they don't need anyone telling them that it's just their imagination or making them feel as if they've done something wrong. When other people cannot relate to what the gifted children can see with their spiritual eyes, often the children will disconnect from those around them.

In every family, I see spiritually gifted children who have spiritual abilities far beyond even my wildest imagination. By talking to these children for a few minutes, I see that they are able to speak to me on an advanced spiritual level and they understand everything happening in the spiritual world. They understand Angels, they understand the dimension where our past loved ones exist—the place we call heaven, they understand God and other spiritual beings, and they also have an understanding of Demons and dark energies.

For years, I have been making radio and TV appearances and doing live seminars and teaching. Doing all of these shows for so many years allows me to see recurring patterns that children talk about and things they experience. It doesn't matter where I am—Los Angeles, New York, Miami, Minneapolis, Las Vegas, Sydney Australia or London, England—everywhere I go I hear stories from children about how they can see Angels, Demons and dead relatives; how Angels give them gifts; how they visit God in heaven and many more.

Hearing these stories over and over again from so many children, I now believe that these children are the biggest misunderstood treasure in our world and we must treat them accordingly. They are gifted and we need to understand and research their gifts. We certainly shouldn't tell them that they have some type of disorder, especially attention deficit disorder. With their natural spiritual abilities, they may gain universal knowledge that could be the key to our future well-being and existence on this planet.

These kids are born with many spiritual gifts. However, their gifts are being ripped away. The gifts are removed by psychiatric drugs, Demon tricks, teachers, parents, peers and mostly a total lack of understanding of who they are and what a treasure they are to all of us. These kids will be a necessity in helping all of us in our natural evolution into a new God planet which does not have darkness and Demons attacking us all daily.

According to God, when we need these very special gifted kids to help us with our spiritual battles against the forces of darkness, they're not going to be around because their natural development has been disrupted. We will have already disarmed them—leaving our planet vulnerable to darkness and dark entities.

This is my biggest concern.

These beautiful, bright light children of the future are being dimmed down every day due to lack of understanding of what and who they are, and what they're really going through. You need to simply open your mind, heart and energy, and be slightly aware of the tell-tale signs of the spiritually gifted child. Learn for yourself to see spiritually, then it will become much easier for you to understand exactly who they are and what they are going through. Even though most people may not yet be able to see all of the things that these amazing children can see, we can, at least, be aware of these special kids and respect them. We must pay close attention, especially in the next ten years-as predicted in many different religions and by many spiritual masters and prophets-to this very bright time in history. We must take advantage and be very aware of the creative dark energies and the tricks that they posses to keep us all dark by suppressing the bright light beings that are being born to all of our families all around the world.

The children are more spiritually evolved than most people on the planet today. If they are not tampered with and their true energy is respected, cherished and nurtured, we will be able to enjoy the beautiful bright energies and the bliss of living on a God planet in the physical dimension in our lifetime. What a great time to be alive!

Now I would like to share a few testimonials ITom parents who are aware of their gifted child and how, being a little more aware, helps them to understand their child.

Testimonial by Paul Cardillo

Hi! My name is Paul Cardillo. I'm an attorney from Tampa, Florida and I've been friends with Gary Spivey for many years now.

Many years ago, I heard Gary on a radio program and decided to make an appointment with him because I had many personal questions I needed answers to.

I was going through a divorce at the time and needed a little insight on what to do. He answered all of the questions about my divorce which helped me win the divorce case, but the last thing he told me when I was leaving was that I was going to get remarried again to a lady named Michelle. Well, a few years later, I remarried and her name is Michelle. I didn't realize how much one appointment with Gary would change my life forever.

So when I started searching for a deeper meaning to spirituality, I made another appointment with Gary. In this appointment, he taught me how to allow God energy into my body, how to receive spiritual gifts, how Demons interfere in our lives, how Angels are there to help us and how to understand the spiritual world around us. I use everything Gary taught me everyday to better my life and the lives of my family members.

Phoenix Cardillo is my 4 and a half year old son. The other day my wife, Michelle, walked into his bedroom in the middle of the day and Phoenix was sitting on the table in front of a crucifix that I had hung in his room by his bed. He was meditating, which surprised his mom because I had only meditated once with him several months before. My wife walked in the room and asked, "What are you doing?"

He said, "Oh, I'm meditating. You have to be quiet so I can meditate."

Michelle said, "Okay." She was quiet for awhile and then asked him, "What do you see?"

Phoenix said, "I see Jesus and God and I have a big sword and I'm fighting Demons and bad guys." Then he said, "Mom you're going to have to be quiet while I meditate." He added, "When I'm finished, what I do is lay on my bed and I look up into my ceiling fan and I can see frogs. Some are bad, some are good, but I kill the bad ones."

Later on when I got home from work, Michelle told me the story. I asked Phoenix about it and he repeated the same story he had told my wife. I asked him, "What does your sword look like?" because he and I had talked about a spiritual sword before. He said, "Well, it's got jewels all over it and it's got a blue circle flame at the bottom and at the tip and it's very sharp. The handle is all silver. There's nothing on the handle, but its all silver and the rest of the sword has jewels and is really sharp." I was amazed that I only meditated with him once and he learned how to do it on his own.

Phoenix is this little kid who sees things spiritually. The other day, he came running into my bedroom and said, "There is a bright light in my room as bright as the sun." I had explained to him many times that when you see God, you will see this bright light. Phoenix got excited and ran back to his room so he could talk to God. Phoenix is always telling my wife things that she's thinking about. He will tell me something I'm doing without me ever telling him and I'm thinking, "How does he know that?"

Thanks for opening my eyes (my spiritual eyes) and teaching me what really exist around us, so that I may better understand and teach my children and now others about God, Angels and spiritual gifts. It's truly a blessing to be able to recognize the spiritual gifts that my 4 year son, Phoenix, already possesses. Being aware of who he is makes me realize even more about who we all are. I learn more from him spiritually than he does from me, as he seems to have a direct line to heaven already.

Paul Cardillo

"And I saw three evil spirits disguised as frogs leap from the mouth of the Dragon, the Creature and the False Prophet."

Revelation 16:13
Bible

Isn't it interesting how Phoenix sees good and bad frogs on his ceiling fan and he kills the bad ones? It's amazing how children can see into the spiritual world and see what's really around us.

In Paul's case, he already had knowledge of the spiritual world around us, so when Phoenix started displaying spiritual abilities, he knew what to expect and how to help him.

This is the reason why it's so important for everyone to understand the spiritual world around us so that, as your child Demonstrates their natural spiritual abilities, you will be able to help them understand what they're going through, rather than telling them their abilities don't exist.

Testimonial by Debra

I first heard you on the radio in San Francisco, and you really blew my mind. The things you said and did for those people really touched me. I'm Catholic and, in the Bible, my interpretation was that anyone who says they can foresee and heal people are the prophets working for the devil. But when I heard you, you brought so much feeling to me and many others. I wanted so much to call and ask you so many questions about me and my family. I have questions about my daughter. I came home at 4:30 am (I work nights) and went to peek in on her and she was sitting up in her bed sleeping. I woke her up and asked, "Are you okay?" She said she was dreaming. She had a smile on her face and said, "It was about God." I told her to go back to bed because it was late.

The next morning, I asked her what her dream was about and she said she dreamed about God. I asked her to give details and she told me something similar to what you said to a caller on the radio. She told me she climbed up some stairs and, when she got to the top, she stepped on a Golden key. She said, "God whispered to me to put the key in the door and open it."

I then asked her what she saw; she told me dolphins and mermaids. Now that put chills up my spine because you were talking on the radio about how there are dolphins in heaven. She said that God met her halfway and took her by the hand and he told her she was beautiful and that he loved her. She said they started playing and God gave her a star and told her she can walk home by herself because she was a big girl. I thought big as in little big girl, but she told me that she was big as in like me. I asked her, "How do you know?" And she said that when she walked into heaven, she looked to the side of her and there was a mirror and she was a big girl. She went back, closed the door behind her, locked it and went home.

Debra

I wanted to share this story with you because many of your children, your nieces and nephews are probably going through the same or similar situations. If you would just take the time to learn about the spiritual world we all live in, you would be able to teach these children what's going on so they can have a spiritual head start in life.

You must understand, children are born awakened to the spiritual world around us and they need guidance. As a parent, guardian and responsible adult, you have the responsibility to also learn what's going on spiritually so you can help guide these children on their spiritual path and so we can all learn from them.

Now I would like to share with you a story about Dalton Hicks, a 14-year-old who lives in Star, North Carolina.

I've known Dalton since he was born. Around the age of 3 or 4 years old, he started displaying signs of being spiritually gifted. He was always talking to his invisible playmates and, when asked by his family, "Who are you talking to?" he would simply say, "My Angel friends." He would tell his parents and anyone who was around him that his Angel friends wanted to talk to them also, but Dalton couldn't understand why his parents and others couldn't see, hear and talk to his Angel friends because it was so easy and natural for him.

Around the age of 6 or 7, Dalton started going into trances very similar to the ones I had when I was a young child. When he would go into the trances, his eyes would roll back and his body would become very stiff and he would start talking in a language that no one could understand. If he was involuntarily awakened from the trance, he would throw a fit—screaming and yelling as if he was in pain—just as I did when I was a young boy. If he was not involuntarily awakened from his trance, he would come out of it and talk about this dark cloud that surrounded and engulfed the earth and how everybody on earth needed to fight together to stop the darkness from destroying the earth. He said that if everyone doesn't fight together, then the earth will blow up.

Around the same age (7) he started displaying his psychic abilities—telling the people around him things before they happened.

Dalton's family never discouraged him or told him his abilities didn't exist. They encouraged him to talk about whatever he was going through and, if he talked about something they didn't understand, they would call me so I could guide Dalton in the right direction.

I taught Dalton about the spiritual dimensions around us and how they affect our everyday life. I taught him how to clear the dimensions, getting rid of dark energy and negativity. I taught him how to receive and use spiritual gifts to get rid of Demons that cause havoc in his life.

Today Dalton understands the spiritual dimensions around us; he's always clearing the dimensions and using his spiritual gifts to get rid of the Demons that cause havoc in his life and the lives of anyone around him.

Dalton was telling me about the time he was trying to help his teacher at school. This is from Dalton in his words; he was about 10 years old when this occurred.

Dalton's story (part one)

One day in school, my Angel told me to get rid of a Demon that was on the teacher. When she was at the chalkboard writing, I started to get rid of the Demon, but the teacher got mad at me because, when she turned around, I was moving my hand around in the air using one of my spiritual gifts on her. She asked me what I

*was doing. I said, "Getting rid of a Demon you have."
She told me to put my hand down. When she started to
write on the chalkboard again, I raised my hand again
so I could get rid of her Demon and she turned around
again and got mad at me and made me stand in the
hall. Later in class, she slipped and fell down. She was
mad. She came into the hall and asked me if I made her
fall. I said, "No, the Demon made you fall. But if you
would have let me get rid of it, you would not have fallen."*
    It was kind of funny.

Dalton sees, hears and talks to God, Angels, Jesus, Mary, Buddha,
The ArchAngel Michael and other spiritual beings, all of whom give
him important messages to share with his family and friends.

    He tries to have a normal life, but as with many children with
spiritual abilities, sometimes what's normal for them may not be normal
for someone else. I would like to share with you another one of Dalton's
stories. This story is also in his own words, is about a reoccurring
vision he had when he would go to sleep at night.

Dalton's story (part two)

    *Well it was at night and I had just gone to bed.
I closed my eyes and, all of a sudden, I saw something
running into something big. Then I opened my eyes and
closed them again and I realized it was a plane crashing
into two buildings. I think it was somewhere near water,
but I didn't know exactly where it was. The next day I
told my mama about my vision. I kept having this vision
for about six months, but the only people I would tell
was my family; I wish I could have told someone besides
my family who would listen and not think I was crazy.*

    *The day September 11th happened, I knew right then
and there that's what my reoccurring vision was about.
I just wish there was a phone number I could have called
and someone would have listen to me. Then maybe
September 11th would not have happened.*

Photo's taken on September 11th 2001 of the World Trade Centers

Throughout this book, I've talked about the damage Demons can do to our spiritual and physical bodies. I've explained how Demons can posses the minds of mankind and make them do things they don't really want to do.

If you look closely at these two pictures taken of the World Trade Centers after the planes hit them, you can see the face of a Demon in the smoke. (These photo's were not altered and appeared in many newspapers the week after 9/11.) As I said before, Demons come in many shapes and sizes. I believe that if everyone had God light inside of them, Demons would not be able to posses the minds of mankind and make them do these horrible things to each other and then disasters like this would never happen again.

This was a horrible act of terrorism. Many innocent people died. My prayers go out to all the families that were affected.

Dalton is not unlike many of your children and even yourself; you all have these abilities, you just need to learn how to use them. Maybe he's right; maybe there should be someone he could call and maybe we should have listened more seriously to his ongoing visions. The reason his family understands and allows Dalton to express his spiritual abilities is because Dalton's mom, grandma and great-grandma are very familiar with the signs of a spiritually gifted child. Dalton's great-grandma is my mom (Eunice Spivey Brewer), his grandma is my sister (Joyce Wallace) and his mom (Myra Hicks) is my niece.

I was able to teach him from a young age what was going on around him in the physical and spiritual worlds so he would not think something was wrong with him. When Dalton started showing his spiritual abilities at a very young age, the same as I did, his mom, grandma and great-grandma all knew what to do and what to say to make him comfortable with his abilities. Dalton knows all about the spiritual world we all live in; he sees, hears and talks to God, Angels and other spiritual beings on a daily basis.

Dalton is growing up with a greater understanding of our physical and spiritual worlds (the big picture) because he has an assistant coach to help him. Every one of you has the abilities and should become an assistant coach to your children and other children because the children are our future.

Dalton does normal activities for a 14-year-old like hanging out with his friends, playing sports and also killing Demons, talking to God and Angels, visiting heaven and receiving spiritual gifts. I know that many of you are probably thinking that killing Demons, talking to God and Angels, visiting heaven and receiving spiritual gifts aren't exactly what you would call normal activities for a child—but, why not?

We are in an age of a spiritual awakening and everyone will have to learn how to carry on with their daily activities here on earth as well as their daily spiritual activities. Everyone on earth is evolving to a higher level of spiritual awareness. Just as people from past generations evolved spiritually and physically, so are we evolving. We are on the edge of a spiritual revolution. Imagine, ten, twenty, fifty and one hundred years from now, how spiritually gifted everyone on earth will be. It starts today with every one of you.

We, as a society, control the future of all mankind. Let us not make the wrong decision and destroy what's suppose to happen spiritually to this world. Every one of you has a decision to make. Let's make the right one and leave this world a little better than it was when we came here.

Think of it this way: We're all going to die and leave this place we call earth and go home to heaven, but we may have to leave heaven one day and come back to earth. Wouldn't you rather come back to a place that's more spiritually evolved like heaven or would you rather come back to the same place you left and go through all of the same stuff again?

Everyone on earth should learn about the spiritual world we all live in so that we, as a society, don't extinguish our children's God light or our own God light which we all have.

I have a follow-up to the opening testimonial in this book.

The opening testimonial was about a young lady who came to a seminar I was having in Portland, Oregon and how she learned about the spiritual world around us and how she went home and taught her children what she learned. After the Portland seminar, she and her children attended my spiritual retreat in Ojai, California so they could further their spiritual training.

It's been a year now since the Scibetta family (Carolyn, David and Brian) attended one of my spiritual retreats and I was looking forward to seeing them this year so I could monitor their progress.

When they showed up, I noticed Carolyn was feeling a little down. When I asked her what was wrong, she said, "I just received horrible news from Brian's teacher." The teacher explained to her that Brian was in danger of failing his class and that Brian had attention deficit disorder and numerous other problems. The teacher had made her feel as if her son was stupid, unable to learn and not worthy of being in the next grade with his classmates. The teacher went on to say that she thought the classmates were far more advanced than Brian because of his disorders. I said, "Don't worry, I'll work with Brian and see what's really going on with him."

Brian told me that he feels pretty good except when he's around other people: Then he feels what they feel. If they're upset, he's upset, if they're happy, he's happy and if they're angry, then he's angry too.

He said, "It feels as if I know everything about everyone all at one time and it gets a little confusing. The only people I have to talk to is my brother, David, or my mom."

Brian then went on to say, "In the spiritual world, I seem to see and know more as I'm hanging out in heaven with God a lot, lately, but in the physical dimension, I'm not doing so well in class. I almost feel as stupid as the teachers keep telling me I am."

I said, "Nonsense you're extremely gifted and your teacher doesn't understand you."

I begin working with Brian to help him clear up his confusion so he could understand what's going on in his life. I realized that he was psychically reading everything going on in someone's life, so I needed to teach him how to distinguish between his feelings and other people's feelings.

Later that day, after I was through with my teachings at the retreat, everyone wanted me to use my psychic abilities to answer some personal questions about their lives. At that moment, I asked everyone if it was alright with them if Brian would help me answer their questions. Everyone said, "Yea" so 13-year-old Brian and I began to answer questions.

In the beginning, Brian seemed a little nervous—not being used to standing in front of a large group of people looking to him for some of his 13-year-old wisdom. But pretty soon he, as well as the crowd, began to change. I started out by telling Brian that, "We are the only one's who are here right now. Pay no attention to the people sitting out there. We are just going to use them for practice as I work with you on developing your psychic abilities." He seemed to be excited about the fact that he was the special one for a change instead of the one with all of the disorders.

I began to take questions from the crowd and one girl asked about her love life, which is a very popular question. She said she had two guys in her life and needed help deciding between them. I started to show Brian how to psychically read the two guys that the girl was asking us about. I asked Brian if he could look into the spiritual dimension where I was looking and see the first guy's energy. Brian quickly said, "Yeah. I do see, but I can't see what his head looks like because it's all black and he has really dark Demons around him." I said, "You see those? Those dark Demons are Drug Demons, so we are simply going to answer her question like this: 'Is one of your guys on drugs?'" The girl said, "Yes. He is." Brian smiled as he realized that he had gotten that one right. I told him he did well.

I asked him to look at the other guy. Brian asked me why he felt really sleepy and bored. I said, "Well, you've got it right! Let's ask her about her second guy." I turned to the girl and asked her, "Is your second guy really boring?" She answered, "Oh my god! He is the most boring man alive!" I replied to her, "So why are you with either of those two guys?" I told Brian that sometimes when people ask you the question, "Is it door number one or door number two?" It could indeed be door number three or door number four which, of course, they haven't considered yet because they are so hung up on the choices they have in front of them.

I then turned to Brian and asked him, "So what would be good advice to give her, Brian?" At that point, he was feeling confident and he said, "Move on. Neither one of those guys is good for you." The crowd applauded and Brian's confidence grew.

As we continued to read, taking question after question, Brian got more and more confident. I would explain to him what the visions were that he was seeing and he was able to interpret them.

We then got to this one lady and, as Brian began to read her, I had no idea what he was seeing or where he was seeing it. I found myself, the teacher, now being taught by the student.

The lady was wondering if she and her aunt were together in a previous life because of their close connection in this life. Before I could say anything, Brian said he could see twenty-two past lives and, yes, she was together with her aunt in more than one life. Brian said, "I see twenty-two little boxes and each box represents a previous life." I had to ask Brian if he could show me where he saw these little boxes. Once he showed me, I realized that he was reading from a DNA level—from a strand of DNA. Brian tapped into the lady's spiritual DNA and was reading from there. It was amazing to me that Brian was able to see this and, more importantly, he was able to teach me how to read from this level. The reason he could see all of her lifetimes so quickly is because your spiritual DNA holds all of the information from lifetime to lifetime.

I then asked Brian if he felt like he has some sort of disorder, he said, "No I feel special and like this is normal." He didn't have some sort of disorder. The teacher had the disorder: SUD (Spiritual Unawareness Disorder). It's not her fault that she has the disorder because most of the people on earth have it. The reason there are so many people with SUD (Spiritual Unawareness Disorder) is because no one on planet earth has been teaching what's really going on in the spiritual and physical world, and how one affects the other—until now, that is!

Once we, as a society, understand what's really going on, I think there will never be another child diagnosed with any disorder ever again.

This is the letter Carolyn sent to me after the retreat.

Testimonial by Carolyn Scibetta

Hey Gary,

Yesterday, the boys finished up the school year and today, they'll begin planning their summer. I wanted you to know that we're very open to continuing their spiritual training. Brian, my 13-year-old, has been practicing doing psychic reading over the phone with some of the folks we met at your last spiritual retreat.He has also been working spiritually with another teen from Vegas who's been "diagnosed" ADHD and has recently been into a lot of trouble. Brian has got him meditating and receiving spiritual gifts and he's hungry for more.

Brian remains in awe of his spiritual gifts from God. He has become the most confident 13-year-old on the planet, I think. On the plane home from Los Angeles, he told me, regarding his new gifts and abilities taught by you (Gary), "Finally, someone 'gets' me."

David, my 16-year-old, seems to struggle with his religious beliefs and his ability to use his gifts from God but I see this changing too.

Truly, I have always tried to be the kind of mom who will do what it takes to help the boys grow and become enriched.

With Love,
Carolyn Scibetta

Brian said it best in the last testimonial: "Finally someone gets me." Imagine how many millions and millions of people from around the world will be saying the same thing. I can guarantee that, in every corner of the earth, there is someone out there wishing someone would understand what they're going through spiritually. I think it is everyone on earth's responsibility to learn about the spiritual world around us and then teach others.

David struggles with his religious beliefs a little, but he knows how to use his spiritual gifts to get rid of Demons and he understands the spiritual world around us. I know that many of you may also struggle with your religious beliefs. I'm not trying to replace your beliefs: I'm trying to show you how everyone can learn these secrets, no matter what your religion or your beliefs are.

Now, the last testimonial in this chapter is from the co-author of this book, Dean Hymel, and a dear friend of mine. I share this testimonial with you because Dean has firsthand knowledge of the torment that happens to spiritually gifted children.

Dean was born a gifted child and has firsthand knowledge of how Demons, dark energies and earthbound spirits cause havoc in your life. He also has firsthand knowledge of being an empath and being diagnosed with mental disorders.

He also has firsthand knowledge of how someone can change their life by using the techniques in this book.

Testimonial by Dean Hymel

I was born May 3, 1968 and was raised in Convent Louisiana, a small town about forty miles west of New Orleans. I remember being a normal, outgoing child— always playing and having fun. Everything in my life seemed normal for a child. Then one day, when I was somewhere around the age of 6 years old, I remember my mom and dad tucking me into bed, as they did every night. But this night changed my life: This was the night that I started seeing Demons and strange people walking around in my bedroom. I remember seeing Demons flying around the room and these strange people walking in and out of the room, but they were not using the doors.

They were walking through the walls. These Demons and dead people came up to my bed and tugged on the sheets and sat on the bed just staring at me while making creepy noises. This scared me, but, for some reason, I never said anything to my parents. I just thought the Demons and dead people would eventually go away and leave me alone. This went on night after night. I have a twin brother, Darren, and a younger brother, Wayne Jr., and, when I got a little older, around 8 years old, I asked them if they could see the Demons and dead people in the room at night. They said they didn't see anything and didn't know what I was talking about, so I never brought up the topic again.

I can recall being woken up on many nights by something pulling on my feet or shaking my bed. I would open my eyes and see a Demon or dead person staring at me or walking around my room. I can remember, somewhere around the age of 12-14 years old, not opening my eyes when I felt them touching me. The next thing I remember was the closet doors being opened and slammed closed until I opened my eyes. But when I opened my eyes, I didn't see anything; I just heard laughter. Needless to say, whenever it was time to go to bed, I was scared to death.

As I got older—in my teens—I started seeing a bright light in my room every time a Demon or dead person would show up. I would feel peaceful and protected by the bright light and I would get so hot that I would start sweating.

My problems as a child were not only with Demons and dead people, but, I was a natural empath. Now, as an adult, I realize what a natural empath is, but as a child I never knew what an empath was. All I knew was that, if I was around someone who was happy, then I felt happy, if they were sad, then I felt sad and if they were angry, then I felt angry, also. This, alone is enough to drive someone crazy, but I always had Demons and dead people to help out with my torment. Making a decision about anything was always a challenge being an empath. I would always empath (feel) what someone else was thinking about the decision that I was trying to make. Many times I would base my decision on what someone else was feeling, not on my true feelings. This caused me to make many wrong decisions in my life.

As an empath, being in crowds of people was painful because I would feel what everyone in the crowd was feeling—causing me to be overwhelmed.

At school, learning was difficult for me—not because I was stupid, but every time I would go to class, I would feel sleepy or I would feel like my brain would shut off and I couldn't understand or pay attention to anything the teacher was saying.

I would daydream in class and, when I would daydream, I would actually be out of my body living my daydream—having no idea what was going on back in the real world in the classroom. Thank God for my mom, Adine, and my dad, Wayne Sr., for having the patience and for forcing me to study when I was younger.

Being an empath in school was really difficult because, after I would come back from one of my daydream trips or one of my sleepy attacks, it always seemed that just at that moment the teacher would ask me a question about what she'd just been teaching to the class. I never knew the answer, and I always felt that the students were thinking I was stupid when I would get something wrong. Eventually, I stopped participating in class because it was emotionally painful.

Throughout my life, I had many strange things happen to me that I could not explain and no one else could, either.

I experienced hearing people talk to me when no one was around; doors opened and closed all by themselves. I would hear people walk around in my house when no one was there but me. When I would go to sleep at night, I would feel Demons bump into my bed and awaken me. I had what I thought were some strange mental things happening to me that I could never explain such as uncontrollable anger. I would get angry for no reason at all. Even though I knew I shouldn't be angry, I couldn't stop it. I would obsess on some things and not others to the point that I thought I could be crazy. I always had a difficult time trying to understand why all of this was happening to me and why everyone else seemed to have a normal life.

Because of everything going on in my life that didn't seem normal, I started doing research to see if I could find out for myself what was wrong with me. After reading many books that provided no help at all, I decided to go to therapists and see if they could help me understand what was wrong with me. After they gave me a variety of tests, they decided I had a higher than average IQ which gave me no clarification why learning in school was so hard. They said I had attention deficit disorder, bi-polar disorder and obsessive compulsive disorder. They tagged me with a bunch of disorders, this made me feel worthless. And then they said that I should be on anti-depressants, lithium and Ritalin so I can cure my disorders. I asked about the side effects of these drugs. My God, the list of side effects seemed worst than what I was going through! So I decided not to take anything and just accepted that maybe no one would be able to help me.

Just when I thought I would have to go through the rest of my life accepting that I might just be crazy, I met Gary Spivey. From that day, my life changed forever.

The first thing Gary said to me was, "You're very spiritually gifted. You have many Angels around you, but you also have many Demons: Your energy is a mess." Gary then said, "You have Obsessive Compulsive Demons around you."

I said, "I went to a shrink and that was one of the things she diagnosed me with."

Gary said, "obsessive compulsive disorder is caused by Demons; let me get rid of the Demons so you can feel better."

All he did was wave his hand and I felt warm energy in my head. He said, "Your Demons are gone: You'll feel better."

I asked, "How did you do that?" Gary said, "I used one of my spiritual gifts to get rid of the Demons." I then asked if he could help with the other problems I was having and he said, "You have spiritual problems—not mental problems." Gary said that he could help me if I wanted to learn. Well, of course, I wanted to learn everything I could and this is how I started my journey into a world I never knew existed.

Luckily for me, Gary needed someone to help answer the phones in his office, so I took the job. I would answer his phones and, when he had the time, he would teach me about the spiritual world and how it affected me in the physical world.

I was like a sponge: I absorbed everything Gary taught me. Gary taught me many spiritual secrets such as learning how to communicate with God, Angels and other spiritual beings; how to receive spiritual gifts; how to heal myself and others; how to clear the spiritual dimensions; how to get rid of the Demons attacking me and all the other spiritual secrets revealed in this book.

All of these things have totally changed my life forever.

I now realize that I was born spiritually gifted and, many times, spiritually gifted people get attacked by Demonic forces. The Demons and dead people don't torment me anymore because I know how to get rid of them. Sometime I still wake up at night with a Demon or dead person standing next to my bed, but, instead of being afraid, I use a spiritual gift to get rid of the Demon or send the dead person to the light. All of the problems that the therapist said I had, even though they seemed mental, were actually spiritual. I fixed the spiritual problem and the mental problem seemed to vanish instantly. All of the therapists in the world would never have figured out what was going on with me. They would have just prescribed drugs.

It was more than ten years ago when I started answering Gary's phones. I'm still working with Gary. I'm not answering phones anymore. I'm now running his business and co-authoring this book.

I teach others how they can change their lives through the teachings that are in this book. I know firsthand that everything in this book really works because I used everything in this book to change my life. When Gary would learn something from God, he would then teach me and I, in turn, was able to teach others. Over the years, Gary has taught many thousands of people how to get rid of their mental, physical and emotional illnesses. I truly have to thank God for putting Gary Spivey in my life path or I would still be wandering around thinking I'm crazy and feeling bad because I'm not like everyone else.

Now I feel like I belong to this special spiritual club and some of the members in this club are God, Angels, Jesus, Mother Mary, Buddha, Ganish and many saints and other highly evolved spiritual beings that I talk to regularly. Based on what they tell me, everyone on earth has the ability to join this special club: You just have to want to.

Thank You Gary for Enlightening Me.
Your Friend,
Dean

When I first met Dean, my Angels said, "You need to help him. He's spiritually gifted and extremely possessed." I thought to myself, how can I help him as busy as I am? And my Angels said, "Offer him a job in your office." I did and he accepted.

From the first day he started working, he began asking questions about how does this work and how does that work, how do you spiritually fix this and spiritually fix that, what about this and what about that. Sometime I thought, "There's no way he could ask another question." But, believe me, I was wrong. Dean listened to everything I said and used every technique I taught him. It didn't take long for his spiritual abilities to shine through. It was amazing to see the transformation in his life.

My Angels were right, Dean was spiritually gifted. He just needed to be taught how to use his gifts. Now I can't stop him. Every day he receives messages from God and Angels, kills Demons, clears the spiritual dimensions and even teaches me new things about the spiritual world around us.

The Complete Woodcuts of
Albrecht Durer c.1498
Dover Publications, Inc.

USING YOUR
SPIRITUAL GIFTS

I wanted to talk to you again about spiritual gifts because I can't express to you enough how important it is to be able to receive and use your spiritual gifts.

If you look at the picture on the title page to Chapter Ten you will see Angels using spiritual gifts of staffs, swords, shields and bow and arrows to fight against Demons. This picture was created in the year 1498, by Albrecht Durer, who could obviously see spiritually, for this is exactly what spiritual warfare looks like in the spiritual dimensions. These are the same spiritual gifts you received or will receive; and the way the Angels fight against Demons is the same way you fight against Demons in the spiritual dimensions. You use your spiritual gifts in the spiritual dimension to rid yourself of the Demons that cause havoc in your physical world.

Throughout this book, you've read about spiritual gifts and the importance of receiving them. By now you should be able to see with your spiritual eyes so you can receive your spiritual gifts. You should also be able to see in all of the spiritual dimensions.

Once you are awakened to the spiritual world, you are going to start feeling and seeing Demons and dark energies around you. You may get a glimpse of a Demon with your spiritual eyes. If this happens, stop what you're doing and use your spiritual eyes to look around you to see what is there. Then, immediately put your hand to your chest and pull out your spiritual gift of a golden staff. A golden staff is one of the first spiritual gifts you'll receive—everyone receives one. When you feel or see the Demon, just take the staff and touch the Demon and it will blow up. You can also take out a sword, dagger or use your bow and arrow to kill the Demon before it causes havoc in your life.

Make sure that you teach your children the simple technique of using spiritual gifts. Tell your child that, if she/he sees a monster (Demon) or feels scared about anything, all they have to do is use their golden staff to fill the room with gold energy and ask their Angels to help them. The monsters will not bother them anymore. If your child is scared to sleep at night or is scared of the dark, then teach your child how to use their golden staff to fill the room with gold energy before they go to sleep. Make sure they do this every night and they will sleep better.

Any spiritual gift you receive can be used to help other people. If you're looking at someone's energy with your spiritual eyes and you see dark energy of a Demon on them, simply touch your chest, pull out your spiritual gift and envision touching the dark energy or the Demon with your spiritual gift. Then watch it explode in gold light. The person from whom you're removing the Demon or dark energy, will experience a warm feeling within their physical body because of the God energy flowing freely into their unblocked body.

I cannot stress enough how important it is to teach your children or any child that you're around, how to use their spiritual gifts. They can help other children at school or play whenever they see Demons or dark energies around one of their friends, and their friends can help them. The same is true for adults: Everyone can help everyone get rid of darkness.

You should always fill your spiritual/physical body with God energy, clear the spiritual dimensions and visit God in heaven daily so that you can remove all darkness and Demons around and in you. When using your spiritual gifts to remove Demons and dark energies from yourself or someone else, always ask your Angels for their help so they can make sure all the darkness was removed

Earthbound spirits often come around people who have a bright God light. You can tell if you have an earthbound spirit around you because you will feel a slight heaviness around you and you will get chills on the top of your arms and throughout your body. If you think you may have an earthbound spirit around you, all you have to do is ask God to send heaven's light to take the lost spirit back to heaven. When you ask for the light, it comes instantly to get the lost spirit. If you look with your spiritual eyes, you'll see a bright light come down from heaven: It looks like a white beaming spotlight with many Angels in it. The Angels will take the spirit back to heaven. You will then feel lightness throughout your body because the earthbound spirit is not in your energy field anymore. When you send a lost spirit back to heaven, you are doing them the biggest favor anyone can do for them. Being earthbound is torture for them because Demons attack them.

This is how simple it is to use your spiritual gifts, but make sure you meditate daily to fill your spiritual/physical body with God energy, clear the spiritual dimensions and visit God in heaven. This will help keep all darkness and Demons away from you and will keep your Angels close to you.

Here's a testimonial from a father and his 11 year old daughter. They heard me on the radio and came to me for a reading, but what they got was much more than a reading.

Testimonial by Mark and Jennifer

My daughter, Jennifer, age 11, and I (father, Mark) had our first reading with Gary in November 2005. After this reading, we were asked to submit "our story" for this book. Because of our experience, we are happy to share and to let people know they can come to Gary for help in their lives. We really had a great time and we look forward to seeing Gary on his next visit to Minnesota.

My Story about Gary Spivey (Father's version)

To begin, I heard about Gary Spivey by listening to the "Dave Ryan in the Morning Show" on radio station, KDWB in Minneapolis. I was fascinated by how accurate he seemed to be in figuring out people's problems.

My daughter, Jennifer wanted to visit him when he came to town. I agreed to see him in November 2005. He was staying over night in "The Castle" in downtown Minneapolis, Minnesota. His room was way up on the fourth floor of this strange and wonderful looking mansion. I was really nervous, but Jennifer seemed excited to finally see him. She had even written down some questions in her note pad that she was going to ask him about.

When we finally got into the room with Gary, I was instantly at ease. After a very limited introduction, Gary began talking to Jennifer. He taught her how to see spiritually, and then he took her on a guided spiritual trip, using their imaginations. They both closed their eyes and soon they were off on their trip together. They were talking to each other confirming what the other was seeing; it was amazing that they were seeing the same things. They seemed like they were actually on a walk together. Gary asked Jennifer what she wanted to do. Well, I was wondering what was going on, so she said she was standing in front of a large pond. She said she wanted to go swimming in the pond. Gary asked me if it was okay for her to take a swim. I said, "Sure, I guess." So, she went swimming and, all during this "trip," Gary kept explaining to me that he and Jennifer were taking this walk and that they were both together in the spiritual dimensions.

I was really amazed that they "connected" so easily.

In the session with Gary, he noticed dark energy in my shoulder and asked Jennifer if she wanted to help her dad. Then they both closed their eyes and my shoulder became very warm. They both said that they fixed my shoulder and it should no longer hurt. Gary asked me if there was anything the matter with my shoulder and I told him about the pains I had been having in my left shoulder and that it felt warm and okay now. He said that Jennifer had just "fixed it" using a spiritual gift. I thought that was pretty neat.

I told Gary that I wish I could go on an adventure with Jennifer in the spiritual dimensions also. He said I could, but, because I was a career person and used to using the analytical part of my mind, that it may take a little time to develop. Gary explained to me that, just because I couldn't see spiritually yet, not to give up because, with practice, I will gain spiritual sight. I will keep encouraging Jennifer to pursue her new spiritual skills.

A couple of days after our session with Gary, Jennifer and I were out driving. I said, "I wonder where your mom is right now." She closed her eyes like Gary taught her and said, "Mom just put on her shower cap and is getting into the shower." I said, "Okay, let's call her on the cell." There was no answer and, when we returned home, I asked her if she got my phone call. She said, "Yeah, but don't call me when I'm in the shower cause I won't answer!" She saw my number on the caller ID.

My Story about Gary Spivey (daughter's version) by Jennifer (age 11)

In the beginning, I became interested in Gary by listening to KDWB, "Dave Ryan in the Morning Show," on the car radio every morning on my way to school with my parents. Dave's radio show had Gary's strange stories on almost every day.

I asked my dad if we could go and see Gary when he came to town. My dad surprised me one day when he told me that we were going to see Gary Spivey in Minneapolis. I already knew some of the questions I wanted to ask him. I wrote them down in my notebook. I wondered if he would be able to answer all of my questions. And he did.

Gary was spending the night in this big awesome-looking castle. It was a mansion. His room was way up on the fourth floor and I couldn't wait until I could see him. When we finally got into his room, Gary, right away asked me if I wanted to take a "walk" with him. I closed my eyes and I could see the clouds and a blue sky in my imagination. I could actually see them and Gary could, too, at the same time. When Gary was thinking something in his head, I could see it, too. And you know *what was cool?   Gary told me that most people can only use five to seven percent of their brains, and I could use seventy-five percent of my brain!*

One funny thing happened when I was talking with Gary that night. My mother was at home because she had the flu or something. Gary asked me if I wanted to fix her up. We both looked at my mother in our imagination and we fixed her up. Then Gary said that my mother should feel really warm right now. Then Gary said, "We need to fix your dad's shoulder." So we did. When we got home, we asked Mom how she was feeling and she said that she was "really warm." We noticed that she did not have the blankets on anymore because she was too warm.

One day, I was riding around with my dad and he asked me to tell him where Mom was. I told him that she was going to take a shower. My dad said, "How do you know?" He called Mom at our home and she would not answer. I said to my dad, "Dad, she is in the shower and she can't hear the phone." When we got home, my dad asked Mom if she got a phone call." She said, "Yeah, I was in the shower and I didn't get out to answer the phone." My dad was really surprised that I actually knew that.

Gary also taught me how to ask my Angels for help with my math problems and stuff. I am really glad that I met Gary and hope that we can meet again some day.

Testimonial Part Two
Follow-up

Gary,

A few weeks ago, I and my little girl, Jennifer, had a reading with you in Minneapolis, Minnesota. We had some neat times bonding afterward. In fact, there is an incident that I would like to describe to you.

In church on Sunday—we go to a church with a famous pastor—he made mention that his eyes were blurry and he might ask someone from the congregation to read the scriptures. Jennifer and I were in the back pews and I looked at her and gave her one of those "go ahead and try it" winks. She closed her eyes and made some movements with her hands and soon the pastor was reading like crazy. He said, that's funny, things are clear now. I asked Jennifer what she did and she said that he had these two black spirit things over his eyes and she "took care of them" with her sword.

The next Sunday, the pastor mentioned, "Thanks for all your prayers and cards and emails for my eyesight." He had gone to his doctor and his doctor said he needed more checks because they couldn't find anything wrong with his eyes. He thought maybe he was getting diabetes or something. I have not talked to the pastor about this experience yet. Should I ask him??????

Talk to you soon.
Mark

This is just another example of the spiritual abilities we all have—not just kids. In this case it was Jennifer, but every man, woman and child on this planet have these abilities: They just need to be taught.

If you have been following along in this book, you have developed your abilities and they will continue to grow day by day. I suggest that, if you have learned anything from this book that you think can help others, please teach them.

MESSAGES FROM GOD
MORE SPIRITUAL SECRETS REVEALED

Since my first encounter with God, he has taught me many spiritual secrets. I shared these spiritual secrets throughout the book such as, how to see, hear and talk to God, Angels and other spiritual beings; how to receive and use spiritual gifts; what makes up your spiritual body; the spiritual dimensions around us and how to clear the Demons and darkness out of them; how to heal oneself and others; how to change your spirit; soul unlocking; how to enter heaven and visit with God, Angels and loved one who have passed away. Now I will share even more secrets with you.

The title of this chapter is *Messages from God and More Spiritual Secrets Revealed* because, as you're reading, this chapter, you will come across messages from God and you will also come across more spiritual secrets revealed on how our spiritual and physical worlds co-exist and how one affects the other.

These messages came directly from God to me and now I pass them along to you.

The first message I received from God was about FAITH.

Faith

Faith is the belief in me (God) everyday through good times and bad, and always knowing I am there for you. The problem I have is that many people's faith is very selective. They have faith when it's convenient for them. There are many people with selective faith; they only need me when they're going through bad times. "Why is that?"

Faith is the belief and knowing that I truly exist. Everyone has the ability to see, hear and talk to me, so why wouldn't you want to? What more proof do you need? Most people want to have faith in the idea of having faith, not actually in the real thing. With true faith, you have the ability to communicate directly to me about anything in the world. With faith and belief in me and my teachings, life would be easier for you, so why wouldn't you want to have faith in me all the time?

Truth and Honesty

Truthfulness and honesty spoken in the physical dimension will clear the spiritual dimensions. When people are being truthful and honest with oneself and others, it creates the vibration of truth in the spiritual dimensions. This vibration resonates throughout the spiritual dimensions with a golden energy attached to it. When this vibration transmits the golden energy into the spiritual dimensions, it clears the dark energies and Demons attacking your spiritual body. The fewer Demons and dark energies that are in the spiritual dimensions, the easier it is for you to live in your physical body. Also, by speaking truthful and honestly, you're helping everyone on earth by clearing the spiritual dimensions. If everyone on earth would be truthful and honest with everyone else and oneself, this would help exterminate the Demons. Remember, people are not evil; Demons are evil and Demons attack everyone's spiritual bodies making you do and say evil, mean and nasty things to one another on earth.

Lying

Lying is part of many people's everyday lives. Lying is as easy as breathing for some people. Everyone, from kids to adults, women and men—everyone, at sometime will lie because they just think it's normal and natural. But if everyone understood the tremendous spiritual damage that occurs to them when lying, they may want to stop.

I will explain to you what occurs spiritually when you lie and then it is up to you to make the decision to stop lying or not. In your spiritual dimensions, you have higher selves; your higher selves are extensions of your spiritual body and your spiritual body lives inside of your physical body. When you lie in the physical dimension, it sends a vibration of untruth into the spiritual dimensions and a vibration of untruth is dark black energy.

I know many of you will say, "I have to lie sometimes." But, you see, no lie is a good lie in the spiritual dimensions. It never has been and never will be. I know that lies are very complex. Lies are in every aspect of your human existence: business, politics and personal. But just because most people lie doesn't mean that you have to.

In the spiritual dimensions, you have higher selves which are extensions of your spiritual body. Your higher selves work on many things throughout the day that affect your physical life. When you lie, it sets off the vibration of untruth which is very counter productive for your higher selves. This is what happens to your spiritual body when you lie; the untruth vibration from telling a lie resonates throughout the spiritual dimensions causing a dark negative energy which affects all your higher selves. When you tell a lie, the untruth vibration penetrates, shakes and rattles throughout your higher selves, so that whatever they're working on for you gets interrupted and shaken loose. Your higher selves may be at a very crucial point of lining up your true love or soul mate or bringing that big business deal that will make you lots of money or maybe just bringing you your dream house that you were looking for.

There is always a truth in every situation, the truth may not be the exact answer you or someone else is looking for, but the truth is much better than lying any day.

Believe me when I say that the truth will set you free; free to accomplish anything you ever dreamed of and more. The truth is the toughest of all my teachings to accomplish and understand because it's so natural for everyone to lie. Most people think that if someone else is lying, then, "So can I." Remember, there is a very old saying, "Two wrongs never make a right."

Lying Is Dying

What do I mean? I mean dying of the spirit for, if the spirit dies, so does your spiritual body. You may be asking, "If I lie, I'm going to die?" Not exactly. If you lie, the physical body will not die, but your spirit inside of you will. You need your spirit to protect your soul.

One of my teachings was about how to replace your warn out spirit through spirit replacement, so you may be thinking, " I'm going to keep lying and just do a spirit replacement as often as I need to." If you keep lying, the spirit replacement eventually will not work because, for the new spirit that is coming from heaven—a place of oneness, honesty and trust—it will eventually not enter into your body because it's torture on your spirit when you lie. When this happens, you are leaving your soul open to all of the Demonic attacks without any protection at all.

The spirit operates on truth and honesty and, every time you say a little lie, a tiny bit of your spirit leaves. When the lie leaves your mouth, the first thing that happens is a little tiny piece of your spirit leaves with the lie. Once the lie has left your mouth, it causes a negative vibration in the spiritual dimensions and the vibration will come back to you. When it does, it attaches to your spirit causing you to lose another part of it.

You must make a mental choice to stop lying because you are hurting yourself spiritually. When a lie is told by you, it is always doing damage to your spirit. Lying, in any capacity, is not worth doing.

Love

Love is a very confusing thing. Many people search for it, write about it and read about it. It's a very simple secret; it's inside each and every one of you. All you have to do is let it out and it will come back to you. Everyone has love inside of them waiting to come out.

Everyone would like to think that they understand love, but the love I'm talking about, you don't understand. I'm talking about the spiritual love between people. The easiest way to show love to other people is not to look at their physical body. If you use your spiritual eyes to see another person's spiritual body and not their physical one, then it will be easy to send and receive love because you will not have any of the negative human qualities to deal with such as: hating people, judging people, being racist or any negativity toward other people no matter who they are. You would just respect and love them because your spiritual bodies don't have negative qualities.

Everyone has love inside of them waiting to come out. If you clear your spiritual/physical body and all of the spiritual dimensions—getting rid of the Demons that are blocking your spirit from connecting to other people's spirits—you will be able to experience love and respect for everyone. Once you do this, whatever type of love you're looking for will come to you. If you're looking for a relationship, you will find it. If you want to be closer to your children, you will be. If you and your spouse have fallen out of love, you will be able to fall in love again. I know this may sound easy and that's because it is easy to find love. The reason you think it is hard is because of all the Demons trying to keep people separated so their spiritual bodies will not connect and become one on earth as it is in heaven.

Relationships

Why is everyone on earth always searching for relationships? Relationships can be in the form of lovers, that special soul mate, very good friends or just that special connection between people that makes you feel good. Everyone is always searching for that someone, but no one really knows why.

Everyone's spirit, before entering the body, lived in heaven: A place of total oneness, a place without judgment of one another, a place of total bliss and happiness and with love and respect for everyone. When your spirit left heaven, it also left that oneness. Once your spirit enters your body, it starts searching for that oneness with other spirits.

On earth, all spirits are separate from each other—living within a physical body. That is why people are always searching for relationships with a parent, brother, sister, lover, close friend or just a companionship, because your spirit needs that feeling of oneness with other spirits to feel complete and whole again.

My goal is to create that oneness on earth as it is in heaven. Many people think of heaven as this wonderful, magical place where everything is possible—a place of total happiness and bliss. If this is what you think, you are totally correct. What I want is for everyone on earth to experience this joy and happiness while living here on earth. There's only one reason you cannot experience heaven on earth and the reason is the Demons, dark energies and negativity that block your joy and happiness.

As far back as you can remember, you probably always had a best friend, were in a relationship and had a special connection with your parents, your brothers or sisters or that special someone you were exceptionally close to. That closeness you felt with those people were the spirits connecting again and being one; the spirits can sense each other and will always try to connect. Everyone has the need for oneness deep inside because your spirits are trying to connect on earth as they are in heaven.

Why isn't everyone on earth one with each other? It's as simple as I said earlier; Demons! In heaven, there aren't any Demons so the spirits can live there as one. In the beginning of a relationship, when you have that special connection with someone, you feel happy around this person because the oneness of the spirits has chased away all of the Demons from your physical bodies. When this occurs, you can feel that special oneness such as it is in heaven. It only takes a little time before the Demons start attacking your spiritual body and playing tricks on you causing the oneness of the spirits to separate from each other. When the oneness separates, then it's only a matter of time in the physical world before your relationship or that special connection with someone will come to an end.

This is an example of what I'm talking about: When you are in a close relationship with someone you love, in the beginning of the relationship it's great. You spend enough time with that person and the world seems like a wonderful place to live. That person means the world to you and you mean the world to that person. Then the Demons start attacking your spiritual body trying to separate the oneness. The Demons' job is to keep people's spirits apart from each other because, when they can keep the spirits apart, the Demons can conquer and rule, but when people's spirits are together, the Demons don't have a chance. Once the Demons start attacking your spiritual body, it's only a matter of time before they will begin to make you do things to the other person in the relationship that you would not do if the oneness of heaven existed on earth.

Demons will cause you to start a fight, an argument, or just do something downright stupid to the other person. Demons may put thoughts into your head; telling you this person is not good enough for you and making you find everything wrong in the relationship. They may make you treat that person really awful and, in return, the Demons may make the other person in the relationship do the same to you. Once this starts happening on the physical level, you may get into arguments and go your separate ways. But on the spiritual level, the spirits still want that closeness and oneness so they come back together and, on the physical level, you make up. Then the Demons come back and, in your physical world, you start arguing all over again. Eventually, what's going to happen is that the spirits will get tired of coming together and then being split up. When this happens again and again, your spirit will eventually search for that oneness with another spirit. When that oneness is found, your relationship will end forever and a new cycle begins.

I talk to people from all over the world who have relationship problems. They all ask me the same question. How do I make my relationship better and fix the ongoing problems we are having? As I see it from my many years of experience, the three biggest problems that relationships face is *denial, drama* and *Demons.* So many people want to live in *denial* that there is a problem in their relationship or they enjoy the *drama* of the problem. If you are honest with yourself and get out of *denial* and stop your *drama* (both of which are the vibration of a lie) the *Demons* will not be able to attach to you. *Demons* attach to lies. They cannot attach to the truth. When trying to make a relationship work, both you and your mate need to check yourself for the three D's: *Denial, Drama* and *Demons.* If you get rid of the three D's you will find that you are now on a truth vibration and your problems will evaporate.

Now you see how important it is to learn how to get out of denial, stop your drama and get rid of your demons-so that you can live in a happy relationship on earth as it is in heaven.

Control

God explained to me that control is one of the biggest "Demon tricks" played on mankind and everyone is guilty of this.

This is God's message about control: Control is the ability to restrict others from being themselves! Someone (a parent, friend, teacher, brother, sister) is always telling you what you should do or not do or who you should be or not be. There is a difference between giving advice to someone and telling someone what to do with their life. Why does everyone feel the need to control others? The answer will probably shock you. No one is really in control of themselves or others, it's a trick played on everyone by Demons. I'll clear this up for you so that you can understand.

When I first created mankind, they didn't have the problems of everyone today because heaven's rules and laws were understood on earth. Everyone was happy and abided by heaven's rules and laws. It didn't last long because, when I created humans, I gave them free will. I gave them the decision to choose to always listen to me and abide by heaven's rules or to use their free will and make their own choices and laws; they chose to make their own rules and laws. They knew that the downside to using their free will and making their own laws was that I had to allow the Demons to influence them as well as the Angels. So you see, humans not only had Angels with them, they now had Demons, also. Now, I didn't leave them helpless against the Demons. I gave them the secrets of how to communicate with me and their Angels for guidance. I also showed them how to receive spiritual gifts and how to kill the Demons that cause the temptations. They chose to make their own decisions and use their free will; they thought the Demon temptations and tricks wouldn't affect them.

The necessity of control evolved out of trying to stop Demon temptations inside of them. In the beginning, when humans were first on earth, they never had to deal with Demon temptations, but they chose free will and, along with free will, came the Demon temptations. When the Demons started trying to control humans, humans, for the first time, had to fight to gain control of their minds and bodies from the Demons. Although the Angels were trying to guide humans in the direction of heaven's rules and laws, so were the Demons trying to guide humans in the direction of their rules and laws which is chaos, corruption, greed, anger, jealousy, killing and anything of a negative nature. The Demons turned man against man and made them try to control each other. Even though humans chose to make their own rules and laws and allow Demon temptations to influence them, they knew the spiritual secrets I gave them. In the beginning, humans used these secrets to keep the Demons away. But, as time passed, the spiritual secrets were lost and the Demons gained control. That is why I say that control really doesn't exist because, if it was not for the Demons, there would not be any control issues; no one trying to control anyone on earth, everyone would be living and abiding by heaven's rules and laws.

If you learn the teachings in this book and get rid of your Demons, you will gain control of yourself. If everyone managed to get rid of their Demons, they would gain control of themselves and no one would try to control anyone anymore. It all starts with you getting rid of your Demons and gaining control of yourself and not trying to control others. It's up to everyone on earth to make the decision to stop the control issues so that everyone can live together as it was meant to be "heaven on earth." But, as I said, I gave mankind free will, so the decision is yours. I can only guide you; but it is your decision to learn my teachings and get rid of your Demons and gain control of yourself again. My spiritual secrets were lost over time, but now I'm sharing them with you. Again, it's up to you whether you to use them or not.

I know that many people think someone has to be in control. Yes, I agree with that for the time being. But it is not correct because you see, if everyone was in control of themselves (free of Demons) then no one would be trying to control others. Everyone would be working together in unity, co-existing as one as it is in heaven and should be on earth. Everyone would be happy with their personal and professional lives because they would do exactly what they wanted. No one would have to be in control. In relationships, no one would try to control the other person—telling them what to do, or where to go, or how do it. There would be no arguments, only love, friendship and happiness because you would be Demon-free and so would the other person. Without Demons interfering in your unity and love, there would be no need for control.

If everyone learns to co-exist as one and get rid of their Demons, then no one would try controlling anyone because control would not exist. The leaders of countries would not want to control other countries causing senseless deaths. Every country on earth would work and live in unity with love and respect for each other and they would only look out for the best interests of every woman, man and child on earth. Remember, everyone has a spiritual body inside of them and your spiritual bodies all come from the same place, heaven. So why not unite and bring heaven back to earth so you can all be home. Imagine everyone on earth co-existing as one, helping one another, loving and being happy. It all starts with being aware of your Demons and then getting rid of them.

How do you get rid of your Demons? By allowing God energy to flow from heaven down your God Cord removing all blocks within your God Cord, then allowing God energy to flow into your spiritual/physical body removing all the Demons, dark energies and negativity within you, then allowing the God energy to flow from your body into all of the spiritual dimensions until they're all clean. By doing this, you will remove all Demons and you'll be Demon-free.

Co-existing

People should live and exist as individuals making their own choices and using their free will without the influence of Demons. Imagine different people with different ideas, goals and dreams all living on earth together happy. I'm talking about the big picture of life: Everyone on earth living as individuals and also co-existing together as one big family—everyone helping one another, not fighting and hurting each other, just living together with love and respect for each other.

Co-existing may be a hard concept for people to understand and many of you will think that it's impossible. If you're one of these people, first get rid of your Demons then show your family members how to get rid of their Demons then show your neighborhoods and, before long, everyone on earth will be Demon-free. Real co-existing is bringing heaven to earth and living on earth as it is in heaven; everyone living as one, helping each other not hurting each other.

There are many Demons and dark energies that exist in the spiritual dimensions and that affect everyone on earth. The only way of co-existing as one is to learn how to get rid of the Demons and dark energies that affect you and others so that everyone can co-exist as one. Oneness is the final goal.

Oneness

Why be afraid of something you don't understand? Everyone has a little bit of fear; fear of what others may think, fear of what is right or wrong, fear of changing your thinking, fear of the unknown. With my guidance, you will learn not to be afraid. You'll realize that fear is only a Demon playing a trick on you—trying to stop you from learning the spiritual secrets that I'm revealing. The Demons don't want everyone on earth to join together in unity as one power fighting against them. The Demons would rather divide and conquer man and have you fight and kill each other. With guidance from me (God), my Angels and other spiritual beings, everyone can unite and win the war against the Demons. Everyone has the ability to learn my secrets and, with a little dedication and practice, you will learn the power of my secrets and the importance of living as one.

Now you see how important it is to learn how to get rid of the Demons and clear yourself on a daily basis so that you can live in peace and happiness on earth as it is in heaven. If everyone cleared their spiritual dimensions daily—getting rid of the Demons— everyone would live free of Demons and oneness on earth as it is in heaven would soon be possible. It has to start with everyone on planet earth. Wouldn't it be much easier to live as one on earth as it is in heaven or would you rather live as you're living right now? It's up to you. Make your decision.

Fear

"Dreams." Everyone has had a dream sometime in their life—as a little boy/ girl, and even as an adult. Everyone at sometime or another has had a dream of who they wanted to be, what they wanted to accomplish, of their fantasy car, of their dream wedding or even their dream life.

What do you think is the biggest reason why people's dreams aren't fulfilled? Has it been because of other people? Many people love to blame others for not having achieved their dreams. Other people are not to blame, and you are not even to blame for not achieving your dreams. I know that many people are probably saying that someone or something has stopped them from achieving their dream. If not someone else and if not you, then who or what? The answer is "Fear Demons."

Fear Demons exist and their main pleasure is stopping people from accomplishing their dreams while living here on earth. Now, when I say fear,

I'm not necessarily talking about shaking in your boots, scared to death to move. For you see fear attaches to you in many areas of your life and in many different forms. Being scared of the dark is a fear, fear of failure or success is a fear or one might have a fear of spiders and snakes. You see, fear comes in many different forms. The fear I'm talking about and the fear you want to understand is the fear that stops you from accomplishing your dreams and stops you from living your life to the fullest. Fear manifests in different places at different times. Fear is different from person to person. But one thing that is the same in everyone is that everyone's fears are from the same Fear Demons. Fear exists in many areas of life; business and personal. Many people say, "I faced my fears head on." What if you didn't have any fears to face head on? Wouldn't it be great if the only thing you had to face was the accomplishment of the task at hand? No more, "I was going to do this, I should have done that." No more wasted time with excuse after excuse.

Many of you would like not to believe me when I say that fear is the biggest roadblock standing in the way of accomplishing your dreams; all I can say is. "It is the biggest roadblock."

The way to know if you have Fear Demons stopping you in any area of your life is to just think for a moment what is it you want in a career, relationship or any area of your life. Think about what you really would love to have or accomplish. Once you think about it, take a look at your life with honesty and see if you are working toward accomplishing your dreams. If you are not working toward accomplishing your dream or you're afraid of trying, then you have a fear Demon. The way to get rid of this Demon is to clear the spiritual dimensions with gold energy. This will get rid of this Demon blocking you from accomplishing your dreams. If you keep your spiritual dimensions clear daily, you will realize that life will become very easy and you will accomplish everything you desire. Every day after clearing your spiritual dimensions and entering heaven, use your spiritual imagination and envision the final accomplishment of your dream while you're in heaven. See it in full detail and then surround it with gold energy. This will keep the Demons and dark energies from causing roadblocks while you're on your path to your dreams.

Nonattachment

Many times you can be the cause of not accomplishing your dreams even though you clear the Demons away from you on a daily basis. Many people develop such strong attachment to the outcome of a situation that it creates a negative energy around what they are trying to accomplish.

You may be trying to achieve a particular goal such as getting a new job, being the number one salesperson in your company, or it may be something as simple as wanting someone to ask you on a date. Developing a strong attachment to the outcome of any goal will cause a negative energy. Many times, you may feel as though your life depends on it, or you can't live without it. It's okay to want things and to have goals, but everything will come much easier to you if you learn this simple lesson, the lesson of "nonattachment to the outcome of a situation." If your goal is to be the number one salesperson in your company, or to find the love of your life, you need to realize that you can live without being number one or without the love of your life. As soon as you realize this, the Demons can not stand in your way and the Angels will bring to you whatever it is you desire.

What occurs in the spiritual world when you have this strong attachment to the outcome of a situation is; you're opening the doors for all of the Demons to come and block everything you have working or everything you're trying to achieve. Demons cannot attach to the outcome of a situation if you have nonattachment.

Setting goals, trying to accomplish things on earth and wanting and needing things is part of what you do when living in your human body. If you keep your God Cord clean, your spiritual/physical body clean and your spiritual dimensions clear, you can avoid many of the roadblocks (Demons) that are standing in your way of the result that you're trying to accomplish. If you clear yourself daily and have nonattachment to the outcome of situations, you will be amazed at how easy you can accomplish anything.

Jealousy

Many people think that jealousy is sometimes good. For example, girlfriends want their boyfriends to be jealous over them and vice versa. Sometimes people are jealous of what others may have such as material things or even happiness and joy.

Can anyone tell me what good comes from jealousy? You can't, because actually nothing good ever comes from jealousy. On the other hand, can anyone tell me what bad things or negativity comes from jealousy? To start with, arguments, not trusting people, verbal fights, killings, family arguments and much more. As you can see, nothing good ever comes from jealousy; only bad things and negativity. Why would anyone want to cause someone else to be jealous of them, or why would you become jealous for no reason? If you guessed a Demon, then you're absolutely right! This Demon hangs around looking for the weakness in men and women, just waiting for its moment when it can infect its prey. No one (man, woman or child) is immune. Some people can just hide it better than others, but everyone is infected with it.

There is a way to get rid of the Jealousy Demons; it's complex, but simple. First, allow God energy to flow from heaven down your God Cord clearing all the blocks, then allow the God energy to enter into your spiritual/ physical body clearing all of the Demons, negativity and dark energies, then allow the God energy to flow out of your body into all of the spiritual dimensions clearing everything. By clearing your spiritual dimensions, you get rid of the Jealousy Demons.

At any time when you feel any sign of jealousy, stop and clear your God Cord, spiritual/physical body and spiritual dimensions, and that feeling of jealousy will go away because you will get rid of the Jealousy Demon. When you feel jealousy toward anyone or anything, it's nothing more than a Demon infecting its prey, and guess who the prey is?

Negativity

Negativity! Why are so many people all over the world negative? The reason is because it's the most contagious of all diseases. Believe it or not, negativity is a disease. How does a disease spread? One person gets it then they spread it to others. So how is negativity spread? By hearing it from others. Before you know it, it takes over your whole body from head to toe. The next thing you know, you're talking negatively and spreading it to others and so on and so on. That's why negativity is the worst disease in the world, because it only takes one person to infect everyone else. When negativity starts, you're totally unaware of it. It's so subtle that it takes over before you know it.

Negativity is the stopping or interfering of energy flowing from heaven through your God Cord into your spiritual/physical body. So you see, when you find yourself talking or feeling negative, stop, clean your God Cord by allowing God energy to flow from heaven through your God cord removing all the blocks. Then allow the energy to flow into your spiritual/physical body allowing the energy to fill your body and remove all of the Demons and negativity from within you. Then allow this energy to flow from your spiritual body into the spiritual dimensions removing all of the negativity that is around you.

If everyone would learn this, then no one would be negative and this disease would stop spreading.

Life

There's nothing worse than being in a physical body and not fully appreciating and using it. What I'm talking about is enjoying life and everything earth has to offer. There are many wonderful things to experience, for example, breathing, as simple as that may sound you should enjoy it, eating is another one of the simple little things that everyone takes for granted, sleeping, walking, talking—all these things are taken for granted. Anything that can be done on earth, such as watching TV, horseback riding, surfing, reading a book, absolutely everything on earth is something great to experience. Life is a miracle to experience.

If everyone would take a moment and think of this; what if tomorrow, you wake up and everything is gone? What if you were left with nothing except the memory of everything you once had? You would say, "I wish I would have taken time to try this and I remember when I enjoyed that." So why not enjoy it now when you are here and have the opportunity to enjoy it? Not everyone enjoys the same things, so everyone should take pride in what they do enjoy. If you don't know what you enjoy, start doing things—taking walks, going to movies, go to dinner—just start doing things until you start enjoying something. Once you find the things you enjoy, then truly enjoy them to the fullest.

People have lost their ability to feel. People have to begin feeling again. Most people go from place to place doing things to please other people or someone else: You're always trying to please other people and not yourself. Everyone has to take time for themselves and enjoy life. You should never put someone else's enjoyment of life before yours because, when you do, you stop living your life

When you were a kid, things were fun and wonderful. As people get older, most people lose their fun and enjoyment of life. You need to take time to take pleasure in every moment of everyday. Then you will start loving life. You should enjoy your work, love-life, friendship, children—everything needs to be enjoyed. Everyone needs to take time for themselves and just love what life has to offer.

Most people on earth treat their life like it's not important. Everything is taken for granted. The most important thing you have is your life, and it can be gone in a second. I can't stress enough to you that your life will end one day; the last thing I want to hear when you get to heaven is, "I regret not taking more time to smell the flowers, or just spent time with someone I love." Remember, you have the ability to live your life while on earth. Simply get rid of the Demons and other dark energies that are stopping you from enjoying life.

The Gift

Life is a precious gift that is bestowed on people, yet most of you, if not all of you, just run around worrying about other people—what they think about you or what they have. Life turned out to be everyone comparing themselves to each other. I want to know, "Why worry about all that worthless stuff?" I see drugs, crime, homeless people, people killing others, wars, children on drugs; all of these horrible things must stop.

The gift of life should start with love for your life, friends, family and all people—everyone on earth living as it is in heaven taking care of one another. Heaven is true oneness. Heaven must come to earth. If heaven were on earth, wars, crimes, drugs, hunger and all the negative things on earth would not exist. With oneness, no one would intentionally do anything wrong to themselves or anyone else. Happiness and love are the true pathways to heaven. Learn to laugh and love one another.

Learn my spiritual secrets and get rid of the Demons and darkness that have been plaguing humans for thousands of years. Allow heaven to come to earth once again.

Tying Everything Together

This will be a tough transition for some and easy for others, but everyone must make it. Whatever your beliefs or religion, everyone must learn God's spiritual secrets.

God said, "My spiritual secrets consist of everything you read in this book." Many of you may not believe what you've read in this book. You may or may not believe in receiving spiritual gifts or that it's possible to communicate directly to God. Most people believe God is this all-powerful being and that one day, if you lead a great life on earth, you may see Him when you die and go to heaven. You're partially correct. You will see Him when you die and get to heaven, but you can also see, hear and talk to Him while you're living. Most people think that you have to be a saint or prophet or someone special such as Jesus, Mohammad or Buddha to see, hear or talk to Him. Well you're wrong! God wants you to know that, in the beginning, everyone was able to communicate directly to Him, but as time passed and the Demons gained control of mankind, only a few were able to communicate directly to Him because they were chosen to spread His spiritual secrets and to see if mankind was ready to learn them. They were not. Now we're in the time of a spiritual awakening on earth and anyone who truly wants to learn His spiritual secrets will have their opportunity.

Learning God's spiritual secrets isn't a complex process. It's rather simple, but it does take a bit of dedication on your part. The spiritual secrets that are revealed in this book are not to be taken lightly. Everyone who makes the decision to learn these secrets is going to receive riches beyond their wildest dreams. I don't mean material riches, I mean spiritual riches and these riches will guarantee you a place in heaven with God.

MORE TESTIMONIALS

I would like to share with you some more testimonials from people that I've helped and how they've helped themselves by believing in themselves, in a higher power (God), and by learning the teachings within this book.

Testimonial by Troy and Esther Baker

As parents of an autistic child, the range of emotions can torment you while you can lovingly search through the exhaustive maze for biomedical, educational and neurological answers from those with and mostly without answers. It's during this arduous journey for the keys to unlock our son's future that we have struggled through the torrent of emotions from joy to depression. Gary Spivey's gifts give loving, caring parents of an autistic child what they essentially crave, filling the greatest need that we all desire...Peace of Mind. Gary's refocusing us on what is truly important cannot be heard enough in a world today that spends more time listening to talk radio strangers than their neighbors, loved ones or God's message. We, like many of today's parents, struggled with the increasing expectations for our young children's education treadmill. Answers to the questions of what can be done to help our son on his life's journey are a priceless gift. Thanks to Gary, we were reminded of what is important from a heavenly perspective and our autistic son's role in our world seen and unseen. I cannot recommend enough, spending time and receiving the gifts that Gary Spivey shares with all who come into his light.

Troy and Esther Baker
Ventura, CA

Having an autistic child creates many struggles that parents with healthy children may never know or understand. With all of Troy and Esther's challenges, trying to do their very best to create a happy life and a wonderful place for their son to live, they managed to make their way somehow to talk to me in a session. I was more than happy to work with them because, if there's anything I care about more than any other one thing, it's that of working with misunderstood children and gifted children. Autistic children certainly fall into that category.

I've had many occasions to work with autistic children. While I don't have all of the answers neurologically speaking or medically speaking, I do think I have some of the answers spiritually speaking.

Autistic children are very spiritually gifted beings; maybe the most spiritually gifted. While seemingly aloof a lot of the time in their physical worlds and sometimes not even talking or saying one word, these children, in the higher dimensions, are performing tremendous tasks and functions for God, eliminating many dark energies from around the earth and beyond. As I worked with Troy and Esther, looking closer at their son's problem, I was able to speak to him in the spiritual dimensions. Understand, he was not present in the session. I was able to speak to him, much like I am able to speak to someone's loved one who has passed on and now lives in heaven (Tenth Dimension). I was able to see what he was going through. He then showed me what his mission was in this lifetime—to eliminate a particular type of dark energy that attacks all of us on a daily basis. He told me that his job was to keep this particular type of dark energy from even coming close to planet earth for it would surely wreak havoc here on earth if it reached us.

As he showed me what he was doing, he started to teach me how to do the same. I realized that this was, indeed, a spiritual lesson for me, as I was seeing a little bit further and a little beyond and certainly over my head with anything I have ever encountered before as far as eliminating darkness in tremendous quantities. As I was talking to him in a very fluent conversation and, as he was absolutely brilliant and articulate in conversation talking back to me, I asked him if he would entertain the thought of entering into his body and letting his higher self, that was so intelligent in the higher dimensions, spend more time in his physical body where he would possibly even talk and communicate with his parents more. He said he would like to do this, but it hurts. I then asked him to explain to me so I would understand. He said, "Well I could show you." So I said, "Okay, let me see." At that moment, he showed me himself, a bright-eyed, beautiful, smiling higher self in the higher dimensions. He then projected down into his physical body. He only stayed in it for a couple of seconds and then popped back out again. In the spiritual dimension, he was bent over and making a face as though he was in agonizing pain. This, of course, was even upsetting to me; for I sensed a tremendous pain that he was feeling as if he'd been punched in the stomach really hard. I started to ask him how he felt; he held his hand up as to say, "Give me a moment. I'll be okay." In a couple of minutes, he went from being bent over holding his knees to standing straight up again saying, "See, it hurts." I asked, "What makes it hurt?" He explained to me that the regular energy that we are used to on earth was so dark and he was, indeed, like an Angel (so highly evolved) that it was impossible for him to stay inside of his body. It was just too painful. This opened up a million questions in my head on what's really going on and if I could possibly clear the energy around his body so that he would, indeed, feel like staying in it a little longer. If we all meditated and cleared the energy around the earth, would the earth possibly have more light and more energy so that he and all of the other autistic children would be able to be inside their bodies?

What spiritual secrets, if he were in his body, could he possibly tell us about what's really going on in the spiritual dimensions? As he explained to me, his job is that he works for God. He works for God diligently daily getting rid of all of the darkness so that our planet is brighter. I asked him if all autistic children do this function. He said, "While we all have different jobs, we all get rid of darkness. Most of us get rid of darkness every day, all day and all night." My head was buzzing with questions, but I sensed that he had to get back to work doing what he was doing. After he spent some time showing me how he kept the dark energies away from our world, I felt blessed that he would share those secrets with me.

I certainly look forward to spending more time with parents of autistic children as I work to understand them more. I believe that some day soon, if enough people would become enlightened and bring God energy/light to earth, that it would be possible for these children to enter back into their physical bodies and that they could live here, too.

This is a follow up letter sent to me a few weeks after I worked with Will.

Gary,

Since our visit to your home with Will, his progress and growth has been extraordinary. Within two weeks of our visit, Will has spoken more words than ever including, "COMPUTER" and written things unsolicited (1,2,3) such as the photo enclosed shows. We cannot thank you enough for your healing touch and further insight into our lives and Will's journey. This past week, he did something he has never done before at school. Within fifteen minutes of his usual departure time, he got up after completing his task, put on his backpack and said, "Home," to his teacher. They nearly cried with joy. You have not only touched our lives immensely, but also those who have been trying to help Will for the past two years. With your healing touch, Will has improved his eye contact and connecting to others, especially us.

Thank you, Thank you, Thank you,
Troy and Esther

As I strive to learn more about the spiritual world and how it affects us physically, I become more aware of how to help gifted children. As an adult, I use my spiritual gifts daily and learn from God and Angels. God tells me that, even though I unlocked my soul and have all the spiritual secrets of heaven within me, if I wanted to learn these spiritual secrets easier and faster, I should unlock the knowledge of my child spirit. As I was asking Him how I unlock the knowledge of my child spirit, He said, "Now is not the time. I will teach you when the time comes." He did say one thing, "Remember, almost everyone was or will be 3 years old at some point in their lives." I gathered from that, that 3 years old must be a key point in our lives. Well just like everything else I've learned from God, I'm sure that when He feels like the time is right, He will teach me how to unlock the knowledge of my child spirit and I will teach you. Until then, remember how you were at 3 years old.

Testimonial by John

My name is John; I was a methamphetamine user for several years.

Toward the end of my habit, I used every day. The only way I could get up for the day was to use. I was unable to stop. My doctor told me I had no chance of quitting on my own, that I would have to enter a rehabilitation program. Even with rehabilitation, my doctor said that successful recovery usually takes a few tries. I couldn't bear the idea of being housed in a clinic for months, but the condition of my health necessitated I do something.

I met with Gary Spivey. He spent about an hour with me removing my Drug Demons. He also drew on paper images of what he saw around my body to help me understand what he was seeing.

I left him thinking, what a waste of time that was. That night, I did not use any drug; somehow I could control my urges, but, before I saw Gary, I absolutely could not control myself.

I stayed clean for six months.

Then I began having dreams of doing speed. In my dreams it was always okay to smoke crystal. The dreams showed me the pleasure of doing crank and told me there would be no harm. So, I started using again. But this time it was different: I wasn't getting high. I used for three days and didn't get the high I was used to. Desperate to fix myself before I fell completely into my old patterns, I saw Gary Spivey again.

Gary said I wasn't getting high because the Demon that used to get high with me wasn't with me anymore. He got rid of some Obsessive Compulsive Demons I had around me and I felt better instantly. He showed me how to get rid of my Demons and keep the God light in my body so I would never have a relapse ever again. This meeting took only thirty minutes. After this meeting, I left him thinking what a gift he is. Today, I'm four years sober

Thank You for showing me the light.
John

In John's case, he had Demons causing him to use drugs. I simply used my spiritual gifts to get rid of the Demons, and his urges to use drugs were gone. As I said before in the book, Demons will come back if you don't clear yourself daily. In John's case, it took six months before they came back, but luckily for John, he knew what was going on in the spiritual and physical worlds and came to me to get rid of his Demons again. He learned his lesson and keeps himself clear of Demons. Now, more than four years later, he is still sober and free of Demons.

Testimonial by Gina

I had an amazing time at your spiritual retreat. I wrote the following a few weeks prior to attending. I strongly feel the need to share it with someone and I believe that someone is you.

When I was 17 years old, I had a nervous breakdown. My mother had always been a complete control freak and had always tried to control every aspect of my life, but, at this time, I decided enough was enough and began to really rebel. In high school,

I had always been kind of quiet and geeky, but I had made a "cool" friend who had really opened me up. I started wearing makeup and became self-confident. Older guys started to notice me; not necessarily a good thing, but pretty cool back then.

I was in my own private hell. I began to think of suicide and wished I had the guts to do it. I stormed off the school grounds one day and went home and wrote what was perceived as a suicide note. I just sat with a pounding headache and a full bottle of pills, but knew I could not go through with it because I could not leave what's known for the unknown. My friend panicked and contacted a teacher, who contacted my parents. They forced me into "family therapy" which was a joke. I didn't want my parents to know anything about my life, they understood nothing. As my depression grew worse, I stopped eating, sleeping, and I spun very quickly out of control. After days and days of this, I had a psychotic episode. I thought people were out to get me, my food was being poisoned and that every move I made was being watched.

I was committed for two weeks in a hospital. My mother came down and told them what medication she was on at the time (Lithium) and so they put me on the same stuff against my will. I was stiff, completely numb, and tired all the time, but was told that if I didn't take it, I would become sick again and that I was a manic depressive and I would probably need to take these meds for the rest of my life. I was forcibly drugged for about eight months, but stopped once I turned 18 because legally, they could no longer force me to take it.

I was okay for about a year, but things spun out of control for me again.

At this point, I was being a slut and slept around for a while. One of the guys I had been with was kind of rough with me. I knew him from high school and always thought he was cute. I ended up at his house. He was very aggressive. I was intimidated and did whatever he wanted. I never considered it rape because I did not try hard enough to stop him even though I told him, no and tried to leave. I felt so ashamed because, even though he forced himself on me, I had to admit, it turned me on.

I had another breakdown and ended up back in the hospital, this time for a week. I had some therapy and got better with no medication at all. My mother demanded they put me back on Lithium, even though I had recovered without it. Lucky me, they refused, even though she went so far as to refuse to pick me up from the hospital unless I was medicated. After all the years of her mental abuse, she forced me to sign a contract to come back home. I was given a big list of rules including the fact that no verbal abuse of family members would be tolerated, but these rules did not apply to her? I also had to agree to talk to their therapist. My mother decided that I was schizophrenic, even though that was never an official diagnosis. I found the "Living With a Schizophrenic" book in her room. She told me it was my entire fault for all my mental problems, for not going out more and, if I didn't get my life together, they would have me committed again. I hated her guts, but at the same time all the years of being told something was wrong with me had taken its toll. I didn't know what was wrong with me, but I knew I was not the norm.

Soon after, my parents divorced and my mother moved out. I started to feel a little bit better. I got a job working retail which paid real low and I was treated lousy, but I had to work so my parents could no longer completely run my life. Being treated like crap from store management, customers and my family was turning me into a monster. I stopped noticing the nice customers and became infuriated by the rude ones. I lost control and told off customers and management. I just did not give a damn. I started smoking pot all the time. Then I graduated to crystal meth. I loved it since it kills your appetite and gives you such a strong high, and most of *the time I was depressed. The only reason I stopped was my friend refused to provide me with it any longer and I was unable to find someone that could.*

I went back to school and got my degree and moved on to an office job. Things seemed to be okay until July 2001. Two people who claimed they loved me had turned their backs on me, even though I kind of deserved it. Anyway, I tried to move on with my life. I met a guy who started out as a dream, but then turned out to be a nightmare. He looked straight in my eyes and told me he loved me. He promised he would not hurt me and asked me to be his girlfriend. He even talked about marriage and having kids with me. The moment he thought I loved him, he showed his true colors very quickly. He demanded to know my whereabouts every second of the day. He complained that I needed to lose weight, even though he was overweight, as well and, even though I had lost weight since I had met him. He was demanding, verbally abusive, possessive and basically a jerk. I was so disappointed. After all of his lies about how much he loved me, he finally admitted he didn't, and that we had to go our separate ways and that we could not even be friends. I was disgusted with myself for having wasted my time on such a rotten demented jerk when, if I had more confidence/respect in myself in the first place, I would not have given him the time of day.

Over the course of one year, I sunk into the deepest darkest hole of my life. All of the stress, anxiety and rejection had taken its toll. I did not realize how badly off I was until it was almost too late. I stopped going out except to go to work. My social anxiety was at its worst. I hated people and wanted to be left alone. I would not even go to the door to pay for my own pizza, I would make my sister do it. I started to wish that I did not exist and was furious at the powers that be for even putting me here in the first place. Now I know you should be careful what you ask for.

My whole life was about just going to work, movies, music and video games. I was alone way too much. Once again, I stopped eating and sleeping and knew it would not be long before I ended up back in the hospital. I went and saw a shrink who gave me a Zoloft prescription and sleeping pills. I had already been told that I now had "Social Anxiety Disorder" but that nice little blue pills make it all better, provided you take them for the rest of your life, of course. What choice did I have?

I had earlier learned about Gary Spivey on the radio station I listened to and decided to have a session with him. I had met him once before and thought that maybe he could help. After all, none of the shrinks or pills or quack therapists had ever done anything for me but gives me pills and a lot of tags always ending in the word, "disorder."

I asked Gary about the Keys to Heaven that I had heard him talk about on the radio. Gary said that, once you have the keys to heaven, you can see God and be healed from all physical, mental and emotional illness. Believe me, I needed a healing. He said that to receive the key, all I had to do was believe, without a doubt, that I could receive it and then ask God for it. Gary then walked me through the steps on how to receive my key to heaven. It was the equivalent of the ultimate baptism. Although I could not see what he could see, I did see a lot of light. He went through and got rid of all the Demons that had me blocked for so long. He said that God "fixed me" and that, in his opinion, I no longer needed my pills. Gary also reminded me that he is not a doctor so I should consult my physician on how to wean myself off of them. He also told me about how those pills block your light and make you numb and dumb to the physical and spiritual worlds. I wasn't surprised at all. So, I weaned myself off my pills over the time period of almost a year. As of April 2005, I'm off them completely.

I feel so alive now and believe myself to be cured from all of the so called mental disorders that I have suffered with my whole life. The only disorder I really had was that I needed to meditate.

Thanks Gary, for showing me how to remove the Demons that have been with me for my whole life creating these disorders. No matter what I have gone through or what I will go through, for the first time I know I'm going to be alright. I have never felt this way before. I can now move on with my life. Through the power of the mind, through meditation, through God and a little guidance from Gary, I've finally been set free. I cannot believe it. It sounds so corny and unlike me, but I know what it's like to be born again.

So, in hindsight, I just wanted to share my story which I have kept inside for so long. Even though some of my closest friends do not know the contents of this letter, I feel the need to write it down and give thanks to the people who were there for me: Gary Spivey, JV, Elvis and Hollywood (the radio show, The Doghouse) that was there for me even when I had nothing else to look forward to in the morning. They always talked about the seven basic principals that we should live by, that I now try to live by, as well. I share this with them since they always put their lives out there on the table and have helped me more than words can say. It may do their hearts some good to know how much they helped someone out. What you've given me is priceless.

I never thought I would owe my life to God, a radio show, a psychic and, the biggest shock of all, myself.

In Gina's case, she had a lot of Demons causing many problems in her life. She was using drugs that were legal and illegal, she was depressed, she thought about killing herself, she had social anxiety, and finally a nervous breakdown. All I did was remove her Demons, then I took her to heaven where God finished her healing.

Everyone's problems/illness will not be the same, but the cure is always the same; get rid of the Demons and dark energies causing the problems/illness and go to heaven so God can heal you.

Testimonial by Jayne Baer

About five years ago, I heard Gary Spivey on the radio and I decided that I needed to see him. My daughter was really struggling; she was getting into trouble at school, and she was also having a very hard time concentrating and sitting still at school. She could not keep any of her friends because she was very loud and bossy. By the time she got home at night, she would be very angry and frustrated. So she was a very angry and unhappy child. Ashlyn (age 9) basically thought that she could not do anything right and that no one liked her.

Ashlyn had seen several doctors and tried many medications although none of the medications ever worked, they only created more issues. She's been diagnosed with ADHD, Oppositional Defiance Disorder, Asperger Syndrome and many other speculated diagnoses over the last several years.

The night I went to see Gary, I brought my daughter to see if I could get some sort of insight as to what I could do to help her. I was at my wits end on how to help her. This is our story of what took place the night we met with Gary.

We met with Gary and he started to tell me some things about myself and some of my life situations and I said that my life is not what I am concerned about right now. I asked that he work with my daughter.

When Gary started to check Ashlyn to see what was going on, he said that she was very spiritually gifted and that she was able to see into the spiritual dimensions. Gary said that she would not even know about these dimensions unless she was spiritual gifted. As Gary worked with her on clearing the negative energy, he started to see that she had many spiritual gifts. He told me that she could hear, see and feel spirits. Gary asked me if she would get real hot at night when she would go to sleep. I told him that she was always very hot and, at night, you could never keep the covers or even pajamas on her. Even in the winter, she would wear summer clothes. That is when Gary told me that the reason she was so hot was because she was such a bright light in the spirit world that the Angels would surround her at night to protect her.

Gary tapped into Ashlyn's energy and found that Ashlyn was hearing voices in her head. He said that it sounded like a crowded room. That is when he discovered that she had 96 earth-bound spirits attached to her and they were all simultaneously talking to her and telling her to do things. Gary sent all 96 spirits to the light. When he sent one of the spirits to the light, he looked at me and said, "Did you feel that?"

I said that I got the chills from that one.

He told me that it was a very angry spirit and that it was cussing at him the whole time he was trying to send him to the light. When he finished, he asked Ashlyn if she heard anything else in her head and she said that it was quiet.

Then Gary said to Ashlyn that there is someone here who wants to talk to you. So Gary said, "Close your eyes and look up. Do you see the light?" She said, yes and he said, "Keep looking up, do you see someone?" Ashlyn then said, yes and she got a big smile on her face. It was Archangel Michael who wanted to talk to her. Michael then said to Ashlyn to reach up, "I have a gift for you." He then gave her a sword and told her to store it in her chest/heart. She asked, "What is it for?" and he said that it is to get rid of the Demons or anything negative. Gary then explained to Ashlyn that the Sword of Michael is one of the best spiritual gifts you can receive. Then Gary said to Ashlyn, "Let me show you how to use it." He told her to look down and she saw a serpent at her feet and he said, "Hit it with your sword," and it exploded. Gary told her to use it whenever she needed to and, when she didn't need it, to keep it stored in her chest.

Then Ashlyn looked at me and said, "Your mom (her grandmother) is here." Ashlyn never met my mother because she had passed over before she was born. Gary said, "Yes, she is here." And he then asked Ashlyn what her grandmother was wearing and she said that she had on a red dress and that she was showing her a room full of shoes. Then my mother went over to Ashlyn and kissed her on the cheek and told her, "I love ya."

Then Gary asked Ashlyn to tell him some things about some of his friends. He would say someone's name and ask her to tell him something about them. I don't remember their names, so I will make up these names.

Gary said, "Tell me something about Jeff." Ashlyn said, "He is really funny." Then Gary asked her about a couple and he said, "Tell me something about them." And she said, "They are going to get married." Gary asked her about several other friends and Ashlyn told him about every one of them. Gary said, "Your daughter is as gifted as I am, except that she doesn't understand it yet." He said that when she is 14 or so it would start to make some sense and that, when she is around 18, she would really start to understand it more completely. Gary also shared with me that the reason she was having trouble in school was because she was traveling out of her body during school. She was also bored and she couldn't comprehend today's teaching techniques.

After our session with Gary, Ashlyn was having less trouble at home and in school. She was learning how to deal with some of the negative energy that was always trying to attach to her. To this day, Ashlyn (now 14) is still off all medications.

About three years ago, we went to a concert to see "The Back Street Boys" with thousands of young people. When we first arrived, the energy was very high and crazy. Ashlyn started to freak out. I had to pull her aside and ask, "What is going on?" She told me that she was freaking out because so many people had Demons on them that it scared her. I gently reminded her to take her spiritual gift out of her chest and to help everyone out and bonk them so they would disappear. So then that calmed her down and, as we were walking by people, she would gently raise the sword in her hand and bonk them on the head. Then she would see the Demon disappear and she would calm down more and more, then she felt better.

There have been so many times that Ashlyn knows what I am going to say before I say it. I sometimes ask her a question and she will tell me the answer before I ask it. For instance, I just got remarried and I was worried that she would not like me getting married again because she was used to having me more to herself. One day I said to her, "I have a question." And she said, "Yes, Mom. I know that you and Thomas are going to get married." Then she even told me where and the time frame.

Ashlyn constantly knows what I am thinking or what is going to happen. She also experiences more things than she shares with me because she feels that I won't understand.

About four years ago, I came home one night and I was talking to her about ascension. I was telling her about what I had just learned that night and she looked at me and said, "I already know that, Mom. ArchAngel Michael taught me that last week when I was sleeping."

Love and Blessings,
Jayne Baer

Jayne's daughter, Ashlyn, was diagnosed with many disorders including ADHD, Oppositional Defiance Disorder, Asperger Syndrome and many other speculated diagnoses over the last several years. She was prescribed different medications for each disorder.

This is where I get angry because this beautiful child has nothing wrong with her except that she is spiritually gifted and misunderstood.

We, as a society, don't have a clue as to what's going on with children and adults like Ashlyn. As I said before in this book, it's not anyone's fault that these people are diagnosed with these disorders because, until now, no one really knew that all of these problems are not physical but spiritual. I believe there is a spiritual cure for all of our physical problems. The cure is to use your spiritual gifts to remove the Demons causing the problems, fill your spiritual and physical body with God energy/light, clear the spiritual dimensions and visit God in heaven. If you do this every day, you will not have any physical problems.

We are all spiritual beings living in physical bodies and, until society realizes this and until people start to take care of their spiritual bodies, then they will always treat every problem they have as a physical problem and keep taking drugs.

The only problem Ashlyn had was that she was born into this physical world with her soul already unlocked and we, as a society, are not advanced enough in our thinking to understand and accept this.

Testimonial by Tina and Richard Zamora

My husband was outside one day working in the yard when he felt this pain radiating from his inner thigh. He thought he pulled a muscle or something, and didn't think twice about it. A few days later, the pain began going down his leg to his knee. Within seven days, his whole leg was in severe pain, and the swelling was unbelievable. His leg was so swollen, it looked like the skin was going to rip open.

He went to a physician, who immediately sent him to an infectious disease doctor. This doctor ran tests, but could not find a thing. He went back to his doctor and was sent to have a Doppler ultrasound. They suspected he had a DVT (deep vein thrombosis), which could be life threatening. This, too, was negative. He did two more of these tests, as the doctors all suspected they must have missed something. He had MRIs, nerve tests, and saw seven more doctors, ranging from primary care to Neurologists. And still, NOTHING. He was put on disability, and started going to physical therapy treatment, which caused the swelling and pain to persist.

After a year of jumping through hoops, the disability ended. Of course, I don't have to tell you how stressful this situation was for us all with a mortgage, three kids and an unknown medical condition. The mental strain was incredible.

One morning on my way to work, Gary was on a radio station, and I thought I'd give it a try. Unbelievably, I got through the lines and asked Gary if he could tell me what is going on with my husband. He immediately began to tell me that he should begin meditating and project positive energy and he would feel better. Well, this was very early in my spiritual journey, and I just didn't understand what he was talking about. I just dismissed this out of my mind.

Maybe about a year after this initial conversation with Gary, I began to seek spiritual answers. I began meditation and have been given the gift of being able to speak with my deceased grandmother.

Gary, again, was on a radio station and I heard that he was having a workshop. My husband and I were not able to pay for the workshop, but the DJ, JV announced that Gary was going to do a healing with some of the listeners prior to the workshop.

I called and spoke to Ruthie, JV's assistant, and asked her if she could ask JV and Gary if we could go to the healing session. I told her a little bit about my husband's problems. At this point, he found it hard to walk. Ruthie called me back and said that we could meet early in the morning of July 25, 2003.

When the healing for Richard began, Gary asked me to touch his heart. I could see all of these black (kind of like bread twist tie) things falling from him. While my eyes were closed, it felt like my eyeballs were just bouncing around like tennis balls. I couldn't control them. I saw so many lights and colors surrounding him. This beautiful emerald green color just completely covered *his entire leg, then his whole body. Gary was surprised that I was explaining what he saw, and told me that I, too, have the gift of clairvoyance and healing, as well as my husband.*

Gary explained that my husband actually had two damaged discs in his back, and they were damaging his sciatic nerve. After all this time, I was hoping that God could help my husband because all of the physicians could not. My husband could barely sit in the chair, as it always causes great pain to his leg. After Gary, Dean, Nils, JV and myself worked on healing my husband, the tears began to flow. Gary explained that, when a healing takes place, all the people around will get teary eyed. That is how I knew my husband was healed. When my husband stood up, he said he felt immediate relief on the spot. He had no pain.

Richard's healing was a few months ago and he just finished ripping out and pouring concrete in our backyard!! (This was a man who had pain when he walked and could not play with his kids!!)

Our whole family would like to thank you, Gary, Nils, Dean and JV for being able to share your wonderful gift with us. It is hard to express just how great this has been. I can't tell you how wonderful the feeling of getting connected is. It's kind of like when you were a teenager and in love for the first time. That's exactly how I feel EVERYDAY!!

Thank You!
    We are believers.
    Tina and Richard Zamora

In Richard's case, he damaged his physical body. He damaged two disks in his back that were pinching his sciatic nerve. When our physical bodies gets damaged, we can heal them. The doctors could not stop the pain by treating the physical body with drugs, but by treating the physical body with spiritual gifts, we were able to heal Richard. In

Richard's case, he had faith and wanted to be healed and everyone around him wanted him to be healed and also had faith, so he was healed.

I would like to give a special thanks to J.V. first for being one of my best friends and for his continued support by allowing me to be a guest on his radio show. Secondly, for taking the necessary steps in his own spiritual discovery. As he found his spiritual way, he shared his experiences with his listeners and helped enlighten hundreds of thousands of people with his own bright light.

Testimonial by Dawn Miller

Gary,

When I talked to you in October of 2003, my husband and I were trying to conceive for over a year and nothing was working. All the doctors told us to keep trying, that nothing was wrong, try using the temperature method, but things were not working.

When I talked to you, you took one look at my body and told me that both my tubes were blocked—one at the top and one at the bottom and that, if the doctors would just clean out my tubes, then I would get pregnant immediately.

On my next visit to the doctors in December, I asked them to clean out my tubes and they decided to schedule me for a Laparoscopy. The procedure was done in January of 2004. The doctor stated that, for sure one tube was blocked and the other could have been blocked, but that they could not confirm it. The great news is that one month later, in February 2004, I conceived and, on October 26, 2004, I had my baby girl.

I truly appreciate you from the bottom of my heart.
Thank you,
Dawn

In Dawn's case, she and her husband wanted to have a baby, but nothing was working, so they came to me hoping I could help. I used my spiritual eyes and looked at her body and noticed Demons and dark energy in her tubes. I got rid of the Demons, but my Angels told me her tubes were blocked. When Dawn returned to the doctors, she had the doctors clean out her tubes and she became pregnant.

We all have the ability to look into our physical bodies and see where the dark energy or Demons are. We can remove the Demons, but sometimes they have already caused a physical problem and this is where doctors come in handy.

Testimonial by Tammy Emerick

Last year in Nashville, I had a personal reading with you.

At the time, I asked you about my mother's brain aneurism, which she was diagnosed with ten months prior. She had decided not to have the surgery due to the risks involved. She was 65 years old. You indicated that, if she did not have the surgery, she would die. You stated that the wall was very thin—less than paper thin. You felt that it was a lot worse than the doctors were saying.

I nervously told my mother about the reading and she actually went back to the doctor and they immediately scheduled the surgery for the following month (the doctor just happened to have a cancellation). After the surgery, the neurosurgeon came out and told us that the wall was much thinner than he thought and, had he known, he would have told her to have the surgery a year ago. He stated that it had already turned red, which meant that it could easily burst.

My family has you to thank for keeping our mother around for many more years.

I cannot begin to express our gratitude.
Thank you very much.
Tammy

Tammy came to me for a reading and, when she asked me about her mom's brain aneurism, I used my spiritual eyes to look at it and noticed that it was a lot worse than the doctors realized. I saw many little Demons and some dark energy around it, so I removed them, but the damage to her physical body had already been done. Again, this is where I did my job by removing the Demons and dark energies and by reading just how serious her condition was, and the doctors certainly did there job by operating immediately to save her life.

Think for a moment how the world would benefit if every doctor in the world was trained how to diagnose patients spiritually as well as scientifically. I bet the number of malpractice deaths and misdiagnoses would drop dramatically.

Testimonial by Mary Anne

My name is Mary Anne and I am the most logical, down-to-earth person you will ever meet, and making the decision to call Gary Spivey was the best thing I have ever done. Thanks to Gary, I saved my niece, Jenna, from spending an eternity earthbound and trapped in a hellish dimension.

Jenna died unexpectedly at the age of 17. No one knew what happened and we were convinced that she was murdered. The pain was unbearable and I knew I needed to find out the truth. I had heard Gary on a radio show the year before and was amazed by his ability. I never believed that anyone could talk to the dead until I heard Gary. Still, my decision to call him was not a hasty one. But thank goodness I did. An appointment was made for him to call me on October 18, 2002.

Gary called me and immediately explained he had an Angel talking to him. I asked him if I could put my sister, Donna, on the other line and he said, "No." He would speak to her separately if she had questions. But, as he was trying to explain his reasoning for this, he suddenly stopped and said that the Angel that was speaking to him said Donna should get on the other phone and he should speak with both of us together.

The only information I gave to Gary was that I wanted to speak to Jenna, who died on September 9, 2002 and that she was 17 years old. He immediately told me that she was still earthbound, but that he could save her. At first, I didn't understand what he meant but I quickly realized that this was a horrible place to be. Jenna was stuck in those last minutes before she died. Gary was able to summon the light so that Jenna could enter and be carried to Heaven by an Angel. He told Donna and me to tell Jenna to go to the light and we did. Several times we said, "Jenna, go to the light. We love you, go to the light." After about a minute, which seemed like an eternity, Jenna went to the light. Gary told us that she was in the light and the Angel had her. I suddenly felt a very warm, almost hot but cozy, sensation in my chest. I thought it was just from the emotion, but then Gary asked if we felt the warm feeling. Much to my surprise, Donna and I both answered, yes. (Donna was in another room at the time and we could not see each other.) Gary then told us that the Angel came back to tell us that Jenna said she loves us. This surprised Gary and he said that never happens. Once an Angel begins the journey with someone, they don't come back, but knowing Jenna the way I do, she was probably very insistent and the Angel figured the trip would be much too long without granting her this wish. It was at that moment that I knew everything was going to be okay. While we waited for Jenna to make her journey, Gary told us what he saw on the day she died. He knew so much even though I told him so little. The bottom line for us was that Jenna committed suicide. (This was confirmed a week later by the autopsy report.)

Gary suddenly asked Donna if her husband, who had died, had problems with his chest or lungs. (We never told him that she was widowed.) Her husband, Bubba, was speaking to him. He was telling Gary to tell her he was doing GREAT. He then showed Gary an older woman whom Gary described as "smelling like fresh baked biscuits or bread." We immediately asked if this was our grandma and he said that Bubba was shaking his head, yes! Our spirits immediately lifted and we began a light banter with Gary as our mediator. With the information he gave us, there was no doubt in our minds that he was speaking to them. Grandma started to cry and said that they were waiting for their baby girl (Jenna) and that she would take good care of her. Gary said the emotion felt from her was incredibly strong. She was crying and he was barely able to relay her message to us. He feels everything they feel and his voice was shaking.

It wasn't long after this that Jenna passed through to the other side. She went straight into the arms of my grandma, which was her great grandma. Gary was once again amazed at this sight. He has seen very few people pass over to the other side directly into the arms of family. To me, this just confirms the strong bond between our family.

I truly believe I was destined to phone Gary Spivey. I had no idea what was going to happen when I called, but I know now that it was meant to be. God knew he wasn't able to save Jenna from herself, but he didn't want her to suffer for eternity and, through this phone call, Donna and I were able to save her.

Thank You.
Gary, you have a truly amazing gift.

In this case, Mary Anne wanted to know if her niece was doing okay after her death, but, much to her surprise, she was not. Jenna, Mary Anne's niece, had committed suicide and was stuck earthbound. I asked the Angels to come down and get her so she would go to heaven where she belonged.

I can't stress enough not to kill yourself because you will not make it to heaven unless someone can see you stuck earthbound and that someone asks the Angels to come and get you or if someone you love prays for you a lot.

Testimonial by Cheryl Cohen

It was summer, 1998. Chris had lived in his new home for about one year. He was so proud to own his first home at age 18. Everything was going quite well for him that year.

Just before Memorial Day, his grandmother passed away at age 86. After this happened, everything seemed normal for a few weeks. One night about 3 a.m., Chris called me on the phone. He was terrified. I asked him what was wrong. He replied, "Mom, I just saw something hovering over my bed. It woke me up! It was holding me down, I couldn't move!" I said, "What do you think it was?" Chris answered, "It looked like a ghost! It was even screaming at me, in a really high pitched voice!"

After this episode, I began to do some research on ghosts. I came to the conclusion that the ghost Chris saw was a Banshee ghost. This type of spirit usually appears either just before or just after someone dies. When Chris first told me this, I thought he just had a bad dream, until I did research. Then I knew what he was describing was very real.

Nothing else happened for at least one year. We had just about forgotten about the appearance of the Banshee ghost. Then one night my phone rang at about 3:30 am. When I answered the phone, it was Chris. I could sense the fear in his voice. I said, "What's wrong?" He replied, "Mom, something keeps waking me up and it is touching me! I can feel the presence of something in my bedroom!" As the days went by, these episodes became more and more frequent.

It got down to where Chris was calling me every night between the hours of 3 a.m. and 6 a.m.; complaining about something was touching him. Chris called me one night and said, "Mom it feels like something is trying to have sex with me. It feels just like a woman." When he told me this, I became concerned. I had some knowledge of the paranormal already. I knew that what Chris was

describing, he had no knowledge. I suggested that Chris
keep his camera in bed with him and, when these spirits
started bothering him, start taking pictures of them. This
is what Chris did. Every time he thought they were
present, he began taking random photographs. I felt
that, even though he couldn't see the spirits, they might
show up on film. When we got the first roll of film
developed, we could not believe our eyes!

In one photograph, there was a man standing
through Chris' waterbed. It looked to me that he was
wearing an old military uniform. Another photograph
revealed an Indian woman sitting in the mirror. He was
actually able to capture spirits attacking him. There was
a Demon-looking creature reaching down toward Chris.
In the background of this photograph, there were several
faces of strange looking creatures. It appeared that they
were watching the attack. Yet another photograph
showed a white tiger lying on Chris' bed.

Things seemed to be getting stranger by the day.
The more I examined these photographs, the more faces
and images I was able to see. I reached the point of not
knowing what to do next. I was getting really frustrated.
I knew that Chris was having a genuine problem, and
was worried for his safety.

In the meantime, I began looking on the Internet for
some help. I found several paranormal investigators that
told me what he was describing was paranormal activity.
The spirits that were trying to have sex with Chris, were
Demons. I tried for about three years to get someone to
come to Chris' house and get rid of these spirits. The
paranormal investigators that I contacted either lived
too far away, or didn't know what to do about Demons.
Most of them were also afraid to deal with Demons.

Once I began looking for help, these spirits started
attacking me while I was asleep. They would wake me
up and hold me down. When I was on the Internet
looking for help, they would either disrupt my Internet
service, or they would make the door open; then slam

shut on my computer. They did this repeatedly. The first time it happened, I almost fell out of my chair! Almost every time I was on the phone with an investigator, we would get disconnected. The spirits made it very obvious to me that they didn't want me to find any help.

There was only one person left for me to turn to. I began to pray to God for help. I also asked Him to protect Chris. I feel that Chris is a vulnerable person because of his medical condition. He has had a seizure disorder since he was 6 years old. I believed what he had been telling me; because he was describing things he knew nothing about. I even asked one paranormal investigator, why this was happening to Chris. He has never done anything bad. The investigator, who is also a psychic, said that Chris is a spirit magnet; she also said that Chris has a very strong sixth sense. This is why he always knew when the spirits were present, and could feel them making contact with him. It is also the reason he was always able to capture them on film.

One day, I was listening to the radio, KLUC in Las Vegas, and I heard Spence announce: "If you have any problems with haunting, call in now. We are going to do a radio show on the most haunted house in Las Vegas, with Gary Spivey." Not thinking anything about what I had just heard, I called in. For some odd reason, I was able to get through. I told Wendy Jo, the producer, about Chris' problems. She was very interested in our story, and told me to send her a detailed email about what had been happening. This is what I did. I also sent her some of the photographs Chris had taken. I really never expected them to pick our story.

The next morning, on my way to work, I was listening to KLUC again. As I was driving, I heard Amy begin reading the email I sent them the night before. I was so excited, I began shaking! Right after Amy read the email, Spence said, "This is the house we are going to do.

This is the most haunted house in Las Vegas! We are all going to spend the night in this house. Friday morning, Gary Spivey will conduct a live séance and get rid of these spirits"

Shortly after this announcement, they contacted me, and we set everything up for the same week. Gary Spivey came to Chris' house on Thursday, October 24, 2002. I was really excited to meet Gary and his assistants Nils, and Dean.

Gary really seemed eager to help us. Finally, my prayers were being answered! As soon as Gary arrived, he told me that a spirit started punching him in the chest as he was approaching Chris' house. It was obvious that these spirits didn't want him to help us, either. When Gary approached the back door of the house, there was an earthbound spirit cussing at him, telling him not to enter the house. The spirit's name was George. He apparently died of a heroin overdose, but didn't know he was dead. George claimed that the house belonged to him.

When Gary walked into the house, the first room he entered was the kitchen. He told us that there was an old woman cooking on a wood stove. The next room we were in was the living room. I told Gary that, when I would come into the house, I would get a very hostile feeling from the spirits just as I would get halfway up the stairs. While we were standing in the living room, Gary said, "This is the craziest house I've ever been in." He then told me to show him where I would start feeling the hostile feeling. Sometimes this feeling was so strong that I would just want to turn around and run out of the house. I proceeded up the stairs. When I stopped at the halfway mark I said to Gary, "This is the point where I feel like running." Gary replied, "You are standing in George's spirit."

Just as we all began walking up the stairs, we all were starting to get a headache. The first room we entered *upstairs was the master bedroom. Gary told us that there was an insane asylum there. Crazy people were there in straight jackets. Then Gary told us that there was also a nine-foot tall monster in the room and a man and a woman fist fighting on the floor. While we were in this room, Gary let these spirits enter his body. I could actually see Gary's face change to look like the spirit, as it appeared in life. The first spirit was an old black woman. The second was George. Then the nine-foot tall monster appeared. I could actually see the monster's fangs. Gary also informed us that this room had a vortex in it and this is how the spirits were-coming in.*

We then proceeded into the second bedroom. As I entered this room, I noticed that my legs began aching. I couldn't lift my feet off the floor! Gary said that this room actually had a hell hole in the center of it. There were hands coming up through the floor and grabbing our legs. I knew then, that was why my legs were aching and why I couldn't lift my feet off the floor.

In the third bedroom, Gary could see a little girl sitting on the floor. He said that she was an earthbound spirit also. When we started leaving the room, she began to cry. She didn't want us to go.

As a result of Gary's investigation, he revealed that there were over one hundred spirits and Demons in the house. He also told me that it was the most haunted house he has ever seen.

Once the investigation was complete, we all had to go to sleep. Knowing about all of the spirits that were present, how could anybody sleep? Needless to say, no one got much sleep that night.

Friday morning came and it was time for Gary to conduct the séance. We all sat in a circle holding hands in the master bedroom, since that was the most haunted room in the house.

Once Gary started the séance, weird things started happening. He was able to make these spirits appear.

During the séance, all of us began to get nauseous, at the same time. Enforcer had to leave the room to check the microphones, since we were broadcasting a live radio show. When he re-entered the room, I saw him fall to the floor, hitting his head. Something had knocked him down. Gary said that two really black Demons kicked him, therefore, making him fall. Enforcer had passed out as a result of this attack.

Gary sent all of the earthbound spirits to the light. Right after he did this, the room turned a green color and became very hot. The temperature in the room had increased by about thirty degrees. Since there was no heat in the house, I knew it was caused by what Gary had just done.

Gary sent all of the Demons away and began to close the vortex, as well as the hell hole. When he did this, the vortex began doing something very strange. I could actually see the air full of colors—spinning around us in the room. It almost looked like one of those spinning tables you would use to paint-shirts or make spin art designs with.

Immediately after the séance, a very pleasant stillness came over the house. It felt so calm and soothing; I knew Gary had removed all of the spirits that had taken over Chris' home.

Things got so bad for Chris before Gary came that he finally had to move in with me. The spirits would keep him up all night long. It became impossible for him to get any sleep.

After the séance was over, I asked Gary if he could try to heal Chris' medical condition. Chris' seizures had gotten so severe that he was having one to three seizures every week: His seizures could never be controlled on any medication the doctors tried. Gary spent a few minutes working with Chris.

The next day, Chris started feeling better. Three weeks went by and Chris didn't have any seizures. Chris began cutting back on his medication to see if he would *have any more seizures. He was down to one-fourth of his normal dose when he finally had one seizure. He immediately went back on his normal dosage*

To this day, Chris has not had any more seizures. Although he still has a seizure disorder, it is now being controlled by medications. This was never possible before Gary worked with him.

Recently, I took Chris to his doctor and she decided to completely take him off of one of his medications. She now believes that Chris doesn't need to take as much medicine as he did before.

Chris is now feeling better and acting better than he ever did before. He is gradually becoming more and more functional. He doesn't feel sick from the medicine anymore.

I thank God for answering my prayers, and for bringing Gary Spivey into our lives. I don't feel that this happened, just by chance. Out of all of the people in the world, Gary is the only one that could actually get rid of all the spirits that were haunting Chris. I think that it was these spirits that were causing Chris so many medical problems.

Now I know why they call Gary Spivey "The World's Greatest Psychic." But he's much more than that, he really is. He has touched our lives in a way that no one else ever could. I just can't thank him enough, for what he has done.

UPDATE FOR CHRISTOPHER

After Gary Spivey came to Chris' house and cleared all of the hundreds of spirits out of his house, he did some spiritual healing on Chris. Since Chris was 6 years old, he has suffered with severe seizures, due to a doctor's overdose of asthma medication.

We saw Gary on two other occasions, when he came to Las Vegas—since the time he came out here to clear Chris' house. Each time we saw Gary, he performed spiritual healing on Chris,

We are very proud to say that Chris has not had any more seizures since the last time we saw Gary. He has been seizure-free for almost three years now, and is only taking half a dose of seizure medication. He is now able to live a normal life. He was recently given a release to get a driver's license, and he has gotten a really good job. For the first time in his life, he is free!

Occasionally, Chris still has spirits bothering him, but it is nothing like it used to be. Chris has the ability to see spirits, and the spirits know it. He is like a spirit magnet. We give Gary Spivey and God the credit for stopping Chris' seizures. The doctor doesn't even know why the seizures stopped. We told her that they stopped after the last time Gary worked with Chris. She was amazed. You did it again, Gary!! I wish there was a way to repay you for all that you've done for us. This is why they call you the "World's Greatest Psychic." You have earned that title, in our eyes.

We love you Gary, and will always keep you in our hearts.

Sincerely,
Cheryl Cohen
Chris Maglish

In Chris' case, he was being possessed by many Demons that were actually crossing over from the spiritual to the physical dimensions. As weird as this may sound, this is a regular occurrence in many people's lives.

Not only was Chris being attacked by Demons physically, they were also attacking his spiritual body causing health problems. I removed the Demons from his house and also from him. After I removed the Demons from his house, he started having a more normal life at home. Once the Demons from his spiritual and physical body were removed, he was able to stop having seizures, take less medication, and now he has a driver's license and a good job.

I know I sound repetitive, but if you remove the Demons from your life, your life can and will change instantly.

Testimonial by Melissa Haro

Not long ago, I had a session with Gary. The first thing he noticed was that there were Demons all around me causing me to be depressed. I was amazed at how quickly he noticed my depression because, before I met Gary, I was always depressed, and swore that there was a ghost or Demon always following me around. I refuse to be alone in a dark place. I was terrified of the feeling that someone was always looking at me. Now that is all gone

After removing the many depressing Demons from around my head, Gary told me to close my eyes. (Through this whole journey I didn't tell Gary anything. I didn't tell him what I felt or saw.) He told me to imagine a big door, so I imagined a huge gold door big enough for a diesel truck to drive through. He said that the door I saw was too big and to bring myself up to that size. As I imagined it, he said, "There you go." The next thing he told me to do was to ask God for the key to heaven. So, with my eyes closed, I looked up and said, "God, may I please have the key to heaven?" And there it was, right in front of me.

I took the key in my hand and put it into the keyhole in the door. I began to open the door. My face and chest were still hot from removing the Demons and letting the light back in, but, as I opened the door, a very hot light came through making me even warmer. Even though the light was hot and bright, it didn't hurt and I didn't have to strain my eyes to see. I walked in, closing the door behind me. In front of me there was a relatively long bridge. Gary told me to walk across it, so I began to step on it, but couldn't help myself and I began to run across. Gary said with a chuckle, "Wow you're running across." At the other end of the bridge there was another gold door. With the same key, I opened the door.

The inside was breathtakingly beautiful. Everything looked white and soft. Over yonder, I could see the golden tops of castles—it looked a little bit like Disneyland. Gary told me to look to my right. Sitting on the floor was a very familiar face. It was Buddha. Gary told me that he sees me running over and hugging Buddha and I was. Buddha told Gary that we're great friends and we go way back. While I was hugging him, I felt extreme comfort almost like a baby being held in the arms of its father. Buddha said there is a blue key in my chest. Gary told me to turn around. He asked if I could see the big round thing which looked like a huge moon setting over the softness of heaven. Gary told me it was the earth. Suddenly, I was floating next to Gary in outer space. I took the key out of my chest, as Gary said to do, and put it into the center of the world. Beautiful rainbows and bright lights began shooting out of the earth and swirling around space. My eyes started to fill with tears of happiness, even though I had no idea what was going on. Gary brought me back into heaven and told me that Buddha had put the key in my chest a long time ago. That's why I had so many Demons attacking me; they didn't want me to find my key. That night, when I put the key into the earth, I had helped the world. I also know that I am not done helping the world, there is much more that I need to do.

Back in heaven, Gary took me over to meet Jesus. He hugged me and then I turned around where I saw a shimmering lake. Gary told me that there are white dolphins in the lake and I could come back whenever I want and swim with them. He said that they will heal me. On the other side of the lake was a man with long white hair and a white robe. He smiled and I walked across the lake. Gary told me that he was God. He put his arms around me and I started crying. An unexplainable feeling of love, comfort, happiness, joy, passion and every good emotion that a human can feel rushed into my body and exploded in my heart. I never wanted to let go and, in a way, I haven't.

Gary told me to turn around again and look across the lake. There was an Angel standing on the other side of the lake. She was glowing. Her wings were so stunning. The closer I got, the better I could see her. Finally, I reached her and she looked just like me; just as Gary said she would. She wrapped her wings around me and put her feet on top of mine. Her feet disappeared into mine. Then the rest of her body entered mine becoming one with me. My Angel is now a part of me guiding me and protecting me everyday. And now I have the wings I prayed for as a little girl. I looked around and there were hundreds of Angels smiling at me and God was by me once again.

Gary told me that I am a special soul, as is everyone who enters heaven, and God has gifts to give to me. He placed different colors of lights on me. He put a crown on my head and then put lots of gold bars in my arms. God joked around saying, "I can't give her too much to carry, she might break the bridge," he laughed. I thanked everyone and gave them all hugs good bye. I went back through the gold doors and across the bridge. When I got outside of heaven, I put the gold key in my chest so I could visit heaven all I want.

Later in my reading, I wanted to know if my uncle, who had passed, was okay. Gary took me back into heaven. It was much faster the second time. There my uncle was dancing around. I have never seen him so happy. After hanging up with Gary, I went to talk to my mom. I am a Christian and I had never been introduced to the Buddhist religion until I was older and had made friends with people who were part of that religion. My mom had told me that, when I was a little girl, she took me into a shop where people got their nails done. On a shelf there was a statue of Buddha and I shocked her when I turned to her and said, "Mommy is that Buddha?"

It has been a few weeks now since I talked to Gary. I have never been so happy, helpful, proud, giving, not depressed, and most of all loving. Gary, I want to thank you for all you did for me. By helping me, you helped *everyone around me as well. I am very grateful for you and please continue to change people's lives the way you changed mine. I wanted to tell you that I went back to heaven by myself the following night. I was able to fly around. Every culture I have ever known and more were inside those castles. It was wonderful and we are all really children of God, no matter who we are.*

Last night I listened to your spiritual gift CD. God gave me two blue balls. I held them out in front of me and a stick appeared between them. I pushed them together and then pulled them apart and there was a screen of light and I could see the Angel inside of me.

Thank You,
Melissa Haro

Melissa had a few Demons causing depression and fear but, after removing them, her depression and fear was gone. After I removed her Demons, I walked her through-step-by-step on how to enter heaven. She saw Buddha, Jesus, God, her Angel and her uncle who passed away.

Everyone on earth has the ability to accomplish what Melissa accomplished. It's really that simple. If you want to get rid of your Demons and go to heaven, don't think it over, just do it!

Testimonial by Eric

In meeting Gary, I have learned a lot, but three things really stand out. The first is that you get what you give. If you put out negative thoughts, your life will reflect that and the same is true for positive thoughts. This has helped me to stay in a positive frame of mind. The second is that there is no one truly mean or evil. When someone acts mean or cruel, it is because they are letting there Demons control them. When you see the world from this perspective, you can truly understand what Jesus meant by, "Love your enemy." It makes it easy to love and pray for everyone. The third thing is to always let your light and love shine in every situation of your life and you will make it through anything.

Peace, Love and Light.
Eric

In most of these testimonials, the one thing all these people had in common was that they or a loved one was possessed with Demons causing different problems in each of their lives.

In all these cases, the problems they encountered were more a spiritual problem than a physical, mental or emotional problem. Of course, our physical body suffers the affects of our spiritual problems. I taught them all how to fix their spiritual problem by getting rid of the Demons which, in turn, fixed their physical, mental and emotional problems. In a few cases, the spiritual problem had already manifested into a major physical problem and they had to go to the doctors for a tune up.

If you learn how to allow God's light into your spiritual/physical body and clear the spiritual dimensions, you can prevent your spiritual problems from becoming a physical, mental or emotional problem.

It's not the fault of these people, nor is it society's fault because, until now, no one was showing you the other side of the coin. We were only shown the physical side. Now that I've flipped the coin over and I've shown the world what's on the other side of the coin, we, as a society, have a responsibility to look at every physical, mental and emotional problem in every person as a spiritual problem first.

Treat the spiritual problem first and the physical, mental and emotional problem will go away.

I can talk about this forever. But, if you read this book and become an active participant, you know for yourself what the truth really is.

This is a testimonial from a good friend who uses the techniques he learned from attending my seminars and spiritual retreats in his every day life.

A Testimonial by Alex Hernandez

Gary,

I am writing to say, thank you for all you have done for me over the past few years.

When I first met you, life was not the greatest. I had just gotten out of a terrible psychologically damaging relationship. I wasn't very happy with myself, and I was very doubtful of myself, many times even feeling like I was crazy! After learning from you how Demons were blocking me and setting me up to fail, I realized that what I was feeling and experiencing was not really me, but these dark energies that were tricking me into thinking that I was crazy and insecure. After my first retreat with you, I was able to get rid of the dark energies myself and begin to manifest the things I wanted in my life, and rid myself of the things I didn't want. In these last two and half years, I have changed my life so dramatically that now I can do anything because I know how to have good intentions and ask God for spiritual gifts. After attending five or six retreats with you, I have come to realize that the short personal conversations that we have are so jam packed with truth and simple information that I don't need to spend thousands on seminars to learn anymore. I can simply apply what you have simply stated and I will have the result I want. If I have questions, you have also taught me how to see and hear God, so now I can ask God and he will either tell me or show me the answer. A good example of your simple statements is at the most recent retreat in June of 2005. You said the most profound simplified thing I have ever heard. It was, "So you think it, so it is," Now, realizing that our thoughts manifest our physical, I know that I don't need to understand the complicated science behind it, only that my thoughts literally manifest my experiences in life. By applying this simple approach alone, anyone can do anything.

Of all the retreats I have been to, the June 2005 was by far the most incredible! I believe it was on the second day of the retreat that you really took it to the next level by meditating in front of us-something you had never done. You had mentioned that you were attempting to meditate that morning, but God told you not to, so you could meditate in front of all of us. As you began to meditate, I noticed that my vision was getting blurry, or so I thought. As I attempted to adjust my eyes, I looked around and noticed many others doing the same- squinting and adjusting. I even felt like the room was shifting from all the energy. If I wouldn't have been there, I'm not sure that I would have believed it myself-you were becoming semi-transparent. Understanding a bit of science myself, I understand that, at an atomic level, we are composed of nothing. So, hypothetically, I understand that this is possible. But to witness it firsthand was absolutely unbelievably amazing! What happened next was the most incredible thing I have ever witnessed in my entire life! Your shape shifted into God! At this point, I had already been seeing God for about two years, so I knew what I was seeing. I was so spellbound that I sat astounded. Your hair changed, your face changed, a white beard and mustache and differentfacial features seemed to be imposed over your body! As I watched, I said nothing. About five pe'ople around me blurted out what I was thinking, so I knew that many others had seen it too! I remember a woman behind me out loud saying," Oh my God, he's turning into God." After a few minutes of witnessing this, I remember you explaining that what we were witnessing was you becoming one with God, and that when you were tapping into heaven that is what happens. I also remember a guy a few rows back from me saying that he saw you turn into Santa Claus, which I thought was hilarious. This was not only an amazing experience, but also a life-changing one. because now I have seen the "impossible" made possible!

Once again Gary, I just want you to know from the bottom of my heart that I owe you a debt of gratitude because I could have spent the rest of my life in darkness and unhappy because of Demons' tricks, as many people innocently and unknowingly do. I now have the choice of living the life I want to live because I can clear darkness, and ask for spiritual gifts that manifest into my life experiences! Thank you for everything!

Blessings, Alex Hernandez

San Jose, CA

A PERFECT WORLD

There is only light and dark.

You can choose a path of light or a path of dark. While the path of light may not always be the easiest or most profitable, if pursued long enough, there's always a rainbow and a pot of gold at the end. It may not be physical golden nuggets or money, but it is an inner peace, a communication and oneness with God. This has a value that is worth more than all of the gold and money in the world. A wealthy soul—wealthy in love, light and happiness—is all encompassing.

I'm asking you, why wouldn't everyone on earth want to join together as one as it is in heaven? While we may be different individuals in every way—religion, color, shape, size and lifestyles—everyone needs to recognize that our core soul, our center and our truth is all the same: We're all light beings. We're affected sometimes by the darkness that attacks and confuses our path, but, as long as we have light in our spiritual/physical bodies and we meditate and pray daily, we can expand that light to every God being on the planet wherever they are so everyone can live in a perfect world. In conclusion, I would like to say that the knowledge in this book came directly from God.

He shared his knowledge of Angels, Demons, Spiritual Gifts, Healing, Spiritual Dimensions and Heaven with me so I could share with others. This knowledge must be spread around the world so that everyone can come together as one. Everyone needs to understand the truth behind spirituality.

It is time to set everyone's mind free from the spiritual trap they've been in for so long. With God's light, anything is possible. Sharing the light is the most important thing you can do.

Now please go out and share the light today.

P.S. God wants me to tell you, "Thank You." But he would much rather tell you himself.

THE FINAL STEP IN YOUR JOURNEY

Now the final step in your journey! You have taken the time and dedication to read this book, so now I ask you to take a little more time and answer these questions. These are the same questions that are in front of the book. After you answer these questions, I want you to compare the answers to those in the front of the book so you can see the difference within yourself.

Complete the following:

1. Religion is…

_____

2. Spiritually is…

_____

3. Heaven is…

_____

4. God is…

_____

5. Angels are…

_____

6. Demons are…

_____

7. Spiritual Gifts are…

_____

Complete the Questionnaire:

Rate yourself from 1-10.
10 = 100% agreement with question or statement.
1 = 100% disagreement with question or statement.

1. __God does exist.
2. __Angels do exist.
3. __Demons do exist.
4. __In history, people have been able to see God.
5. __I can see, hear and talk to God.
6. __God has spiritual gifts for everyone.
7. __In history, people have been able to see, hear and talk to Angels.
8. __Only select people can see, hear and talk to Angels.
9. __Angels can help guide your life.
10. __Demons cause havoc in everyone's lives.
11. __I have the ability heal myself from physical, mental or emotional illness.
12. __I can see, hear and talk to Angels.
13. __Heaven does exist.
14. __I have to die to see heaven.
15. __Demons cause mental illness.
16. __In history, people have been able to hear God.
17. __I can visit heaven whenever I choose to.
18. __I have a physical and spiritual body.
19. __No one can see God and Angels.
20. __Demons cause physical illness.
21. __I have a spirit and soul within me.
22. __Spiritual gifts are given to you by God.
23. __I can receive spiritual gifts.
24. __There are a limited number of spiritual gifts that I can receive.
25. __Everyone on earth belongs to the same spiritual family.
26. __Spiritually is a waste of time.
27. __In history, people have been able to talk to God.
28. __Given my past, I can't be spiritual.

29. __I don't have time to be spiritual.
30. __God doesn't exist.
31. __Angels don't exist
32. __Demons don't exist.
33. __Spiritual gifts don't exist.
34. __The only way to heal yourself is through medication.
35. __Spiritual healing is for suckers.
36. __I don't need to be spiritual.
37. __Demons cause emotional problems/illness.
38. __No one can see, hear or talk to God or Angels.
39. __Children are spiritually gifted.
40. __I don't want the responsible of being spiritual.
41. __My religion is the only correct religion.
42. __There are other dimensions that I can't see with my physical eyes.
43. __There are other dimensions I can see with my spiritual eyes.
44. __Someone has to be specially selected to see, hear or talk to God.
45. __I have a physical illness.
46. __I have a mental illness.
47. __I know everything there is about spiritually and religion.
48. __Meditation is a waste of my time.
49. __I never meditated in my life.
50. __I meditate every day.
51. __I don't know how to meditate.
52. __I can't find my soul mate.
53. __Soul mates don't exist.
54. __I have fear.
55. __I have anger.
56. __I have guilt.
57. __I believe luck has to do with spiritually.
58. __I live in denial.
59. __Truth is important.
60. __Truth is important in being spiritual.
61. __Faith is important to me.
62. __Being in a relationship is important to me.

63. __Spiritually is important in relationships.
64. __I have problems I need to fix in my life.
65. __I know everything about everything.
66. __Everyone who is diagnosed with mental disorders should take medication.
67. __Everyone who is diagnosed with emotional problems should take medications.
68. __I believe that people have the ability to diagnose physical illness with their spiritual abilities.
69. __In medical school, doctors should also be trained in diagnosing physical, mental and emotional illness with spiritual abilities.
70. __Earthbound spirits exist.
71. __The only way to stop being a drug addict is to go to rehab.
72 __I can see, hear and talk to my dead loved ones in Heaven.
73. __I can manifest my dreams and desires.
74. __Children can see earthbound spirits.
75. __I can see earthbound spirits.
76. __I think this questionnaire was a waste of my time.
77. __God loves everyone.

...Coming soon

YOUR KEYS TO HEAVEN

BOOK TWO

DIMENSIONS ELEVEN THRU TWENTY-TWO

Share your experience with Gary.

If you have an experience that you would like to share with Gary, please email it to

MYSTORY@GARYSPIVEY.COM

or you can mail it to

Gary Spivey
P.O. Box 9
Star, NC. 27356

Become One with
GARY SPIVEY

Add Gary as a friend, follow Gary, Watch Gary's Videos!
Daily Updates! Leave Comments! Rate Videos!
Come see what Gary is doing right now...

 www.myspace.com/garyspivey

 www.facebook.com/garyspivey

 www.twitter.com/garyspivey

 www.youtube.com/garyspivey

www.garyspivey.com

Join Gary Spivey's Enlightenment Club!

Gary Spivey's Enlightenment club is an online experience like no other! Usually, one class with Gary Spivey costs $50.00, but now for only $4.16 per month you get access to all of Gary's online video tutorials of Gary himself teaching you all of the Spiritual Secrets within Your Keys to Heaven and many more not in this book. That's only $49.92 a year! When you join Gary Spivey's Enlightenment Club you will have access to Gary's teachings any time you have time. Gary himself will be with you guiding you through the teachings. The online video library consists of Gary teaching you how to:

- Discover your psychic ability ● See, hear and talk to God and Angels
- Receive Spiritual Gifts ● Heal yourself and others of all illness
- Manifest all of your dreams and desires ● Receive your spiritual eyes
- Get rid of Demons that cause havoc in your life ● Find your soul mate
- Get rid of demons causing all addictions (drugs, smoking, eating etc...)
- Improve your relationship and bring back your lost love for each other
- Remove the spiritual blocks from your children

Subscribe today and you also get...

- Subscription to Gary's monthly online newsletter "FREE"
- Discounts on private readings, seminars, and Spiritual Retreats
- Spiritual online community chat room where Gary will have a weekly chat and you can ask him questions!

Only $4.16 per month!
(That's only $49.92 per year!)

To join Gary Spivey's Enlightenment Club, logon to: www.garyspivey.com

Get up to $1000.00 OFF
Gary Spivey's
Spiritual Retreats!!

Gary's Spiritual Retreats take place in the beautiful Ojai Valley of Southern California as well as other beautiful spiritual locations throughout the world. People come from all over the world to learn spiritual techniques that Gary Spivey has spent a lifetime discovering through meditation, talking to God and his Angels and doing thousands of personal readings!

By attending one of Gary Spivey's Spiritual Retreats you will learn how to:

Understand Energy	• *Get in touch with your angels*
Remove dark energy	• *Meditate / Pray*
Clear Negativity	• *Receive Spiritual Gifts*
See God and Angels	• *Manifest your destiny*
Trust your inner voice	• *Get out of denial*

...and much more!!

To redeem this coupon or to find out more information about Gary Spivey's Spiritual Retreats, please call :

1-800-827-4279

Order other products from
Gary Spivey

The Enlightenment Series

Meditation CD   Depression CD
Spiritual Gifts   Depression is in your head

To Order, Call: **1-800-827-4279**

or order online at www.garyspivey.com

Quantity		Book or Cd Title	Price (each)	Total Price
		Gary Spivey's Meditation CD - Spiritual Gifts A meditation a day... keeps the dark energy away	$14.95	
		Gary Spivey's Depression CD Depression is in your Head	$14.95	
			Shipping	1 item - $3.50 2 items - $5.00 3 items - $7.00
		Add 7.25% sales tax for California residents		
			Total	

Name: _____

Address: _____

City: _____ State: _____ Zip: _____

Make check or money order payable to G.S. Limited Inc.

Visa/MC/AE/Disc #:_____ Exp. Date: _____

Signature: _____

Mail to: Gary Spivey Meditation CD's
P.O. Box 9
Star, NC. 27356